WHAT'S THE BIG IDEA?

What's the Big Idea?
Copyright © 2020
Robert G. Lee

ISBN: 978-1-952474-29-3

Cover design by Jonathan Grisham for Grisham Designs.

Published by WordCrafts Press
Cody, Wyoming 82414
www.wordcrafts.net

WHAT'S THE BIG IDEA?

A COMEDIAN EXPLAINS GOD, THE UNIVERSE AND OTHER MINOR STUFF

ROBERT G. LEE

WordCrafts

For my daughter and my son.
The only truly good things I've ever accomplished on this blue dot.

Contents

The Bible

Follow Who, Exactly?

Section III–The Conundrum

The World Is Broken

I Don't Wanna Believe!

An Eternal Evite

Introduction

Let me be straight with you: I am not a scientist. Nor am I a theologian. I'm that guy in the back row of class who spent most of his time looking for any opportunity to throw out a funny line. Teachers tended to think I was rude. As a comedian, I considered it on-the-job training.

Despite my total deficit in the PhD department, this is a book about the intersection of science and faith. To be clear, this is not written for either scientists or biblical scholars. This book is for everybody else who is interested in either of those areas but find their eyes tend to glaze over while trying to listen to the experts endlessly pontificate about their area of study.

Think of me as the smart aleck who's been waiting for the opportunity to comment on the lecture. Scientists and biblical scholars are certainly invited to read this, but be warned: excessive eye rolling may cause undue optical strain.

You should also know I tend to be an equal opportunity offender. The role of the comedian is to look at *all* nonsense and call it out for what it is. Which means, more often than not, that I tend to step on toes, whether the person is two-stepping to the right or leaning to the left.

If you're curious, the way I came to write this book is that I was *Slumdog Millionaired.*

The plot to that movie is simple: a young man wins a game show and is suspected of cheating, but we come to see how the obscure questions from the show seemed to pop up in his life just before he was chosen to be a contestant.

1

It was the same thing with this book. Events happened in my life that, on the outside, would seem to have very little in common, but looking back, all appear to be tiny pieces of a much bigger puzzle.

Random events, from the books I was reading, to being called in for jury duty, to having lunch with a lesbian, all contributed to what you're reading now.

That being said, I think it's probably important to fill you in a little about me and why I'm audacious enough to think I can tackle subjects as unwieldy as God and the universe.

For years I made my living warming up the audiences for television sitcoms in Hollywood. I started off on *Golden Girls, Designing Women* and *Perfect Strangers.* I did the pilots for *Frasier, Everybody Loves Raymond* and worked on the historic last episode of *Cheers.* I closed out my career in TV working on *Becker, The New Adventures of Old Christine* and Norman Lear's reboot of *One Day at a Time.*

It was a great job, it kept me in town with my family and as a result, no one living outside of Los Angeles has ever heard of me. Truth be told, I'm pretty anonymous in Hollywood, too.

About two decades ago I took a job at my church as their interim part-time drama director. When they dangled health care in front of me, that job became a full-time position and I spent the next 16 years working with some of the most wonderful, talented people I have ever known.

That job ended when a new pastor was hired who disbanded the drama department on Ash Wednesday.

That's right, my church gave me up for Lent.

So now I'm back in the comedy game full-time. Which, it turns out, is the absolutely perfect time for a man in his sixties to break into show business!

Over the years, I made some eight comedy video/CDs, wrote and directed an ultra-low budget feature (*Can I Get A Witness Protection?)* and even wrote a handful of episodes for *Veggie Tales*!

You've got to love a career where you get paid to write punchlines for vegetables.

That's my work resume. On the private side, besides the 38 years of marriage and kid stuff, over the last three decades I have been involved in a men's covenant group and have taught a weekly Bible study.

These last two experiences, beyond the friendships they have cultivated, have, by sheer osmosis, steeped me in God's instruction book.

As you may well imagine, as far as the world is concerned, I am a walking contradiction: a professional mocker who loves both Monty Python and God (but not necessarily in that order).

I see no conflict between my profession and my faith. I believe God has a sense of humor. All you need to do to believe that is get out of the shower in the morning and look in the mirror. Personally, with me, He's getting funnier every year.

As someone who looks at life from a slightly askew angle, I spend my days writing material, going on stage and pointing out the absurdities of our common existence.

Quite simply, that's how I came to write this book. I have spent a lifetime listening to and working for some great people on both sides: those who love God and those who don't so much. My secret wish is to be instrumental in getting these two polar opposite camps to meet somewhere in the middle.

It may well be a pipe dream, but who better to lead a discussion on the big issues of life than a smart aleck?

So that you don't get overwhelmed by the tsunami of facts front loaded at the very beginning, I want to lay out the book for you.

The first third is about the universe, the world and your body. These chapters contain the bulk of head-banging scientific information that I've tried to present in reasonably fun, bite-size bits.

The middle third offers an introduction as well as explanation of a lot of the confusion surrounding the One who claims to have created everything.

We wrap up the book with a variety of reasons why you would naturally want to resist everything I've laid out, countered by a lot of personal reasons why I've come to wholeheartedly accept it.

I think that about covers it.

A woman in my Bible study says every week we "learn through laughing." That's probably the best label I could come up with for what I'm about to embark on.

I will take many side trips on the way to our final destination, but at the end of the day, even if you end up disagreeing with me, if nothing else, I hope you enjoy the journey.

Full disclosure: the main reason I'm writing this is for my daughter, my son, their spouses and my eventual grandchildren. As I am one of those crazy people who actually believes in a benevolent Creator, I wanted to give them, in one book, absolutely every reason I can possibly come up with as to why I have staked my life on the very simple premise that God does exist.

But before you jump in, let me address the elephant in the room: for those of you who are ready to check out because of my confessed faith, I will leave you with a quote from theologian Dallas Willard:

"We live in a culture that has, for centuries now, cultivated the idea that the skeptical person is always smarter than the one who believes. You can almost be as stupid as a cabbage as long as you doubt."

Here's to the faithful, the skeptics and the cabbages!

Section I
Creation

Such a Gift!

I come at this subject as a fan. When I take more than a minute to contemplate the complexities of the universe, it rocks me back on my heels. I stand in amazement at our miraculous cosmos, this particular planet and the myriad of humans scurrying around on it.

Maybe it doesn't freak you out, but I'm a little concerned that the planet on which we currently reside is floating in space held up by nothing.

I repeat, nothing!

You can say that we're in the gravitational pull of the sun, and that sun is in the orbit of a galaxy, but what holds all that up?

It's like that moment in the *Superman* movie where Lois Lane dramatically falls off the roof of the Daily Planet, Superman flies up to catch her and says, "Don't worry, Miss Lane, I've got you." Stunned, she says, "You've got me? *Who's got you?*"

I feel like that every day.

As a fan, I find the "how we got here" explanations from both the scientific and religious communities to be somewhat lacking.

If this subject were a test, scientists would be great at showing their work, but they can't seem to agree on the logical conclusion of those facts. Meanwhile religious people like to skip straight to the correct answer, but tend to push people away with their overly simplistic explanations about how they arrived at their solution.

Scientists have spent lifetimes describing the astounding creation around us but, because of personal beliefs, lean toward the rather absurd answer that everything happened by sheer chance.

Conversely, people of faith confidently say that their God made everything but won't listen to reason when science points out rather rational explanations of how things came to be.

Faced with these two differing opinions, I find myself in the uncomfortable position of disagreeing with pretty much everyone. Your instincts are right on; I'm not invited to a lot of parties.

Regardless, I challenge both scientists and theologians alike to imagine they're back in school, ready to turn in their final assignment, when the teacher takes a cursory glance at their work and says, "Since your whole grade counts on this, why don't you look over your paper one more time before you turn it in?"

With that in mind, I reluctantly take the unpopular stance of an obstinate contrarian mainly because I wholeheartedly believe the subject at hand is of the utmost importance.

That, and I think *Obstinate Contrarian* would make a great T-shirt.

Common Ground

One of the goals of this book is to take a good look at what we've all seen our whole lives but haven't taken the time to unpack.

To my mind, the best way I can lay down the ground rules and attempt to explain the enormity of what we're facing is to give a tip of the hat to the High Priests of irreverence, Monty Python, and their opus, *The Galaxy Song*.

I reference this song for two very important reasons:
1. It sets up the enormity of the essential problem I want to address.
2. If you don't like Monty Python, you might as well stop reading now.

From where I sit, the world seems to be inextricably divided over so many things today, from politics to gender, that it seems the only thing we can agree on is that we don't agree on anything!

Is it even possible to find any common ground today?

I humbly submit there's one fact that everyone, regardless of political persuasion, can agree on: Cindy Crawford is still one fine looking woman.

Okay, two facts.

Regardless of your political, religious or sport affiliations, all scientific evidence points to the fact that…

The universe is expanding.

If that is true, then it stands to reason that at some point, it had a beginning. A beginning that was apparently named after the popular TV sitcom, *The Big Bang Theory.*

Assuming that's true, then there should be no conflict between our communities, right?

The point I need to make here echoes the timid refrain of Rodney King, "Can't we all just get along?"

I believe that while the biblical and scientific communities seem to be at odds, the reality is that they are looking at the identical reality of the wonder of creation—but from vastly different perspectives.

I believe both have very valid points to make and hope to unpack both viewpoints in this book.

Succinctly put, science gives us the all-important 'how' while religion does its best to give us the potentially life-changing 'why.'

Astrophysicist and prolific author Hugh Ross states there are two kinds of questions. One is purely scientific: we want to know *the way* things work. The other is spiritual in its origin: we want to know *why* things are the way they are.

Famed author C.S. Lewis agrees and says there are two views that are widely held. First are those who he would call 'materialists.' These people believe that matter and space just happen to exist and nobody knows why.

Other people take the 'religious' view. They believe that a great mind is behind the universe and, as such, they spend much of their time trying to figure out not so much the 'what' but the 'how' and the 'why.'

C.S. Lewis says, "We want to know whether the universe simply happens to be what it is for no reason or whether there is a power behind it that makes it what it is."

In his attempt to address this problem, scientist Gus Speth says, "I used to think the top environmental problems were biodiversity loss, ecosystem collapse and climate change. I thought that with 30 years of good science we could address those problems. But I was wrong. The top environmental problems are selfishness, greed and apathy... and to deal with those we need a spiritual and cultural transformation—and we scientists don't know how to do that."

In a nutshell, that's what I intend to focus on. My aim is to give an overview. I'm a big picture guy. As you will soon discover, there are more than enough astounding facts to relay to you, and as such, it is my intention to skip over a lot of the dull parts.

You're welcome.

Think of me as the guy who took a bullet for the team. I dove into very deep scientific waters, tolerated tons of geek-speak and am coming back with a report on things normal people can actually understand. Well, normal people who don't wear Lab Coats. I think that crowd sort of gets off on technical jargon.

So here we go...

We Won the Lottery!

The fact that you are living and breathing and have the ability to procrastinate a long list of To-Dos in order to slice out a little 'me' time in an attempt to comprehend words on a page is absolutely astounding.

So much so that it's not out of bounds to declare that everyone alive today has won the cosmic lottery in an 8-billion-way tie.

Seriously, the odds are so stacked against the human race it's unbelievable. If any one tiny little factor changed over the past 14 billion years, we'd be nothing but stardust.

Not only did we win the long odds of the Big Bang, but after that we got the winning electromagnetic force ticket, the strong nuclear force Powerball and the strength of gravity scratch off!

Don't let anyone tell you otherwise; we're all winners, baby!

American theoretical physicist and Nobel laureate Professor Steven Weinberg says, "Life as we know it would be impossible if any one of several physical quantities had slightly different values. One constant does seem to require incredible fine tuning."

That's a phrase we'll go back to again and again: 'fine tuning.' It's the song of the universe.

According to people who actually studied in school, if the energy of the Big Bang was different by one part out of 10 to the 120th power, there would be no life.

To translate this math-speak to something mere mortals can understand: the odds of creation existing as we know it has the same odds as that of a short, bald, out-of-shape, broke man with three rotting teeth hooking up with a different supermodel every single day for the rest of his life.

And yet here we are.

Astrophysicist Michael Turner says, "The precision is as if one could throw a dart across the entire universe and hit a bullseye one millimeter in diameter on the other side."

Why not toss in 'while blindfolded,' just to make it really difficult?

Stephen Hawking in his book, *A Brief History of Time*, said, "It would be very difficult to explain why the universe should have begun in just this way, except as an act of a God who intended to create beings like us."

Physicist Freeman Dryson said, "The more I examine the universe and study the details of its architecture, the more evidence I find that the universe in some way must have known that we were coming."

The fuzzy haired but clear-thinking genius, Albert Einstein, said, "The most incomprehensible thing about the universe is that it is comprehensible."

So, there you have it; several very smart people have looked at the vast nature of the universe and have come away, to a person, believing that there must be some sort of design, or better yet, a Designer behind everything that we see and experience.

But I'm getting ahead of myself.

Fun Fact: There are more than 200 billion galaxies in the observable universe. Each galaxy contains about 200 billion stars, bringing the total to 50 billion-trillion, or the approximate number of followers Chrissy Teigen has on Instagram.

Living in the Past

As I begin to lay out some of the building blocks of the universe, don't be overly concerned about whether or not you fully comprehend all of it. I certainly don't.

This is not an exhaustive study by any stretch. Think of me as your creation docent guiding you through a whirlwind tour of the museum of existence.

And we're walking… we're walking…

When astronomers study the skies, they are at a distinct disadvantage as everything they're looking at happened a long, long time ago in a galaxy far, far way.

That, in and of itself, is mildly mind-blowing. I'm always tempted to walk up to astronomers, and in my best surfer Bill & Ted voice, say, "Dude, live in the *now*!"

The light from our closest galaxy, the Andromeda, took over two million years to reach us, give or take an eon.

That's right, the most current, up-to-date information we have about our closest galaxy falls so far outside the statute of limitations, it wouldn't even hold up in court.

"Your honor, my client's over two million years old! I ask that Ms. Andromeda be released under her own recognizance."

"Before I set bail, I must ask, can she still move at the speed of light?"

"She can, but every time she enters a solar system she forgets why she went there."

The reason we can observe all of this is that we just happen to live in the darkest location in the Milky Way, which just happens to be in the darkest location of the universe.

One of the big benefits of our current home is that we are able to look out into space with a minimum of cosmic dust obscuring our view. Since we are living near the cosmic darkness on the edge of town, we have a much better view of the heavens surrounding us.

Which is how we're able to see and measure the light coming to us from so far away. Fairly convenient, I must say!

Since we can measure light's speed, we can estimate where that light came from and how old it is. And by 'we' I mean people with PhDs following their names. Personally, I couldn't measure light if my life depended on it.

Astronomers are like snooty wine connoisseurs, "The universe has a deep, dark texture, with a full body. Robust in taste with subtle undertones of space debris."

The actual birthday of the universe is hard to pin down. Most scientists put it at 13.73 billion years. Young Earthers say it doesn't look a day over 10,000 years. Genesis says it took six days, and God took Saturday off. Debate amongst yourselves.

The Big Bang

If you were pitching the origin story of the universe, like every fledgling screenwriter, you'd need an elevator pitch. Something you could spit out to a producer between the first floor and the penthouse suite.

It might go something like this…

"Picture this! After the initial totally cool CGI explosion, the universe expands for a million years, and atoms and nuclei form. Matter comes together and forms galaxies under the force of gravity. Hydrogen and helium are drawn together like a magnet under the force of supernovas and their nuclear fusion! That's when our hero walks in. The rest writes itself. I'll have my people call your people. Let's do lunch!"

Here's one fact that's irrefutable: the name Big Bang started off as a joke. Some guy was trying to belittle the theory and thought of the most demeaning name he could give it—and it stuck.

About a decade ago People in Lab Coats (from here on simply labeled as PiLCs) estimated the Big Bang exploded from a mass the size of a basketball. Evidently that was just too big.

The most up-to-date theory is that it all started from a tiny, tiny speck. A speck so small, in fact, that, according to author and astrophysicist Neil DeGrasse Tyson, it was originally less than one trillionth the size of the period that ends this sentence. That is one small font!

Close your eyes and try to imagine every galaxy, star, planet and comet coming from something as small as that!

When the Big Bang banged, it let out masses of radiant energy. The unimaginable heat formed stars that, as a side benefit, cooked up several elements.

In case you're thinking of making a universe of your own someday, the chemical compound is about 74% hydrogen, 24% helium and 2% various heavy elements. Stir and set aside to let rise for several billion years.

To give you an idea of the power of the Big Bang, *one second* after the initial bang, the universe had grown to a few light years across and tipped the thermometer at a billion degrees.

That's around *12 trillion miles* in a single second and was *way* hotter than anything that has ever been created (with the possible exception of a cheese pizza right when it's taken out of an oven).

This event was a one-time only spectacular. There was no afternoon matinee. I guarantee you have no way to wrap your head around this information. We have nothing to which to compare it.

After that initial ka-boom, it took about *half a billion* years to form the first stars. Those stars and existing gasses around them in turn formed billions of elliptical and spiral galaxies. You read that right, *billions*!

The fun part here is that all those literal super-stars, each with a mass about 10 times that of our sun, would cook up dozens of new elements in their hydrogen powered pressure cookers and then...explode!

By doing so, they scattered their contents across the galaxy, new stars would form from that and they'd start the cycle all over again.

To give you an accurate image of how our universe started, think of billions of ovens cooking up a storm, and when each individual dish was done, that oven exploded.

Sunday dinner with the universe for the first several billion years was a very messy affair.

After that, the universe kept expanding and cooling until you have what you have today: a nicely comfortable, not as hot as it used to be, middle-aged universe.

If our universe expanded too rapidly at the outset, then matter would have dissipated without forming the necessary gas balls that eventually turned into stars, planets and galaxies.

But if it expanded too slowly, everything would have collapsed into a super dense lump or black hole.

The rate of expansion was so precise that the odds have been compared to that of a *billion* pencils all standing on their sharpened points all at once on a glass surface.

Sure, that could happen.

Here's where we enter the world of *probability* versus *possibility*.

It's entirely *possible* that the universe happened by chance, by some random act of nature, but it's not *probable*.

It's also entirely *possible* that monkeys are going to fly out of my (choose any available orifice), but it's not *probable*. Actually, that one may have a higher chance of probability than the Big Bang happening on its own.

Physics

Before your eyes glaze over any further, let me de-mystify the word 'physics.'

This is a word referring to the physical laws of the universe. The wonderful thing about our particular home is that the rules apply to everyone, everywhere, whether or not you or some random galaxy choose to believe in them.

When you hang around physicists, you may well be intimidated. Don't be. They're smart but they didn't actually invent anything. They're just very bright voyeurs. They look at the way the universe operates and then report it back to the rest of us.

When they report something that's particularly astounding, react like Forrest Gump, "So we can't violate causality laws. Okay, one less thing."

For example, gravity is a constant force to be reckoned with, no matter where you are. The surprising twist here is that it may be lighter or stronger, depending on a variety of factors, but it is always there.

Remember the footage of our astronauts bouncing around on the moon? That's a perfect example. The moon's gravitational pull is much less than that of the earth's, so Neil Armstrong could win the Olympic long jump even while weighted down wearing his space suit!

But make no mistake; there is still gravity on the moon. If there weren't, Neil would have floated off the surface the second he stepped out of the lunar rocket.

Gravity is like most younger brothers. They come in varying degrees of annoying, but they're always there.

While gravity can increase and decrease, there is a group of rarified members in an exclusive club called 'The Constants.' These are members of a superhero team known only for their ability to never change. They are…
1. the conservation of mass and energy
2. the conservation of linear and angular momentum
3. the conservation of the electric charge.
If you're not a physicist and can't keep the constants straight, try to think of them as you would the Beatles: mass and energy are

John and Paul, George plays both linear and angular momentum and the electric charge is Ringo.

As in, "I loved the early constants, but clearly they were more powerful as a group than when they separated."

A Tsunami of Knowledge

Right about now I suspect some of you are ready to raise your hand and ask, "Is this going to be on the test?"

There is, in fact, way too much information to impart to you. You don't have to memorize and retain everything included here. I'm presenting it so that you can not only get an overview of the world in which you live, but also as sort of a Cliff's Notes version of the science class you skipped out on when you went to make out under the bleachers.

It must have been so much easier to get an education thousands of years ago…

"This fire. It hot. Don't touch. This food. It good. Eat. This poison. It not good. Don't eat! This tool. End be sharp. Don't touch. This animal nice. Can pet. Those animals not nice. Don't pet. That about it. Any questions?"

"Which part be on test?"

Until the year 1900, human knowledge doubled about every century. Just 50 years later, our cumulative information doubled every 25 years. By the time we hit 2000, it doubled every year. Now, our knowledge/information is doubling almost every day!

It's exhausting just thinking about it! There is now officially so much information in the world that no one person or group can hold on to it all.

Which is why we rely so much on computers. Fortunately, there's not a single science fiction scenario in which the computers of the future are anything but kind and altruistic towards humanity. Let's hope our good luck holds!

And now back to class.

Matter vs. Anti-Matter

At the very, very start of the Big Bang, say, in the first one hundred thousandth of a second, we had a variety of quarks and anti-quarks, which are also known as matter and anti-matter.

As quarks are likely to do, they all exploded.

Fortunately, when the positive quarks faced off against the anti-quarks, the optimistic quarks won. According to a variety of talking head sports commentators, the two teams appeared to be equally matched, but when the score was tallied, anti-matter had 10 billion anti-particles, but matter snuck in for the win with 10 billion and *one* positive particles.

The reason why is obvious. In stories like this, the good guy always wins. Evil tries, but no matter how hard they try, they're just doomed to failure.

If anti-matter had just come up with a different name, it might have been a different story, but, c'mon, if you put 'anti' in your name, you're just asking for trouble.

For us, it's a good thing the quarks won, because if it weren't for that one particle out of 10 billion, the whole universe would have been one big gaseous experiment. Our universe would be filled with radiant energy but no particles on which to build a playground.

Why do I mention this? It is merely for your edification. It is also useful to fill in during awkward lags in the conversation. You'll be the hit of any party when you drop in a non-sequitur like, "I don't know about you, but I sure am glad our universe has more quarks than anti-quarks! Am I right?"

Dark Matter and Dark Energy

Then there's (ominous theme music, please) dark matter. Please note that this is not to be confused with matter or even its arch enemy, anti-matter. No, this is something even more elusive.

We can't see dark matter, but we can deduce it's there. PiLCs describe it as, "a ghostly class of undiscovered particles that interact with matter via gravity."

Dark matter is thusly named for a very good reason: it's everywhere, but it's so dark we can't see it. However, this is not to be confused with dark energy, which is so named because we don't understand it!

Our old friend gravity and dark energy have been in a cosmic tug of war since the beginning of time. Gravity was winning for the first seven billion years, but as the universe expands, it's winding down as dark energy grabs the baton for the victory lap.

That's right, when the universe was young, gravity ruled the roost. It kept the neighborhood from expanding at too great a pace. But dark energy was holding back, biding its time. It sat in the dark, doing push-ups and whatever else dark energy does to get in shape, waiting for gravity to get complacent.

And now, after some 14 billion years, dark energy is now officially stronger than gravity.

To put it in superhero terms, Marvel's the Hulk just caught up and passed DC's Superman. Or as Darth Vader, the official mascot of dark energy, would say, "the apprentice is now the master."

What does this mean to you? Absolutely nothing. The result won't be evident for a least another billion or so years as our universe expands into nothingness. If it ever gets that far (which I highly doubt).

The fact that the universe is expanding at an ever-increasing rate and that gravity is powerless to stop it may well give you a moment of white-knuckle fear. That is, until you remember how old we are and how long it will take for dark energy to push the universe to the edge of extinction.

According to the best estimates, it will happen long after you are gone, but well before your student loans are paid off. So, there's an upside.

The best thing about dark energy is how much science geeks giggle like little school girls over this. Evidently PiLCs have figured out that the sum total of dark energy is no bigger than a billionth of a trillionth of a trillionth of an electron's mass.

It may be diminutive in stature, but man, it sure seems to be able to kick some serious heinie.

The bottom line here is that evidently dark energy takes some off-the-charts fine tuning. Our universe needed to expand at exactly the right rate of speed or, as I have previously stated, catastrophe would ensue.

The fight between gravity and dark energy was really more of a wonderfully choreographed dance, with each one taking the focus when it was necessary.

PiLCs are so obsessed with dark energy that they've spent billions of dollars building a 17 mile underground super collider between Switzerland and France. They send protons through the tunnel, hoping they will smash into each other in order to produce measurable dark energy.

In my humble opinion, this grand experiment may not make a healthy return on its investment.

Because I believe what they're looking for is, in fact, the Designer. Not to get too religious too fast, but in both Colossians 1:17 and Hebrews 1:3, the New Testament claims that the Creator holds the universe together.

While scientists stare in amazement at galaxies that should, according to all of our data, fly off in a million different directions, the Bible sits quite comfortably in its declaration that the Force that created the cosmos is also the very One who holds it together.

Regardless of your thoughts on who's behind it, you've got to admit that the proof is pretty overwhelming that some kind of very powerful and meticulous Designer went to a lot of trouble to put together a rather magnificent home for us.

I'm good with that!

Fun Fact: 99.73 percent of everything that exists in the universe is 'dark.' It's like God's running around the universe blowing out stars, saying, "Does anyone have any idea what it takes to keep these stars on all day and night? What am I, made of money?"

The Speed of Light

Something we all know from experience is that light moves extremely fast. So fast, in fact, that there is nothing in our universe that is faster. Gossip comes in a close second, but at the last Olympics, light edged it out at the tape.

Light is considered another member of the 'constant' superhero squad. You can depend on light. It always moves at the same speed. Imagine what a crazy world it would be if we were constantly waiting for light to arrive.

"Did you turn on the light?"

"Yes!"

"Then why is it still dark?"

"I don't know, it must be moving slow this morning!"

The speed of light in a vacuum is 186,282 miles *per second* (or, 299,792 kilometers per second). Let that sink in.

In miles per hour, light speed is almost as fast as the Millennium Falcon. It goes about 670,616,629 mph. If you could travel at the speed of light, you could go around the earth 7.5 times in one second. Now that's without any luggage or carry-ons, but it's still pretty impressive!

We call a billionth of a second a nanosecond. If you need to go smaller, a picosecond is a trillionth of a second. Personally, I've never needed to measure anything down to the nano or picosecond, but I'm not a professional light timer.

Beyond its speed, light is full of practical applications. There's the light we can see, of course. Basically, think of any rainbow (not to insult the LGBTQ version, but that only has six bands of color. The original has seven).

But there are bands of light outside the visible spectrum that do us a lot of good as well. There's infra-red light on one side and ultra-violet on the other.

Once we move down the electromagnetic spectrum we get radio waves, microwaves, X-rays and gamma rays. If Bruce Banner were a ham radio operator he never would have been exposed to gamma rays and, as such, never would have turned into the Hulk. Isn't it funny how fate works?

The other thing you need to know about light is that it is both a wave and a particle—at the same time! Who would have guessed that?

The wave part allows us to measure time over cosmic distances. I have absolutely no idea what the particle part does, but without it light just wouldn't feel complete.

The other amazing aspect of light is that it's how we measure time, yet, surprisingly, light is outside of time.

Here's how PiLCs explain it: the faster one travels relative to another object, the slower time flows for the traveler relative to the flow of time measured by the stationary observer.

I could say that slower, but it wouldn't help.

This statement is the reason most of us were sent to shop class. "How many understand what I just said? Fine, those three of you stay in class. The rest of you gather your things and head over to the career center."

Einstein says that if you could travel at the speed of light, time would cease all together. The time of all events would become compressed into a never ending *now*.

No past, no future, just *now* all the time until the end of time. This could well be a clue about how a being of light could, in fact, transcend time. Something to hold on to for a later discussion.

Space

Trust me, no matter how attractive deep space may seem, you don't want to go out there. It's literally freezing! Think going-out-to-get-the-paper-in-the-middle-of-winter-in-Wisconsin-naked.

And then having the door slam behind you, locking you out.

And then falling through the ice.

Times ten.

To be comfortable in space, you have to wear so many layers that once you're out in it, you can barely move. Inevitably, the minute you're outside the capsule, you have to go to the bathroom. It's so much nicer in the space station next to a warm fire.

The universe has a normal temperature of 3 degrees Kelvin. That translates into -270 degrees Celsius, or a whopping -450 degrees Fahrenheit. That's *negative* 450 degrees! Even with no wind chill factor, that's flippin' cold!

On top of the lack of warmth, there is no atmospheric pressure, so if you absent-mindedly wandered outside the starship Enterprise, you'd suffocate in a matter of moments. Before you could say, "I'd better pop back in and get a scarf," your blood cells would burst and your eyes would pop out. Yech!

But if you managed to survive all that, you've got to deal with the constant bombardment of cosmic rays. Yeah, that's a real thing. Granted, they're subatomic particles, but they're almost as fast as the speed of light. That just can't be good for you.

Not to mention space debris like comets and tiny asteroids whizzing by willy nilly.

What all this means is that in any movie where the hero survives in space for more than three seconds, it's a load of hooey.

The next time you're in a movie theater and one of the Guardians of the Galaxy or Princess Leia are jettisoned out into space, yell out, "One, one thousand…Two, one thousand…Dead!" Everyone in the theater is bound to appreciate your efforts to hold Hollywood to a higher standard of sound scientific realism.

Regardless of the unrealistic aspects of shows like Star Trek, I still love them. As a kid back in Indiana, I loved watching Kirk and Spock and their crew wander around California's Mono lake, pretending they were on another planet.

Science fiction writers love to throw in just enough science to give their fiction an air of authenticity, but pretty much everything breaks down under tighter scrutiny.

The most obvious example is always the fashion. If the Federation is some 200 to 400 years in the future, why do all the women wear the same beehive hairdos they wore in the nineteen sixties? Why do all the men look as if they could land on any planet in the universe and immediately start selling life insurance?

There was a famous space movie from the fifties where all of the rocket ship's communication devices were attached to curly telephone cords. Really? Nobody thought we'd ever evolve our way past that?

The point here is that good science fiction always uses the science as a springboard to tell a story that echoes our current tumultuous times.

Because with the hindsight of time, the vast majorities of stories set in the future end up being laughable. That's why science fiction is best enjoyed by several grains of salt, shaken onto the top of a huge tub of popcorn.

Density

One very big problem people have with our universe is its size. If you had a dime for every one of those stars in the innumerable galaxies, you could buy Amazon and Apple like they were chump change.

Specifically, Hugh Ross estimates that those dimes, when stacked together, would cover the entire North American continent and be over 1,500 feet high.

I don't know if he's factored in the Grand Canyon, or the simple problem of theft, but even with that, it's an impressive word picture.

I'm unsure why Dr. Ross feels it's okay to squish the entire population of a country under a mountain of dimes just to prove a point, but that's a scientist for you!

It's hard to comprehend how big our universe is when most of us have a hard time grasping the size of our planet. Any time you have to travel across our globe in a plane, you may well think to yourself, "Surely this orb doesn't need to be this ginormous!"

Despite its relatively massive size, our planet is nothing more than a mere speck when compared to the vastness of the emptiness of space.

Surely our cosmos doesn't need to be *billions* of light years across? Imagine taking a flight to the next galaxy! Especially if there's no meal service! You wouldn't make it past Mars!

Here's one reason PiLCs believe the universe needs as much space as it has: it's a question of the right mass and the right elements.

To quote Marty McFly's dad in *Back to The Future*, "You're my density!"

It's not all about the bass, it's all about the density!

If the density of all the protons and all the neutrons in the universe were much lower, then, you guessed it: nuclear fusion would be less efficient and, because of that, the cosmos would be hard pressed to generate any elements heavier than helium.

I'm sure you can see the problem. If the heaviest element we get is helium, then everyone would talk in really high voices and eventually everyone you know, after laughing themselves silly, would get monster headaches. It's just not practical.

On the other hand, if the aforementioned protons and neutrons were even *slightly* higher in density, then nuclear fusion would be entirely too productive! Again, your instincts are right on; all the hydrogen in the universe would fuse into really heavy elements like iron.

You can't have a universe made of nothing but iron. All you'd have would be heavy metal music. Can you even imagine a world with nothing but Ozzy Osborne and Iron Maiden but no Captain and Tennille or the Carpenters? The horror!

A Brief Lesson in Gravity

The other reason PiLCs think the universe needs to be as hugely stupendously massive as it is centers around its expansion rate.

The closer two massive bodies are to each other, the more powerfully those bodies attract each other.

On the flip side, Hugh Ross says the further apart those big, massive bodies are, the less 'braking effect' gravity has on cosmic expansion.

In other words, when the universe is flying down the road at 600 million MPH, we need something more than your paranoid mother sitting in the passenger seat pumping on invisible brakes. We need gravity to slow it down before it hurts itself.

To summarize, a universe with less density wouldn't form stars like the sun and planets like the earth.

To quote Bill Murray in *Ghostbusters*, that would be "bad."

But adding more density just causes a myriad of problems on the other side. As previously stated, if we had just a little more mass, the universe would expand so slowly that all the stars would turn on themselves and become black holes.

If that were to happen, the density of those gigantic stars would exceed, get this, *five billion tons* per teaspoon.

Imagine trying to bake a cake using that teaspoon set! You'd get a hernia before you even started on the icing.

And that's just the issue with density! There are a myriad of other ingredients that had to be perfectly measured and timed for us to be where we are.

Amazing stuff, huh?

Fun Fact: It takes eight minutes and twenty seconds for light to travel from the sun to the earth. That's the freshest light you're going to get.

Fun Fact: The temperature on the surface of the sun is around 10,000 Fahrenheit. At its core, however, it's a nice and balmy *27 million* degrees! While it's good information to have, the potholders and thermometer we used to get it are totally ruined!

It's Elemental, My Dear

Imagine for a moment you're on the panel representing your High School in your local 'Exercise in Knowledge' program. Your parents had to spring for a very itchy, expensive wool sportscoat that has your High School emblem sewn on the pocket, so the odds of returning it are slim.

At the end of the program, for the win, they ask you, "What was the first element ever created?" And for a bonus, you can also tell the judges which element came in second place.

You came to the contest with heroic dreams of your teammates carrying you out of the gymnasium on their shoulders, forgetting for the moment the four of them combined can barely lift anything heavier than a slide ruler.

You shake that off, center yourself and think back to your science class, trying to picture the poster of the periodic table behind the teacher's desk.

Unfortunately, your teacher falls in the Van Halen category of *Hot for Teacher*, so you've never actually seen the poster behind her impressive décolletage.

As such, you blurt out "Silicon!" and when you slink back on the bus in abject humiliating defeat, your other teammates pummel you with their tiny fists.

Had you answered "Hydrogen," you would have been a hero. If you then stated, "And helium is second on that list," your teammates would have attempted to carry you on their shoulders until they succumbed to a group hernia.

The bottom line here is that, to live, we need just the right amounts of various, diverse elements as well as a perfect expansion rate of our cosmos. Without these things, along with our aforementioned density being perfect, there is no possibility for life.

PiLCs estimate that for the first 365 million years, our universe had only five elements. This changed over time, of course. Otherwise our periodic table would be the size of a Post-it note.

I will admit that I did not know we started out with so few elements. I doubt if many of us are even conscious on a daily basis of things like the elements or our current heart rate. But without them, very few of us would be alive today (excepting, of course, a handful of corporate raiders).

I seriously can't remember the last time I shouted out, "Thank the Lord for boron!" But I should.

Evidently for life to exist we need over 20 different elements heavier than boron. I doubt if this question will ever come up on a SAT, but it's good to know.

Our original five elements were mixed and sautéed in the nuclear furnaces of our first big stars. When one star burned out, another one was formed, and more elements mixed and mingled until we got our current list of 100+ elements.

As it happens, the elements we need for basic survival took nine billion years in the oven before they were ready.

Coincidentally (please read this with a heavy dose of sarcasm), just when our elements were ready, the earth was formed. Imagine that! Scientists peg this at about 4.5 billion years ago.

As a comedian, I love timing. When a piece works, be it a play, joke or song, it comes off as effortless. But we can all smell bad timing a mile away.

Each part of our cosmic recipe had to be done at exactly the right time with just the right amount of each particular ingredient or the whole thing would've fallen like a bad soufflé.

The Original Carbon Footprint

Of all the elements, the most important for us, and all life, is carbon. It's our #1 BFF. Without it, life is a moot point.

Let's take a closer look at carbon, just so you can shake your head in amazement.

To form carbon, you need one part of element #4, which, I'm sure you know, is radioactive beryllium. That element has to absorb the nucleus of element #2, which is helium. When those two elements combine, you get element #6, our life-giving carbon.

Sounds simple enough, right? Introduce the two elements, hope they hit it off and eventually become an item.

But wait! It's more complicated than that! One little known fact is that beryllium (specifically, its unstable cousin, #8 isotope), when you can find it, has a shelf life of 10 to the negative 16 seconds.

Say what?

To make carbon, helium has the impossibly narrow window of opportunity of 0.0000000000000001 seconds to hit on radioactive beryllium.

That's one ten *quadrillionth* of a second.

The pressure is enormous! Imagine a coach rubbing the shoulders of his number 2 element, trying to give him a pep talk…

"Okay, helium, go out there and hit on—Nope, missed it. Okay, shake it off, you're not a failure, you just have to wait for the right opportunity to—Nope, missed it again. Okay, helium, this is your chance—Nope, missed it. Wake up, helium, we need carbon—Nope. Come on, you're my number 2 guy! Put some effort into—Nope! We need carbon to make life! What have you been training for? Get out there and—Nope!"

Without some kind of intervention and guidance, this conversation could last for all of eternity!

But wait! It's even *more* complicated! Not only is the short shelf life of beryllium a problem, but the only way the helium nucleus can be absorbed is for it to match the beryllium's exact level of excitation.

Married couples will understand the impossibility of this phenomenon perfectly.

And so, once elements #2 and #4 are in sync, excitement-wise, then they can collide—as long as it's all over and done within 0.000000000000001 seconds.

Talk about performance anxiety!

What's truly amazing here is that carbon just happens to be the fourth most abundant element in the universe! Do you know how many times helium and radioactive beryllium had to do their special little quickie-excitement collision for that to be true?

The timing had to perfect millions and millions of times! And this is just one element! There are dozens and dozens more elements that had to be cooked up exactly right. How does that just happen by chance?

This is just one of the exceedingly long list of razor's edge fine-tuning that, if you think about it for too long, will make your head explode.

To close this section, I want to give you the lyrics to Tom Lehrer's song, *The Elements*. As you read over the list, try to imagine how each one was miraculously made.

As you sing along, warble as if the tune were written by Gilbert and Sullivan (because it was).

There's antimony, arsenic, aluminum, selenium,
And hydrogen and oxygen and nitrogen and rhenium,
And nickel, neodymium, neptunium, germanium,
And iron, americium, ruthenium, uranium,

Europium, zirconium, lutetium, vanadium,
And lanthanum and osmium and astatine and radium,
And gold, protactinium and indium and gallium,
And iodine and thorium and thulium and thallium.

There's yttrium, ytterbium, actinium, rubidium,

And boron, gadolinium, niobium, iridium,
There's strontium and silicon and silver and samarium,
And bismuth, bromine, lithium, beryllium, and barium.

There's holmium and helium and hafnium and erbium,
And phosphorus and francium and fluorine and terbium,
And manganese and mercury, molybdenum, magnesium,
Dysprosium and scandium and cerium and cesium.

And lead, praseodymium and platinum, plutonium,
Palladium, promethium, potassium, polonium,
And tantalum, technetium, titanium, tellurium,
And cadmium and calcium and chromium and curium.

There's sulfur, californium and fermium, berkelium,
And also mendelevium, einsteinium, nobelium,
And argon, krypton, neon, radon, xenon, zinc and rhodium,
And chlorine, carbon, cobalt, copper, tungsten, tin and sodium.

These are the only ones of which the news has come to Harvard,
And there may be many others but they haven't been discovered.

Exquisite Timing

I feel this whole chapter is starting to resemble a late-night infomercial; as in, "But wait, there's more!"

Building the elements over nine billion years is amazing enough, but while that was happening, as we all know, gravity had to slow down and dark matter had to speed up.

Then two generations of stars had to die out before our current third generation sun was created.

Not to mention the perfect solar system had to form in the Milky Way.

On top of which, a lot of dangerous radiation had to burn itself out in order to leave us with just the right amount of radiation. Yes, there is a 'right' amount of radiation.

By all estimates, the universe wasn't even close to ready for life to exist for the first nine billion years. Still, our home wasn't quite in move-in condition.

After our world was formed, it took another billion years for it to cool down.

Then the continents had to gradually shift to their current locations and a planet full of plants had to work overtime to provide us with adequate oxygen. And then our moon had to be delivered. All of that took another five billion years to accomplish.

Finally, a mere 14 billion years after the Big Bang, everything was ready for the premier of *Guess Who's Coming to Dinner?*

Mind you, if humans arrived any earlier on the timeline, we'd have either suffocated or died from radiation poisoning. It took that long to get our house in order.

As I lay out these facts, you're perfectly welcome to think to yourself, "How the heck am I even alive? The odds of the universe working are incomprehensively slim!"

How right you are!

ET, Where Are You?

In what I'm sure will be a blow to everyone who wants to meet an Extra Terrestrial, PiLC's have determined that it would take the average alien a minimum of 25,000 years to get here—from our galaxy alone!

You don't even want to estimate the needed travel time to and from any galaxies that happen to be in the back forty.

Face it, if there is life somewhere out there, it's not realistic to think that it started any earlier than our life began here. Each planet in the cosmos has to fulfill a long list of requirements before it can even start to think about raising a bunch of children.

PiLCs have been searching a long time for our twin lost somewhere out among the stars and, up to now, have come up short.

It may disappoint our SciFi readers, but the reality is, in our galaxy anyway, we are totally alone. Yes, it appears you memorized the entire Klingon alphabet for nothing!

But if, by some outlandish miracle, there are other races of beings out there, and if they felt the need to pull a Christopher Columbus and explore what's across the ocean of space, they'll still run up against one irrefutable fact: no one can fly faster than the speed of light.

Which means, even if space visitors can navigate around the constant barrage of space debris, they'd still be a minimum of 25,000 years older than when they first started.

Which would obviously suggest you need automation because no one, even in suspended animation, can survive that long of a trip. Most families want to murder each other after three days on the road. Can you imagine being stuck in a cramped space ship with someone for 25,000 years?

The bottom line here is that if Kal El (Superman's given name) had been put in a rocket ship back on Krypton when his red sun was ready to blow up, by the time he got here, he'd be dead. And not just sort of dead. Ma and Pa Kent would find nothing in his rocket ship but dust wrapped up in red, blue and yellow blankets.

The good news is that the Avengers can relax. If Thanos ever does manage to try and take over earth, he'll be so old I doubt if he'll even be able to lift the Infinity Gauntlet on his own.

So, rest easy, Earthlings, we are safe from being attacked from outer space.

All that being said, infiltration by beings from another *dimension* is another matter altogether (cue reprise of dark matter ominous music).

Fun Fact: It took about 3.8 billion years for the plants on our continents to raise our oxygen levels from 1% to our current level of human-life-sustaining level of 21%. The next time you get angry about the weeds in your backyard, get down and thank their ancestors for making this planet livable!

The Sweet Spot

Here are a few more facts that should push the possible thought of alien life forms out of your imagination…

At the center of the Milky Way, deadly radiation radiates (which is what radiation does) out for 20,000 light years from the galactic core, which happens to be a black hole. Not something you want to get close to.

Fortunately, our little planet happens to exist a little over 26,000 light years from the center, putting us 6,000 light years in the safe zone, give or take.

Coincidentally, if we were any further out than 26,000 miles from the galactic center, the elements would be noticeably lighter and we'd have to deal with cars too buoyant to stay on the road.

Other galaxies across the universe are either too dense or have other supergiant galaxies as their neighbors, rendering life and the occasional BBQ all but impossible.

Most galaxy clusters have up to 10,000 galaxies bumping into each other. Our Milky Way has about 40. All that elbow room is what makes life worth living—and even possible.

And another tidbit of amazing information; did you know that stars bounce? I didn't! But the majority of stars bounce up and down above and below the galactic plane.

Before you clutch your pearls, know that our sun bounces no more than 228 light-years above or below our galactic plane. Which, in Baptist terms, is about the same as having a sun that's not dancing, but merely tapping its toe to the music.

You can imagine what it would be like if our sun bounced in and out of view on a daily basis, "It's going to sunny today—wait, no, now it's not. Prepare for sub-zero freezing conditions—wait, no, it's back again. So, we're back to a beautiful sunny—wait, darn it!"

But rest assured that will never happen because, guess what, all the planets in our solar system bounce right along with our sun! It's as if our galaxy is one big trampoline, and we're all bouncing to our heart's content.

The big point here is that we never bounce too *high* or too *low*! If we did, we'd lose the protection of our radiation shield and get zapped by all the bad stuff we're currently protected from in our sweet little softly bouncing pocket.

I'm sure it's not a shock but still worth reporting that we're in the perfect sweet zone of our galaxy, with a sun that stays relatively still and elements that have just enough heft to them.

Our gravity's perfect for our needs, we have an adequate amount of radioactivity that won't melt our faces off, the magnetic field keeps our refrigerator magnets attached and our volcanic activity enhances tourism in Hawaii instead of wiping out all of civilization.

With all of these essential puzzle pieces fitting perfectly in place, it's enough for some of us to take this whole life thing for granted. Beyond that, the point is simple: the chances of another planet having even a portion of our good fortune is slim at best.

What Are the Odds?

Specifically, PiLCs have determined that the odds of all the above conditions being met anywhere else are less than one chance out of ten to the power of ten to the power of 123.

Spelled out in human terms, that's one out of a billion, billion, billion, billion (repeat the word 'billion' one billion times).

I'd print out the odds here, but paper is a precious resource. I'll give you a moment to wrap your head around that.

The fact that we are alive is absolutely, without a doubt, no two ways about it, flat out impossible.

And that's our starting point.

The creation around us is way too complex and convoluted to even contemplate that it all happened as a freak of nature. Nature's just not that freaky.

Now that I've filled your head with more information than you can possibly absorb, let's take a moment to look back at a few of the superstars who brought us to this point.

Major Misfits

Before I dive into the lives of a few of the geniuses who helped lead us all to the scientific promised land, I want to pause with a word of caution: even if it's totally natural, don't let the following accomplishments make you feel insecure in any way.

"Man, that guy discovered the theory of relativity! What have I done?"

While the world is littered with people who have accomplished major achievements, there are probably just as many who just missed reaching their full potential.

Stephen King was rejected over 30 times before his first novel, *Carrie*, was published. In fact, his wife had to fish it out of the trash and encourage him to submit it one more time. That book's paperback edition went on to sell four million copies. Stephen went on to be one of the best-selling authors of all time and today he has to struggle to get by on a mere 40 million dollars a year!

It's well documented that Vincent Van Gogh only sold one painting in his lifetime. Now any Van Gogh is worth millions of dollars. If I ever stumble across a time machine, I will immediately go back and snatch up *The Starry Night*.

David Bowie's teacher said the young man needed to learn that music would never make him a livable wage.

But the ultimate booby prize here goes to Albert Einstein's teacher, who told his parents their son was too ignorant to learn!

I point out these facts to inform you that regardless of what you've been told, there's always a chance you just haven't found your niche yet!

God Bless Einstein

Every man, woman and child should be in absolute awe of Albert Einstein. He was a once-in-a-lifetime freak of nature .

This one man used pen and paper and a massive imagination to figure out that light moves at a constant speed, that there's a thing called gravitational waves and eventually acknowledged that the whole she-bang had a definite beginning.

The thing is, he was only a part-time physicist! He was an engineer who studied physics in his spare time. Some men like to hunt or play with trains. Albert dropped out of the canasta club because he liked to use his leisure time measuring the velocity of light.

And if you need to respect him more, here's a not-so-fun fact: because Mr. Einstein was Jewish in an Aryan based society in pre-WWI Germany, he wasn't allowed to work in any of the local labs. He was relegated to the 'theory' room with the other Jewish physicists.

But that's where the story gets good.

See, Albert's sweet spot was using his imagination! If he had to prove his theorems, who knows how far he and his theories would have advanced. But because all he could do was brainstorm, he was able to ponder his way to the Theory of Relativity.

To use a biblical reference, his oppressive government intended their plans for evil, but God used them for good.

Originally, he called his observations the Principle of Invariance, but that label didn't pop. The marketing people rebranded it as the Theory of Relativity, and it just took off.

Years later, after Edwin Hubble, the telescope guy, proved that galaxies are expanding away from each other, Einstein dropped his theory of self-stretching space and acknowledged that the universe must have had a beginning and, in his words, "the presence of a superior reasoning power."

That's another reason to admire Einstein. He followed the evidence rather than his own suppositions. Smart guy.

What makes Dr. Einstein even more amazing is when he made his discoveries.

It was a century ago, around 1916, right in the middle of World War I. Compared to the tools available to scientists today, Albert was using a slide-ruler made out of toothpicks and a toaster.

So, at a time when people still had to crank their cars to get them to start, could only call friends and family on a *land line*, and movies were silent, this young upstart with crazy hair and one suit made some observations that stood science on its head.

Makes me want to encourage people to give up bowling and take up cancer research as a hobby. Who knows what could come out of that?

Specifically, his Theory of General Relativity predicts that any spinning massive body will drag or twist the space-time fabric in its neighborhood.

To put it another way (that may well make even less sense), if a disk of material orbits a very dense body (say, a neutron star or a black hole), the dragging of the space-time fabric by the dense body will cause said disk of material to wobble like a child's top.

That wobble will then generate oscillations in the intensity of the radiation emitted from the gas in the disk.

It's amazing how it all comes down to how much gas is emitted. Thus, proving my own personal theory that the majority of humor usually comes down to something as base as a fart joke.

What we have here is an engineer looking up in space and figuring out that large dense objects will affect the space-time fabric around them, and in doing so, will cause planets around them to wobble.

He did this by using math! I will never mock the plastic pocket protector crowd again. Well, not to their faces, anyway.

Einstein's Theory of Relativity may have started with pointed questions about his observations, but eventually they led to where we are now. It was sort of a, 'If this, then that…' kind of scenario.

Can you imagine Albert's home life? His wife would ask, "What did you do at work today, dear?"

Then he'd say, "Nothing much. Figured out that dense objects cause lesser dense objects to oscillate. They affect the space-time fabric."

"That's nice. More kielbasa?"

His theory was that gravity, in the presence of matter and energy, actually curves the fabric of space and time.

Where's the explanation from Doc in 'Back to the Future' when you need him?

From that observation, other PiLCs (who were allowed to work in labs) figured out how the universe worked. Simple, huh? Class dismissed!

Specifically, from these observations, Einstein then postulated his famous Theory of Relativity. Like me, I'm sure you can recite his famous equation, E=MC squared, but don't have a clue what it means.

Albert's discovery is that *energy* (E) actually equals *matter* times the *speed of light* (MC squared). Meaning, they are two forms of the same entity.

Say, what?

He's saying that matter can be made from energy and that the flow of time is not constant.

Again, what?

How he got from point A to point B is beyond me. Some people make huge leaps in logic that take the rest of us mortals an entire lifetime to fully comprehend.

He says all matter came from energy. Time began when that energy created matter. Sure sounds like the Big Bang to me!

Stop for a moment to consider that all the matter we see around us in the universe, from the moon to the ocean, to your fingernails, was created by some type of energy.

Some type of energy outside of time.

This is where we cut to Reverend Jim from the sitcom 'Taxi,' and he says, "Whoaaaaa! Mind blown!"

Could it be that energy was created by, I don't know, a thought?

A really powerful, concentrated thought.

By a very intelligent and unbelievably powerful Creator?

If you've got a better explanation of the Big Bang, send it over. But as of this printing, that's the best theory we've got. Otherwise, it apparently came from nothing. And that, my friends, considering the complexity of the final result, is a little hard to swallow.

As a side note, Einstein actually proved the Theory of Relativity in his own lifetime by marrying his cousin.

Ba da dum! (Insert rim shot here.)

Fun Fact: The Theory of Relativity has gone from a 10% possibility of error to .000001% of any chance of it being wrong. In other words, you can expect a blizzard down in Satan's homestead before this will be disproven.

The Universe VI

Time is Relative!

I apologize in advance that this next section is a real head spinner. Sit down, put on your thinking caps and prepare to be amazed!

A big part of Einstein's theory is that if our universe had a beginning, then so does time itself.

I love the concept that time itself is an invention. Before time there was no time.

If it didn't exist, I wonder if people would be more relaxed?

"You're late!"

"Maybe in your world. In mine I'm early!"

Einstein figured out that time passes at a different pace depending on where you are. Another mind-blowing concept. Time is relative!

Evidently changes in gravity will affect the velocity at which we travel which, in turn, will affect the rate at which time flows.

If we were to compare our system's passage of time to another system's passage of time, we would have to first understand that each system most likely has their own system of time. Say that five times fast.

But seriously, everyone has experienced this. When you're in a rush, time moves twice as fast as it usually does. Conversely, when you're stuck in a boring classroom praying for the bell to ring before the teacher gives out a homework assignment, time comes to a full and complete stop.

This is where Einstein coined the term, *relativity*.

46

The law of relativity tells us that the flow of time at one location with high gravity or high velocity is actually slower than the flow at another location that has lower gravity or a higher velocity.

For those of you planning on interplanetary travel, here's a simple equation…

Gravity strength + traveling velocity = rate of time.

It's no 'rightie—tightie, leftie—loosie,' but hold on to the nugget that time is affected by gravity. In other words, your calendar must adjust to the amount of gravity in your current location.

Just as gravity will affect the weight of an object (the reason you don't just float off of this planet and the reason Astronauts can pole vault on the moon without a pole), gravity also affects the flow of time.

If we ever do connect with extraterrestrials, imagine the confusion we'll have trying to meet up.

"We've got you penciled in for a meet & greet on Thursday, but on your planet, that's 400 years from now. Maybe we can reschedule for a more convenient decade."

And I thought traveling through time zones was difficult!

From this theory Einstein theorized that the speed of light actually exists outside of time. It makes sense if you think about it; how would light be able to tell time? It can't wear a watch. It has no pocket in which to hold a smartphone. For better or worse, light is time intolerant.

But here's where light and the concept of time gets interesting metaphysically. Because if the universe and time had a beginning, what came before the event that kicked off their creation?

Many physicists reluctantly agree with the concept of a time before time. Alexander Vilenkin said, "With the proof now in place, cosmologists can no longer hide behind the possibility of a past eternal universe. There is no escape, they have to face the problem of a cosmic beginning."

I hope you can grasp the problem here. For people who tie themselves up in pretzel logic to deny a Grand Designer, the very real problem of a cosmic beginning implies a cosmic Beginner.

Ouch!

Even Stephen Hawking originally agreed with this. In his *A Brief History of Time*, Mr. Hawking says, "Many people do not like the idea that time had a beginning, probably because it smacks of divine intervention."

Gerald L Schroeder has theorized in his book, *The Science of God*, that from our perspective, the universe is 14 billion years old. But he then hypothesizes that, from the cosmic clock's perspective, since time is relative, the universe could well be just six days old!

According to him, *both* science and the Bible are correct!

Gerald says that the Bible uses a few hundred words to explain events that took several billion years to unfold.

It's definitely a strong example of 'Creation for Dummies,' but if this is correct, I can understand why the God of the Bible would have explained His handiwork this way.

The creation story is the opening of a long and wonderful book explaining who God is and who we are, with lots of interesting, poignant stories along the way.

The whole thing would have gotten hopelessly bogged down if God spent too much time explaining the endless details of His creation. He simply wanted His people to know He did it and let it go at that.

Is Mr. Schroeder's version true?

Are science and religion in agreement, but just coming at it from different perspectives?

There's no doubt that our own personal prejudices affect what we ultimately believe, no matter which side of the fence we ultimately fall.

Let's examine the opinions on either side of the fence, shall we?

Grasping at Objects Used to Suck Up Liquid

I apologize up front if what follows is offensive, but it often feels as if those firmly entrenched in the secularist camp react to the news that everything in our universe was exquisitely designed and the subsequent idea of an actual Designer behind that design like this...

"La la la la la! I can't hear you! There are infinite universes! It started on its own! You're all haters! Help, help, I'm being repressed!"

The amount of work non-theists go to, to deny the reality of the logical conclusion of a Creator behind the Big Bang curtain, is, to my way of thinking, quite astounding! On the other hand, you've got to admire their dogged persistence!

They've postulated the existence of multi-verses, an oscillating universe (denying the 2nd law of thermodynamics) and a host of other obscure theories. All with one purpose in mind: find any theory that leaves out a Creator.

Not to be unfair, but it's the scientific version of, dare I say it, grasping at straws. The irony is that these unsubstantiated theorems have sprung from PiLCs who claim to be people who follow the clues of nature to their natural conclusion.

The problem is simple: when you start with the prejudiced view that God doesn't exist, then it naturally follows that all your conclusions will be tainted by that particular world view.

These far-reaching theories are first cousins to all those monkeys sitting in a room banging away on typewriters, hoping to eventually come up with the collected works of Shakespeare.

Of course, that's patently absurd, and so is the idea of a multiverse.

The comic book fantasy of the multiverse goes like this: ours isn't the only universe. Rather, it's one of billions and billions of other universes that somehow exist side by side in other dimensions without managing to bump into each other.

The obvious appeal of this theory is the random aspect of it. Otherwise it makes no sense, nor does it have a shred of proof of existence.

Stephen Hawking, in his later years, is the poster child for this particular brand of blind faith. I will admit here and now that I'm not worthy of tying the bootlaces of Mr. Hawking. He was far more intelligent than I, but that doesn't necessarily mean his final conclusion was correct.

He missed the boat for one very good reason: he ignored where the evidence was pointing.

According to his ex-wife, he refused to even consider an Intelligent Designer. He was bound and determined to prove that the universe was created without cause. Whether or not he created the idea, he latched on to the infinite multiverse.

Mind you, the Big Bang has been proven to .000001% accuracy, but Stephen Hawking supported something concocted out of pure imagination because it supported his presupposition.

Sure, the infinite multiverse is *possible*, but as I've repeatedly stated, it's not *probable*.

The final blow against the multiverse is the very same one that the single universe atheists run up against: who or what started the multiverse?

Just because there's a bajillion of them still doesn't mean they started on their own. In fact, the idea of a multiverse is even more complicated! Think of all the co-existing dimensions you'll need just to keep everything in order!

Try as they may, scientists have yet to discover one complex thing in the entire universe that has ever put itself together.

There's a famous case where a scientist from the Smithsonian found some 60,000 fossils on a dig, but hid them in his office for over six decades because they didn't fit his worldview.

Seems the fossils showed fully developed fins and skeletons which contradicted Darwin's theory that we started as single cell organisms.

It's as if a number of these physicists are police detectives who are willing to look the other way. They have the criminal at the scene of the crime. He's confessed. He has the motive. But they keep looking for clues that might better explain who killed their victim, since they all hold on to the belief that people are inherently good—despite evidence to the contrary.

While I admire astrophysicist Neil DeGrasse Tyson, even he likes to play both sides. Against all reason and our observable law of causality, he wonders if perhaps our universe was always here, or just popped into existence from nothing!

Nothing? Really, Neil? Are you really suggesting something as intricate as our universe came into existence without rhyme or reason?

If you insist on staying in the non-theistic camp, here's what you're saying...

- All living things came from chance from a non-living event.
- Consciousness came from a void which is not conscious.
- Our emotions, intellect, spirit and will came from something that has no emotions, intellect, spirit or will.
- The impossibly intricate fine tuning of the universe was a complete accident.
- Jesus was either completely delusional or a world class liar.
- Mickey Mouse is a lousy, stinking Commie!

Personally, I think it takes more faith to believe in the list above than it does to accept the concept of an intelligence behind our creation.

For our universe to happen by total random chance has been compared to the odds of a Boeing 747 being formed as a result of a tornado hitting a junkyard. I actually believe the odds are stronger for that to happen than for the universe to happen by itself.

Can anyone recall a single higher functioning machine or life form coming from complete chaos?

It's just not how life works.

Simply put, the second law of thermodynamics states that the entropy of any isolated system always increases. Which is just a fancy way of saying everything, everywhere, will eventually break down.

Against all scientific reason, this appears to be exactly the opposite of what the non-theists have come to believe.

Fun Fact: Nicolas Leonard Sadi Carnot is considered the father of thermodynamics. Though he died at the age of 36, his work on understanding the properties of heat and perfecting the steam engine (attempting to increase its efficiency beyond a paltry 3%) not only led to the discovery of the 1st and 2nd laws of thermodynamics, but also to the diesel engine. Because he died in a cholera epidemic in France, his writings on his discoveries were feared to be contaminated, so they were buried along with him at his funeral.

The Universe VII

Unearthing Young Earthers

On the other side of the aisle, Young Earth Creationists seem to really have a problem with science claiming that the universe might possibly be older than Moses' grandma.

They get very tied up with which day things were created and how the big bang is an atheistic view of creation.

As someone who lives a life of faith, let me say in the strongest terms possible, "Baloney!"

Here's how I reconcile the Bible and science: when God told Moses how He created everything, He was talking to a man who had a very limited education. Writing had been invented, because Moses eventually wrote the story down, but I doubt he knew cursive.

Think of God as a college professor talking to a bunch of slightly dim preschoolers. He's a deity who exists outside of time trying to explain complex physics to people who only had a passing knowledge of basic math.

On top of which, the Egyptian's written language consisted entirely of emojis, for goodness sake!

I've always wondered what it would be like to be a court reporter back in ancient Egypt.

A lawyer would ask, "Read that back."

The court reporter would say, "Man with bird head, snake, water, man, woman, Sun God Ra, big eye."

"Your honor, I rest my case!"

53

To say God dumbed down the complexity of the creation would not be a gross exaggeration. Common sense suggests He simplified it and relayed it in six easy-to-understand steps.

We may not understand black holes or thermodynamics, but we can grasp light and dark.

Pastor Tim Keller says the very first chapter of Genesis should, in actuality, be interpreted as a song!

While this may be considered heresy in some circles, I don't believe that God created the universe in six of our days.

The most logical reason I can come up with for my belief is simply light.

We know how fast light travels. Measuring light and looking at the expansion of the universe ultimately gave us its age.

When we look at stars, we're actually looking into the past because it's taken, sometimes, billions of years for that light to get to us.

I know that God could have magically made the whole universe and back-timed the light from stars, but why would He? We get back to our possible/probable conundrum.

This is an 'observable' universe. We've landed in a unique position where we have a clear view of our surroundings and can make intelligent decisions based on that view. If we were in a constant fog, we'd have to make a lot of this stuff up.

God wants us to use our brains and all the scientific knowledge available to understand Him and how awesome His creation is. That's why He gave us intellect instead of just instincts.

Another point is that God is outside of time. Even He says that a thousand years is like a day to Him.

In Genesis, the Creator's not giving an exact measurement or accounting of His creation. He can't. It's too much for us to take in. All we need to know is that He did it.

So, God told us what happened in steps. It so happens those steps more or less line up with science. Maybe not in the exact order, but is that really so important?

First there was dark and the universe began.

Check.

Stars in the heavens were created.

Check.

The planet was formed and covered with water.

Check.

Then the land masses appeared and vegetation sprang up.

Check.

Eventually your relatives started walking around, wars were fought, books were invented and here we are!

Check!

Still, there are people who reject what the PiLCs have discovered and insist on hanging on to the belief that God made the whole thing in a week.

The way I see it is that young earthers have the very same problem a lot of non-theistic scientists have: namely, they start off with their preconceptions set in stone and are unwilling to consider any other options.

To clarify, physicists like Hugh Ross would be "creationists," or people who agree with the basics of science and believe God made the universe in His own sweet time.

In an entirely different camp, Ark Encounter owner Ken Ham is the poster child of someone who clings to the belief of a physically young earth that's somewhere in the neighborhood of 10,000 years old.

Scientists who refuse to believe in a Designer/Creator look at the facts, yet deny any logical conclusion that even suggests the very obvious outcome that might exist outside of their worldview.

Young Earthers appear to be in the very same boat. They won't listen to what scientists have discovered because the facts with which they are presented seem to be in conflict with their firmly held beliefs.

To be so thoroughly pigheaded and insist that the world had to be made in six straight days, is, to my mind, the height of hubris.

You might as well stand on a street corner and throw a tantrum, screaming, "This is how God did it and I won't listen to any other facts, ever!"

I believe with all my heart, mind and soul that our world was exquisitely created by a loving Benefactor. To me, all of our most recent discoveries don't diminish what the Designer/Creator did. I believe they actually enhance it.

I'm stunned by how much work it took to get us here. Sure, six days would have been amazing, but to take 14 billion years is, to me, even a greater testimony of a loving, caring, nurturing Creator.

Still, ultimately, it's not the main issue, so I'll leave it here.

When we get to the other side, we'll be able to see how He did it and all our questions will be answered. Until then, let's continue muddling through with the best information we have.

Details aside, most religious folks believe that an intelligent entity outside of space, matter and time created a Big Bang from which all blessings flow.

And if that's not enough for you, or if you believe I'm going straight to hell for dissenting from your firmly held convictions, I'll just pack my handbasket and go saddle up the horse I rode in on.

Astrology

As I came to grips with the amazing complexity as well as the size of the universe (the study of *astronomy*), it struck me that people who actually buy into *astrology* (the baseless belief that stars control our destinies) are neck and neck in the gullibility marathon with folks who send their money to prosperity preachers and Nigerian princes.

People who buy into this mess can't even determine how many people are in their camp. Their own numbers range from 22% to 73% of the population, which roughly tracks with its percentage of accuracy.

Let's look at the facts. Except for the moon's glow, all the light we see in the night sky is actually from the past. Many stars from which that light is emanating may well have already blown up.

So, say some star wanted to influence your life. To do so, it had to know who you were more than a million years before you were even born. Then it had to time its life-influencing light to hit the earth just as you were ready to read your horoscope that very day.

The odds are off-the-charts amazing!

Since we get hit by similar light by the Sun, which doesn't seem to influence anyone's behavior except around the equator, there must be something super special about all the stars out in the universe.

And how does their magical power work, exactly? If one constellation has a billion stars and another only has, say, half a billion, isn't that horribly unfair to those of us controlled by the lesser galaxies? I suppose the lesser galaxies get the undesirable traits, like stupidity or stubbornness, while the larger ones get charity and altruism.

As there are twelve different astrological signs, it seems to suggest that somehow all of these constellations, that just happen to be millions of light years away from each other, with no communication devices, somehow worked with each other to split up all of humanity into twelve different very distinctive groups—and then keep track of each group through all of time!

"Hey, Sagittarius! Have you seen my Cancer? He was supposed to look out for a new business opportunity today but I can't find him anywhere!"

"Can't help you! I'm trying to see if Gemini is still influencing the moon in my seventh house! How it got into my house I'll never know!"

And if all of that isn't ridiculous enough, the universe is expanding! So, the stars that were thought to control the destinies of humanity have moved on from their original locations in ancient times and have left no forwarding number.

Where we see them right now isn't even close to their current address. If they're sending out signals, they're several million years late and a couple of billion dollars short.

I am truly sorry if dashing your scientifically unfounded, wishful thinking fantasy is too mean for you, but most of us live over here in a place I like to call reality. Come visit. Eventually you get used to it.

A Creative Designer

That apostasy aside, let's take a deep breath and look again at a few facts that support a Creative Designer...

If the universe expanded a trillionth, trillionth, trillionth of a second faster or slower, it either would dissipate into gas or collapse into a black hole. In other words: no life.

- If the nuclear force was manipulated to either increase or decrease the number of elements by just five percent; no life.
- If the balance between the electromagnetic force and the gravitational force was adjusted by just a hair: no life.

Nobody touch our universe! It could collapse any second!

Fun Fact: When ancient Babylonians created the zodiac over 3,000 years ago, they were working with a 12-month calendar— but there were 13 constellations, so they ditched Ophiuchus. To further complicate matters, NASA pointed out that the earth's axis doesn't even point in the same direction as it did when the original constellations were drawn, so all birth signs now have different date ranges. When astrology lovers got upset their new signs were no longer in alignment with their tattoos, NASA responded, "We study astronomy, not astrology. We didn't change any zodiac signs, we just did the math."

The Universe VIII

Other Things I Can't Explain

Before I close out this section, I'd like to share a few events from my own life that defy explanation. Take them all with a shaker full of salt, but the fact remains that, just like the creation of our cosmos, 1) they really happened and 2) they should have played out much differently.

The first involves flying glass.

Back when we first were married, my wife and I were like ships in the night. She worked a nine-to-five job, while I took the day shift looking after our daughter and writing unsuccessful screenplays before heading out to wait tables at night.

On one of those days I planned to make a nice Chinese dinner. I took out the frozen package, put the skillet on the stove and set the glass lid next to it. But when I turned on the stove, I mistakenly turned on the electric burner under the lid rather than beneath the skillet. I went about my business, thinking nothing of it, until I smelled something funny. I looked over and saw my mistake. The burner was red hot, and the lid above it was starting to smoke.

I moved to the stove, turned off the burner, and, like an idiot, looked down at the lid. Which, at that very second, exploded into a hundred pieces.

Hot glass. Flying directly at my face. Shocked, I grimaced and braced for the worst.

Somehow, it all missed me. The glass flew all over the counter and up to 10 feet behind me, burning holes in both the carpet in the dining room as well as the linoleum of the kitchen floor.

I got one small cut on my thumb. Nothing else. It was if someone or something stood in front of me at the moment of the explosion, shielding me from the impact.

Weird, huh?

The next involves a falling garage door.

When my son was a toddler, he loved lawnmowers. Every time we went on a walk, he always begged to stop at any neighbor's house who happened to be mowing their grass. We got him a toy lawnmower to push around our house, lawnmower socks and investigated an internship with the local Blow-N-Go landscapers.

On this particular day I was getting ready to mow our lawn, so naturally our three-year-old son was out in the garage with me.

On this windy day, the spring-loaded wooden garage door was up as I moved in and out of the garage. It was something I'd done a hundred times without it ever falling down once. I had just pulled the lawnmower out of the garage when I heard a loud bang.

Evidently the wind had slammed the garage door shut. I turned, looked down and saw a picture that haunts me to this day.

I saw my young boy's hips and legs sticking out from under the garage door, looking like the wicked witch from the *Wizard of Oz* when Dorothy landed a house on her. I ran over, grabbed the handle and threw up the door. There was my son, on his back, crying.

I made the mistake of picking him up to comfort him. I was later told it would have been best to not move him in case there was some kind of spinal damage.

We called the paramedics, they came and took him to the hospital to have him checked out. Miraculously, he came out of it entirely unharmed.

To give you a picture of the severity of this accident, a friend came over later that night. He picked the garage door up a few feet and let it fall. The sound of the heavy door crashing closed was frightening. He said, "There's no way your son could've survived that."

And yet he did. The door didn't hit him in the head, or break his leg. It landed directly in his stomach, and somehow the weight of the door was absorbed by someone or something taking the brunt of the impact.

The last example involves a traffic accident.

In my current job, I fly around the country, telling jokes and stories to various groups. On one such day I was driving to the airport at 4:30 in the morning.

While I generally don't love getting to the airport in those dark hours, those flights are almost a pleasure because of the lack of L.A. traffic.

This morning was no different. The pre-dawn freeway was wide open. I was literally the only one on the road.

Just as I passed a freeway interchange, a car came out of nowhere, flew across several lanes and tried to merge into mine. I heard the engine roar off to the side, saw something barreling toward me out of the corner of my eye and a moment later, I felt it.

I was going the speed limit (well, maybe 5 miles over, but that's within the legal range) when a literal bat-out-of-hell flew across three lanes, ran into my car, then bounced off like we were both bumper cars and burned rubber out of there.

The strange thing was, I felt the car hit me, but at the same time, I knew it didn't. Something or someone acted as a buffer, taking the brunt of the impact.

Against the laws of physics, a car had come out of nowhere, attempted to occupy the space I was in, then subsequently bounced off of my car without causing any damage to me or my vehicle whatsoever. That'll get your heart racing!

Not to go all holy roller on you, but in each case, I felt an immediate spiritual presence that I couldn't explain away.

I am not protected from everything in life. More often than not, my prayers seem to bounce off the ceiling. But on my darkest days, these events bubble to the surface of my memory, helping curtail my litany of complaints over whatever injustice I am experiencing at the moment.

Knowing I was protected at least three times in my life somehow helps me get through the tough times.

I have no doubt in my mind that when we cross over to the other side, to a person, we'll all be shocked and amazed by two things:

1. the 'making of' video of the universe showing us once and for all how He built every galaxy down to the last molecule and
2. all the ways the One who I believe has the whole world in His hands guided and protected each one of us throughout our lives.

Why?

If your head is about to explode from the long list of fun facts and theories I've laid out here, I totally understand.

As I close out the universe section, I am reminded of a brilliant bit Mel Brooks and Carl Reiner started many years ago called *the 2,000-Year-Old Man*. On one of their albums, Carl Reiner asked Mel (playing the 2,000-year-old man) about the invention of religion.

Mel goes off with a very reasonable explanation. He talks about a very strong caveman named, of course, Phil. Not only was Phil the strongest man in the village, he was also the smartest, and everyone worshipped him as a god.

One day Phil was climbing a tree and he was struck by lightning. When Phil fell out of the tree, dead as a doornail, everyone looked up and said, "There's something bigger than Phil!"

And that's my belief. There's something bigger than Phil.

My bottom line in all of this is simple. I may have over or under emphasized a few of the facts regarding the creation of our universe, but the eventual conclusion is rock solid: someone or something went to an awful lot of trouble to make our home.

I, for one, appreciate it.

Recipe—One Universe

1. Set oven to billion, billion, billion degrees.

2. Speak universe into existence.
3. Let expand to taste.
4. Begin with 5 elements. Cook separately.
5. Add gravity, then slowly mix in dark matter.
6. For decoration, add 50 billion trillion stars.
7. Make large stars, explode. From debris, form second stars, explode. From debris, form sun.
8. Form Milky Way. Set aside.
9. After 9.5 billion years, form earth and moon.
10. Create life.
11. Rest.

Fun Fact: While Sigmund Freud and his cronies believed religion was a pathological malignant social force that encouraged
irrational thoughts, today's American Psychological Association
says that since 85% of the world's population embrace some sort
of religious belief, they theorize it may just be a byproduct of the
way our brains work. We've been downgraded from 'crazy' to 'it
appears we're just made that way.'

For What It's Earth

Hopefully you can agree that the stunning complexity and wonder of the universe in which we live is beyond our wildest imagination.

I put it to you that our planet may well be even more amazing!

Not that it's a competition. If it were, the universe would probably take the evening wear category, but earth is a slam dunk for 'Miss Congeniality.'

So many factors had to come together in perfect synchronicity for life to have reared its shy little head on this puny rock that to lay out the odds of our appearance is beyond staggering.

On the outside chance that you think I'm prone to exaggeration, I'll point out that in high school I placed third in the state in the 100-yard hyperbole.

Our privileged planet sustains life for countless plants and animals and close to 8 billion people. Half of whom are currently trying to make it as actors in Los Angeles!

One of the wonders of this planet is that it's basically one huge scrapbook, providing tons of clues as to what went on before we arrived on the scene.

We've got fossil records, isotope records, geological layers, sediment cores, ice cores and tons of old men who eat lunch at Wendy's every day who are more than willing to tell any passer by what it was like back in their day.

Basic Planetary Requirements

FYI, the most basic of requirements for any planet attempting to support life is that it must be close to a star that can provide the minimal conditions for said life.

It's estimated that only about 0.001% of all stars are capable of that task. But as there are hundreds of billions of stars, our universe should be packed to the gills with ETs, right?

Not so fast, buckaroo! Once the stars align, you've got to place them in the right galaxy, as not just any galaxy will do. It has to be a spiral one. None of those elliptical or irregular ones you find at second hand stores. About 6% of our non-dwarf galaxies are spirals. The other 94% have recently been voted off the island.

It also has to have just the right amount of radiation, because, let's face it, wearing those bulky HazMat suits 24/7 would get real old real fast.

You can't be too close or too far away from the center of the galaxy or your oxygen and carbon would be waaaay off! Then you'd be light headed and write bad checks. Society would collapse.

The bottom line here is that there are a million and one things that could have gone wrong before we sprang into existence, so, as you go about your daily activities, try to appreciate the fact that, regardless of how it all got here, the current reality that we are alive and able to pitch a bitch about politics, the environment and our neighbors is truly a wonderful thing!

Copernicus and His Pals

Before we jump into a long list of fascinating facts and figures, let's take a peek at some very smart people who were instrumental in getting us to where we are now, information-wise.

When the 1500's rolled around, Nicolaus Copernicus decided it was high time he discovered something that would get his name in the history books.

Back in 1492, an upstart named Columbus stole his thunder when he had a catchy little ditty written about him when he sailed the ocean blue, so Nicolaus knew he needed a big attention grabber.

His big contribution was to suggest, gasp, that our home actually revolves around the sun, not the other way around. At the time this was, to hit the nail on the head, earth-shattering.

When people are fed wrong intel their whole lives and are then faced with the truth, it doesn't always go down well. Think Neo and *The Matrix*.

Regardless of how many powdered wigs were knocked askew at this new notion, Copernicus stuck to his guns, and eventually science won out.

The issue here was not with the Bible itself, but rather, with the church. Assumptions had been made and history has shown that religious types are never particularly keen on being proven wrong. Additionally, if those religious types happen to hold any kind of political power, the truth-sayers are often excommunicated, or worse—barred from the weekly potluck!

Not to be outdone, in the early 1600's Johannes Kepler trotted out his three Laws; the third of which states, "the square of the orbital period of a planet is proportional to the cube of its mean distance from the sun."

As a side note, his first two laws were, 'Measure twice, cut once,' and 'Maidens; can't live with thee, can't live without thee! Be I right?'

There's a reason you've never heard of Kepler. It's his formula. Einstein's theory popped. It had legs. But no one is going to write a romantic ballad based on the squares of this, or the mean distance from that.

No matter the theory, you've still got to sell it to the tweens. They drive the market no matter in which century you live.

Regardless of its lack of marketability, later in the century Isaac Newton used these discoveries to lay the foundation for his more general and generally more understandable theories of motion and gravity.

Fortunately, Newton was not only a mathematical genius, but was savvy enough to wrap up his theories around home spun stories like, "there I was, sitting under an apple tree…"

More than two centuries later, Einstein came up with his Theory of Relativity, using the foundations postulated by both Kepler and Copernicus.

Basically, this is the mathematical version of rock & roll. Just as gospel music laid the foundation for Little Richard, who then laid the foundation for the Beatles, who then paved the way for pretty much every garage band after that, these geniuses built on the foundation that was presented to them by the scientists who came before.

Rarely does inspiration happen in a vacuum. Even though I don't understand how the math brain works, I appreciate the fact that people on that particular wavelength get each other and use one discovery to leapfrog over to the next.

Anyway, after a lot of work by a lot of very smart and dedicated PiLCs, by the early 1930's, we had most of the basic information about our local address fairly well worked out.

Now on to the really juicy details!

The Marvelous Mrs. Milky Way

I feel it may well be impolite to give a galaxy's size, but we're all friends here, right?

Ms. Way consists of 100 billion stars flattened into a spiral shape. It's 80,000 light years in diameter and 6,000 light years thick.

Currently we're hidden off in a corner in the only habitable zone of our galaxy.

Another thing you need to know about our planet is that, even though it's not the biggest or the strongest of the planetary bodies, for our purposes, it's the absolutely perfect size.

If we were smaller, our gravity wouldn't keep our atmosphere in, resulting in the entire planet having to be on inhalers.

If we were larger, our core would probably cool quicker, resulting in a weaker magnetic force, causing the sun to burn us to a crisp and everyone's To Do list to slide off the refrigerator.

Not only that, but if we were on a planet, say, twice our size, our surface gravity would be 3.5 times higher. I don't have to tell you what that would do to jump balls in the NBA.

Another problem with larger planets is the fact that they tend to attract more asteroids and comets. People, Bruce Willis can only save this planet so many times!

It may not need to be said, but we need to be satisfied with the size we were born with. Regardless of what the other planets have, for us, either a surgical augmentation or reduction would end up a total disaster.

We're a nice B cup. Anything more or less would be a waste.

Placement

It turns out that everyone on earth totally lucked out in what appears to be the only location in the entire universe that not only encourages life, but can sustain it as well.

For you to be reading this, we had to land in a solar system that resides in a galaxy that lives in a supercluster of galaxies exactly like ours.

See, the universe expanded for several billion years. During that time, explosions were pretty much a daily occurrence.

The reason no one wants to live next door to a Meth Lab is that there's a very high likelihood that one day their roof is going to go up like a fireball. Plus, Meth-heads rarely keep up with proper lawn maintenance.

Before we could move in, we needed the universe to calm down a bit. It also had to expand enough so that we wouldn't be in constant danger. Nothing will kill a family's vacation plans quicker than running into another galaxy. It's a mess!

This is also the reason you don't want to be the first one to move into a new neighborhood. Our solar system's fine now, but for the first 740 million or so years, it was downright dangerous!

Asteroids and comets were bombarding our little system on such a regular basis that they tended to literally melt the planets they came in contact with.

However, this is good news for us, as it's where we got some of our rich deposits of uranium, thorium and the like, while, at the same time, the barrage of space debris managed to kick up and remove much of our atmosphere's chlorine.

When the dust settled, our home was great—but you certainly wouldn't want to live here while those elements were being delivered.

Secondly, at the start, our sun would have regular tantrums of solar flares and bursts of intense X-ray and ultraviolet radiation. It has, thankfully, matured, and doesn't behave like that anymore.

As I stated earlier, we also desperately needed our sun to be a non-bouncing one! Otherwise we'd all be exposed to tons of dangerous cosmic radiation, and it's hard to have a neighborhood picnic when everyone's face is melting off.

It goes without saying that we had to be in a spiral galaxy and reside within that galaxy in a very narrow habitable zone.

Thankfully, our Cosmic Real Estate Agent was able to find us a home that met all of our minimum requirements in a neighborhood with reasonable association fees.

It also helps to have big brother planets nearby like Jupiter and Saturn to either attract or deflect all the comets and meteors away from us. Think of those planets as our first line of defense.

Oh, one more thing: we need a planet tilted just so, that rotates at our exact rate, with the right amount of gravity so that methane escapes but oxygen stays. Otherwise, when you light a match, the whole planet's going up. Our tilted rotation rate is also instrumental in facilitating things like rainfall and seasons.

Then we need a moon to stabilize that tilt and exert enough gravity to control our tides.

Finally, we can't be too close or too far away from the sun.

Too close and all of our water evaporates. Too far away and everything freezes.

I'm sure you can see by just a few of these examples that we are extremely fortunate that all of these issues were worked out before we even knew what we were getting into.

Nine Zones

All of the above requirements are necessary before we settle down in a neighborhood that possesses the nine known Habitable Zones.

I'm sure you can guess most of the zones needed: water, oxygen, a good school, anchor retailers, reasonable restaurants, plus easy freeway access.

Miraculously, our little earth is the only planet we've found that hits all nine zones. It's location, location, location, people!

Specifically, our UV radiation has to fall within a certain range to allow life. If we don't get enough, we don't manufacture vitamin D. If we get hit with too much, we can get cancer. It's estimated that only about 3% of all planets in our galaxy could possibly hit this particular standard.

Another zone involves photosynthesis. Without this amazing wonder, we wouldn't have large warm-blooded animals like cows, which means we'd have to eat Chick Fil A all the time, and they're closed on Sundays, so how would we get around that?

Another habitable zone necessity is a protective ozone layer. This regulates the amount of radiation that gets down to the planet. Currently our ozone layer absorbs 97 to 99 percent of the sun's damaging UV rays, while allowing the good radiation to pass through to our surface.

The question of balance here is of paramount importance. Too much ozone—large animals can't breathe. The inevitable implication being that Shaq could never have played for the Lakers. Too little ozone—we all burst into flame.

Bottom line, let's do everything we can to keep our ozone layer!

To round out the final habitable zones, we need a breathable atmosphere and to possess a strong magnetic force. This force is best if the planet has an outer core of molten iron surrounding an inner core of solid iron.

There has been discussion in the scientific community as to whether or not having access to a strong WiFi signal falls in the habitable zone category, but the jury's still out on that particular topic.

To my mind, it's not whether or not there's life on other planets, but rather, *How Did We Get Here?* The odds of all of these very particular, extremely specific, list of demands being met are outside the realm of chance.

We currently reside in miracle territory.

Thankful

Just living life on this planet in our universe is beyond amazing. One of our greatest gifts is that we just don't know how lucky we are and how protected from disaster on a daily basis.

If we made a list of everything that could go wrong at any moment, I don't know if any of us would ever get a good night's sleep ever again.

With that in mind, I'm including a very simple non-denominational prayer here that anyone can pray, especially if you never want to be asked to pray again.

"I'm thankful today that my skin didn't melt off from excessive radiation and that our atmosphere isn't made up of dangerous chlorine gas and that we are not constantly bombarded by planet-killing asteroids or comets and that gravity keeps my relatives from floating off into the freezing cold abyss of space and bless this food and our bodies for thy service. Amen."

Fun Fact: The earth weighs 6 sextillion metric tons and is gaining weight every year. To be fair, most of that is water weight.

Our Privileged Planet II

Here Comes the Sun

One of the reasons our planet took so long to be finished, is that along with George Harrison, we were waiting for the sun.

See, for you and your family to survive, we need a very particular type of sun and that took a looooooong time to work out.

When listing the requirements needed for our perfect sun, you'll need to insist on a middle-aged third generation class G bachelor star. If it's not, swipe left! This is very important!

First generation stars are huge and carry entirely too much radiation for anything to survive, let alone get a nice, healthy tan.

The second-generation star is a bit better, but it doesn't know its own strength, so those stars will kill you as well.

The only star we can stand to be around, the only star who is fit to orbit, is our very own class Three, Pop I star. Thank the Lord we found each other!

Then there's the light emanating from the sun itself. Visible light is actually an extremely ever-so-small part of the electromagnetic spectrum. Somehow, we got lucky with our particular atmosphere in that we can actually see light.

Blue skies and white fluffy clouds? They're unheard of anywhere else in our solar system (and probably our entire galaxy).

Saturn would kill for a sunset like ours! Mercury hasn't had dew since their planet started! We'll get to Mars and Venus by the end of the chapter, but suffice to say, no one's standing on the surface of those planets singing, "Oh, what a beautiful morning..."

To show you how hard our sun works, every second of every day, 4.5 *billion tons* of hydrogen are turned into helium in the *fifteen-million-degree* core. If anyone ever asks you how the sun manages to float in the middle of space, the answer is obvious; lots of helium!

I don't want you to skip over the previous fact. We're talking 4.5 tons *every single second*. That's 270 billion tons every minute, or a rough average of 16,200 billion tons of hydrogen is turned into helium every single hour. Why? How many balloons can the sun possibly fill up?

Not only that, but every single day the sun loses a million tons of its surface material every single second. We call these high energy particles 'solar wind.'

Again, I want you to try to absorb that fact. Our sun loses 86,400 million tons of surface material every day. I don't know how long the sun can continue to lose so much weight. That, combined with the endless manufacture of helium, makes me wonder when it's going to up and float away!

Still, the main question on everyone's lips usually revolves around the issue of "When's it going to burn out?"

PiLCs estimate our personal star has about four to five billion years left before it burns out, so I think we're good.

Built for Speed

Here's where it gets amazing. Again! We circle the sun in an elliptical pattern, not in a circle. Evidently when it comes to orbiting a sun, circles are so last eon!

But, and this is a very important 'but,' we're only off of a perfect circle by three degrees. If it were any more we'd either freeze or fry to death.

The three degrees lets us brag that we're in the elliptical club, but it's not enough to throw our entire population into chaos. PiLCs have determined that if our orbit were a circle, when you went on a trip, you'd have to pack for both Antarctica and hell. Thankfully, an elliptical pattern saves us from having to drag around excessive luggage.

Since I'm talking about orbiting the sun, I'd love to know if any of you have any sensation of movement? Because even if you don't feel it, you are definitely bookin' it, baby!

For the earth to make one complete rotation, it has to spin around at something like 1,000 mph at the equator. If you live in the Midwest, you're practically cruising along at 875 mph. The people standing on the North Pole are merely dizzy.

Not only are we spinning, but to get around the sun in a year, we're flying through space at 20 miles a second. That's 72,000 mph without even shifting into third gear.

Do you feel like you're flying through space at 72,000 miles per hour? I don't, but every time we go outside we should all throw up our arms and yell, "Wheeeee!"

But wait, there's more! While we're racing around the sun, at the same time, our entire solar system is careening around the center of the Milky Way at ten times that speed! That comes out to 720,000 miles an hour.

Man, whatever you do, do *not* step off of this planet! If you turn your back for just a second, this bad boy will disappear over the horizon.

If all of those speed estimates are true, every single one of us should look like we've just parachuted out of an airplane, with our cheeks flapping back like a pair of basset hound's ears.

But somehow, we're oblivious to the speed at which we're traveling. What a great gift!

The next time you get pulled over for speeding and the Cop asks, "Do you know how fast you were going?" Say…

"Well, Officer, I know I'm rotating at close to 900 mph, while flying around the sun at 72,000 mph and around the Milky Way at more than 720,000 mph. Which should all make the 50 I was doing in the school zone feel fairly insignificant, don't you think?"

Personally, whenever I'm bored, I like to jump up in the air just to see how far the planet will rotate underneath me. Last week I jumped up in Los Angeles and came down in Fresno. Things just tend to move faster out here.

Our Moon

Along with our sun, the moon is another perfect addition to the party.

Our moon is 1/400th the diameter of the sun. But in a weird coincidence, it is also 1/400th as far from us as the sun, making the pair often appear to be the same size in the sky.

This may not seem like an important piece of information to you, but to PiLCs, it's another barnstormer.

It's all about our eclipses. Which, because of their relative size in the sky, can be 'total.' That is, our tiny moon entirely covers up our sun, leaving only its surface aura visible.

This is important because that's the way scientists can figure out what elements and light the sun is giving out.

It was during such an eclipse back in the 1800's that a scientist was first able to see the light spectrum. Add that to the long list of strange coincidences that help us observe our surroundings.

Now, how our moon got here is subject to much debate. The best minds figure a huge asteroid collided with earth, causing no small amount of destruction, and the debris formed our moon.

As in life, sometimes the worst thing somehow, eventually, can turn into the best thing. The earth getting rammed by some mysterious rock early on helped us tremendously. Before the moon event, our atmosphere was too thick to breathe. Now it's just right.

The collision also brought us iron and a few other critical elements. It stabilized our rotation axis tilt and lowered our rotation rate to a level where life can exist. All in all, a good thing.

Surprisingly, when comparing the mass of our planet to our orbiting satellite, our moon is 50 times larger than any other moon in our solar system. Must be for a reason.

The moon is physical proof that two are better than one. Not only does our wonderful moon stabilize our tilt and rotation, it also controls our tides and has a supporting role in dozens of romantic songs and movies, not the least of which is my personal favorite, *It's A Wonderful Life.*

See, if our tilt were any larger, our climate would wildly fluctuate. You wouldn't know when to wear a bikini or a parka. A smaller tilt would lead to very mild seasons, but it would also prevent any wide distribution of rain. My wife would hate that because she lives for any day she can wear her colorful rubber boots.

The bottom line here is that if we didn't have our moon, and if it weren't its exact size and placement, then we wouldn't exist. So, don't thank your lucky stars, thank your lucky moon!

And do it soon because the moon may well be slightly miffed at us. PiLCs have discovered that the moon is gradually moving away from us at a rate of 3.82 centimeters a year! That's approximately two inches! A year! In about ten million years this might actually turn into a problem.

Until then, as long as George Bailey can lasso it for Mary, we're good.

The Lunar Landing

If you've yet to hit your fifties, you missed the great television event of 1969: man's first landing on the moon. While every eye was glued to every available fuzzy black & white set, PiLCs in NASA were sweating bullets. And for good reason! Something of that magnitude had never been attempted before.

The problems of getting to the moon are myriad. First, it's out in space. End of list.

To get a ship to land on a moving object from a moving object is difficult enough, but you've also got to factor in Newton's law of inertia. Well, obviously!

In space if you hit a golf ball, it will travel onward forever. But on earth, gravity and friction will cause it to eventually stop. Since the rocket will encounter friction when it takes off, but none when it hits space, how does one account for that?

To quote Yul Brenner *from The King and I*, "Is a puzzlement!"

Then you have to factor in steering, sub-zero temperatures, artificial atmosphere, food, how to protect the crew from the heat of reentry and the very real problem that there's just no room to squeeze in a toilet on such a small capsule. I have no idea how Neil Armstrong held it for such a long trip.

With modern computers able to bang out facts and figures, you may think all of this was child's play. But the reality back in the sixties was that all of the calculations needed to make that miraculous trip a reality were hammered out with a number two pencil and people counting on their fingers.

In one year, we had both the lunar landing and Woodstock! Nothing of that magnitude happened again until we all watched the final episode of *Friends*.

Fun Fact: The gravity on the moon is about .17 of ours. To put that in layman's terms, if you can dunk a basketball here on earth on a regulation 10-foot tall basket, on the moon, you could leap over Michael Jordan with LeBron on his shoulders with a 59-foot jumper!

What We're Made Of

Beyond location, we need the right building materials to sustain life. Which leads us right back to the question as to why the universe is so big; we need it to be incredibly immense in order to provide us with the right construction materials.

Earth is the home owner. The universe is a massive hardware store with free home delivery.

The earth is positively *loaded* with Thorium (610 times more abundant than the average thorium content on other planets in the Milky Way) as well as Uranium (a close second, with it being 340 more times more abundant than other planets). Fortunately, these super-enriched heavy radiometric elements have been propelling our planet's tectonic activity for four billion years.

The more you dig down into it, earth is a very complex recipe. Regardless of how much trouble this planet is, we don't have the time or the tools to make one from scratch, so I guess we should just learn to live with this one.

Water

Now we get to that wet stuff! We need an abundance of water that has yet to be found on any other planet. Without it you don't have Hawaii, and that means no Hula girls, and what fun would that be?

But we can't have too much water! If we were covered with it, we'd have *Waterworld*, and anyone with a memory remembers what a bomb that was!

Water needs to be a small enough proportion of our total mass (less than 0.03%) to allow for continents to form. From those continents come rivers and streams which trickle down to smaller tributaries, which we in Indiana call 'cricks.'

Water is our miracle solvent. It dissolves many types of molecules, while it's also able to transport other molecules while still preserving their integrity.

I can't tell you how important it is to me that molecules preserve their integrity. Otherwise we'd have a world full of skanky molecules, and we all know where that eventually ends up: trailer parks full of white trash molecules drinking beer who set off fireworks at all hours of the night.

The absolute miracle about water is that it stands apart from the crowd by being denser as a liquid than as a solid.

That way, when it freezes, it floats, providing a layer of insulation to the water underneath on lakes and streams, preventing any further loss of heat, thus protecting the little fishies who, I'm told, totally take this for granted.

If ice were heavier than its liquid version, it would sink to the bottom, the sun's warmth couldn't get to it and we'd eat a lot of frozen fish in the winter.

Water provides another great service: the chemical reactions of water with the minerals in our earth's crust at the bottom of the ocean evidently weakens it, providing lubrication that allows the crust to bend without breaking. This, in turn, helps our plate tectonics move and stretch on occasion without cracking.

So, if the question, "Hey, why are the oceans so big?" ever comes up, you can look super smart when you answer back, "Obviously, to keep a lid on excessive earthquakes."

Water's also great fun to ski on, scuba dive under, drink from a hose and soak in with soothing bubbles after a hard day at the office.

Water is our ecological BFF. Without it we wouldn't just be up a creek without a paddle, we'd be up a long dry dirt gulley without a paddle and with no discernable need for one.

Thank you, water!

Just Keep Swimming

My personal love of water started early on. While I loved the obligatory midwestern sports, I was entirely too uncoordinated to master baseball and basketball, but I took to swimming like, well, a fish takes to water.

In the summer, I basically lived at our local YMCA and when I was eight-years-old, I swam my first mile. On purpose. It was by far the hardest thing I had ever done. (This dropped to second place after I screwed up my courage to pass a "Do you want to go steady—check box A or B" note to Joan Kennedy just a few years later.)

The entire class of much older kids were out of the water and dressed and had moved on to the prom by the time I finished the required 62 lengths of the pool. I later added it up and discovered a mile in a 25-yard pool should actually be 72 lengths, so I'm pretty sure my instructor at that time took pity upon my flailing skinny little arms and legs.

Since that day, I have never been out of the water. I was on our high school swim team and, to this day, in memory of my eight-year-old accomplishment, I swim a mile every year on my birthday. When the Pandemic hit, all of our gyms and pools shut down. I had to fly to Tennessee for a gig just to get in some laps!

Part of the appeal of swimming is that I hate to sweat. In truth, I dislike exertion of any kind. But when I'm in the water, if I do perspire, I don't feel it, so I'm okay.

My goal is to live until I'm 90, then join a Masters Swim Team and finally win state. If I have to wear floaties to make it to the other end, so be it.

Dirt

I want to give a big shout out to the amazing properties of dirt. And not just because I'm from Indiana, where it sometimes seems as if that's our best attribute. 'Indiana Dirt—From Corn to Cows, We've Got You Covered!'

Dirt is all around us. It helps our crops grow, it buries our dead (except in horror movies), it keeps Tide detergent in business. But what is it and why is it so darned important?

First off, it's the only substance on our planet that contains both the water and nutrients needed to help our plants grow.

Think about where we'd be without acres and acres of good old dirt! Without dirt, there would be no crops of grain or corn. There would be no trees! We couldn't grow grass, which means there would be no picnics! No baseball diamonds! No place to hide Easter eggs!

Specifically, dirt's a blend of cyanobacteria, fungi, algae, mosses, sand, clay and other various and sundry organisms. It aids in photosynthesis and cushions your fall when you trip. Concrete doesn't do that.

It gradually reduces greenhouse gas levels and cools the earth.

The record shall reflect that I was never a dirt man until I got to know it. Now I realize I can't live without it!

Isotopes

Along with my previous opinion on dirt, I've never been partial to isotopes. I'm more of a leg man, myself. But you have to give it up for the i'topes.

If you're like me, isotopes and their cousin who works at the FM station, radioisotopes, don't come up very often in casual conversation. It's a rare day when I hear, "I was driving to the store to pick up milk when I was hit by an overwhelming urge to discuss isotopes!"

In college or high school, if you studied things like math, business, art, communications, psychology or pretty much any other subject under the sun that kept you out of the science building, you may also find yourself asking, "Say, just what is an isotope?"

Here you go…

Isotopes are the atoms in an element that have the same atomic number but a different atomic mass; that is, the same number of protons and thus identical chemical properties, but different numbers of neutrons and consequently different physical properties. Isotopes can be stable or unstable or radioisotopes. In the latter, their nuclei have a special property: they emit energy in the form of ionizing radiation while searching for a more stable configuration.

Now do you understand why people beat up science nerds in the cafeteria? Because they not only talk like this, but they can also understand it!

From the definition above, what I get is that isotopes are atoms that spend an inordinate amount of time looking for stable relationships.

Evidently, they're just like us, only much smaller. And radioactive. Got it.

Stephen White (a very funny man who tortured our great nation for years writing for *Barney*—the dinosaur, not the sitcom detective) says that a radioisotope is one that isn't good looking enough to become a televisionisotope.

PiLCs say it took some nine billion years for enough supernovas to explode to provide us with the needed number of radioisotopes.

Somehow these little buggers generated enough heat to blast away the perpetual fog earth was encased in. They also helped us establish our magnetic field. This is important because that particular field protects us from deadly cosmic and solar radiation.

Who knew? And here I thought they were just an overly needy lot who constantly complained about their unstable relationships.

Even though radioisotopes are not sexy and most of them die

off entirely too quickly, if you leave them out, the whole planet will collapse in on itself.

With respect to the isotope's usefulness, may I present carbon-14. This isotope (and its measurable half-life) helps PiLCs determine the age of objects from cave men discovered buried in ice to the Shroud of Turin.

In medicine, radioactive iodine-131 is used to test for thyroid activity. And for you wine drinkers, measuring cesium-137 in any vintage made before 1950 is proof that someone's trying to pawn off a current wine as something older than 70 years old!

Radioactive isotopes are also helpful in discovering leaks in pipes, as long as you happen to have a handy Geiger counter in your tool kit.

In these and other cases, hats off to our helpful friends, the isotopes!

Fun Fact: It's estimated our planet only started off with about
250 distinct minerals that have, after years of bombardment, now
topped 4,300 (3,800 of which are named)! Surprisingly, the most
common mineral in the earth's crust is silicon (insert joke about
earth's bouncy crust here)!

Our Goldilocks Planet

Perhaps you're one of those people who take our little blue dot for granted. Well, get ready to have your socks rocked!

For life to exist here, our planet needs to rotate in a full circle every 24 hours. Everyone knows that; otherwise all of our clocks would be off.

But did you know it took about 4.5 billion years of tidal interaction with the Moon and Sun to achieve that?

Way back when, it only took us two to three hours for one full rotation. That would never work out today. We'd only have a five-hour work week and salaries would have to be through the roof to afford decent housing! Not to mention late night TV could only last about ten minutes. That's barely enough time for Jimmy Fallon to introduce the Roots.

We should also be grateful for dinosaurs, and not just for providing fodder for so many monster movies. Those decayed bodies fermented under the ground for about 543 million years until they became petroleum and natural gas.

It's almost like someone knew mankind would, at some point, be inventing cars and we'd need some kind of propellant. Now, how a T-Rex transformed into unleaded gas is beyond me, but given bacteria and half a billion years, I guess a lot can happen!

Coal started as mighty forests some 300 million years ago! And while it's dirty to burn, without it we wouldn't have had the Industrial Age, so there's that.

The bottom line here is that everything, from our oxygen levels, to the tilt of our planet, to the amount of water we have, to our location in the Milky Way, to the over-abundance of raw materials at our disposal, to the gift of large reptiles transforming into petroleum products, seems to point to not only a Designer, but one who appears to be very concerned about the endless details of making a planet that fulfills our every desire.

When you line up all the very specific needs we humans have, and look at the millions of other planets that don't even come close to measuring up, it becomes apparent that we are either the absolutely luckiest species in the universe or that something *out there* did it all on purpose.

In an attempt to put it into perspective, let's say you're tired of this planet and have decided to move on to another one. You give your realtor your list of basic planet requirements and wait for the possible listings to crash your email inbox.

Here's what you might ask for...

"I don't want our new home to be too big! But big enough to have an ocean, for goodness sake. Oxygen's a must. We'd prefer a neighborhood that's not in danger of another galaxy crashing into us. We like our sun to be nice and hot, but not melt-your-face-off hot. The days can be long, but nothing over a week. Seasons are a must. A few of the land masses can be forming, but we prefer our continents to be stable. If possible, we'd like to avoid excessive radiation. We can live without all the elements. If we need a few extra, we can just bring whatever we've got left over at our old home, right? I'm afraid an unstable molten core's a deal breaker. Animals are a must, but I can live without the poisonous ones. Or ones with big teeth. Or ones that slither. And none of those little yapping dogs who all seem to come with their own purses. Do you have anything like that?"

Realtors, being who they are, listen carefully and then send along what they've got. At which point, you spend years and years looking at billions of potential planets. And here's what you'd say as you looked at each and every listing...

"Not that. No. Not that. No. No. No. No. No. No. Did they even listen to us? No. Absolutely not! This one's covered in ice! This one's five feet from a super Nova! No. No. No. No. No. No. I swear, this is depressing. No. No. No. No. No. No. No. No. No! Did our agent even listen to us? This is a disaster!"

Other PiLCs have labeled this planet 'Goldilocks' for the very reasons I've listed above. It's not too hot, it's not too cold, it's just right.

Hopefully, this information will spur us on to take better care of our orb, because the odds are slim to none that we can find a replacement planet that's half as good as this one.

Life!

Once our house was ready to move into, we jumped on it. Almost out of nowhere, life began. We see the explosion happen during the Cambrian period, about 530—542 million years ago.

Don't you love science? PiLCs throw out figures like "530 to 542 million years ago" as if it's nothing. I have to count backward in my head before I can figure out how long I've been married, and that's not even close to a million years yet (although on my off days my wife might argue that time is, indeed, relative)!

All we can do is hope the people in Science Club are checking each other's math because I'd hate to insult the Cambrian period by overestimating its age.

The start of life has a discrepancy of some 12 million years. Eternity-wise, that's a drop in the bucket, but a lot can happen in 12 million years. Some star could go totally supernova on us. Or a new species could be introduced. But invariably the cable repairman will show up the very second you leave to go check on another solar system.

One fun fact (or disturbing, depending on your point of view) is the speed with which life appeared. Years ago, biologists were quite fond of espousing evolution as the primary method in which life began, postulating that it took place over billions and billions of years.

Astrophysics took care of that. Once we figured out when the Big Bang happened and when the earth was formed, the window of opportunity for classic evolution was unceremoniously slammed shut, forcing biologists to reevaluate.

The facts are these: life exploded.

Out of nowhere.

Almost as suddenly as the Big Bang.

And we're not talking single cell organisms. The fossil record shows that we've got full skeletons showing up—from all kinds of animals.

Suffice to say, if you don't come from a faith-based background, this causes a lot of head scratching.

Richard Dawkins, the uber atheist evolutionary biologist, says of this period, "…It is as though they were just planted there, without any evolutionary history."

Yup. Funny how that happened.

After all that pent-up life exploded onto the planet's surface, you'd think we were on our way. Nope. Just as soon as it popped up, life was extinguished. Don't worry, because soon after, life happened again. But, wouldn't you know it, right after that, life was extinguished.

It may seem a bit depressing that life couldn't seem to catch on, but each extinction period left us with something important, and each new beginning brought us closer to where we are today.

Which is something only someone from our vantage point would say. This viewpoint would not be popular in the least when making small talk with dinosaurs.

Way back when, in the Devonian period, we got trees with good strong bark and seed-bearing plants. This led to a slowing of erosion and eventually to forests. It was only a matter of time before tree forts were invented.

Unfortunately, 250 million years ago we had yet another mass extinction caused by a handful of nasty volcanos. They spewed smoke in the air, released tons of carbon dioxide and subsequently raised the temperature of the entire planet.

Finally, we got to the Triassic and Jurassic periods. You know what that means: theme parks and dinosaurs!

It appears that the T-Rex didn't make his debut until years later in the Cretaceous period, but I'm not going to goof up the timeline of 'Jurassic Park,' so don't hold me to that.

Just before any volcanos could belch out their filth yet again, we were hit by an asteroid. This one hit in Mexico. It missed the United States by a smidgen because of the ancient wall that had been erected to keep undocumented asteroids out.

This particular asteroid was six *miles* wide. It hit with the energy impact of *three billion times* two atomic bombs. I'm surprised we don't still feel the aftershocks of that today!

This behemoth instantly killed everything for thousands of miles, setting off earthquakes, causing tsunamis over 325 feet high and releasing 550 billion tons of sulfur into the atmosphere. It was as if one huge stink bomb blocked out the sun.

At this point all the volcanos were saying, "Who do you love now, huh?"

Because of this massive asteroid, a minimum of 75% of life on earth was destroyed, leaving the remainder gasping for breath and saying, "Whew, what died?"

And do you want to know who survived, who kept their collective heads down and eventually lowered the deadly carbon dioxide in the atmosphere? Ants. That's right, ants!

Somehow those industrious little insects enhanced the weathering of calcium and magnesium, which is somehow important when it comes to cooling the earth's atmosphere.

Flies and snakes I'll never understand, but I now have a new appreciation for ants.

Finally, after all of this, the planet stabilized enough for Mr. and Mrs. Neanderthal to show up. They were top dog, sloping foreheads and all. The couple made stone tools and even went so far as to bury their dead.

Some believe that Neanderthals observed the ritual of burial as a sign of respect for the dead. It could also have been because they didn't want grandma's carcass to be eaten by a saber-toothed tiger.

Eventually the Neanderthal lost out to the Cro-Magnon crowd. The new gang had higher functioning motor skills, which translated into better tools, stone lamps, and eventually, farming.

Evidence suggests that the cruder and more simplistic Neanderthals simply died of embarrassment. "Me not know how to farm. Wife say me not a real man. Me die now."

Early Life

While it is widely agreed that human life started somewhere in Africa, the Cro-Magnon apparently settled down to a nomadic existence in southern France.

From a family grave that was discovered in 1868, we know that life for the first, more highly evolved, humans was difficult, at best.

Almost all of the skeletons appeared to have fused vertebrae in their necks, and at least one female had a fractured skull. This indicates not only that they got bopped in the head a lot, but also that their casual days of drinking wine, eating cheese and looking down their collective noses at Americans was years away!

Fragments of necklaces and ornaments were found in the grave, including a very small keychain of what looks like a crudely carved facsimile of the Eiffel Tower.

The discovery of flax fibers as well as weaving baskets has led many experts to declare this particular branch of modern man as the first practitioners of haute couture.

Fun Fact: As of this writing, we know of 700 different species of dinosaurs. The longest and heaviest of the bunch was discovered down Argentina way and was named, you guessed it, the Argentinosaurus. It clocked in at 77 tons, which is roughly the weight of about 17 African elephants or me after I totally stuff myself at Thanksgiving.

My Dear Watson, it's Evolutionary!

I love National Geographic specials for so many reasons; they're gorgeous, fascinating and go into deep dark places that scare the pants off of me.

My problem with these specials is how they throw out half-facts, assume we're all in agreement and then quickly move on to some amazing footage of an eagle in flight.

Will Smith narrates one of their series and basically says, "Everything was ready for life in the ocean, it got hit by lightning, some rudimentary creatures crawled out onto the beach and here we are!"

It's as if our only frame of reference is the movie *Frankenstein*! We all accept the fact that if you hit something with a billion volts, instead of frying it to kingdom come, it will magically come to life!

How life came to be on this rock is a bit more complicated than that.

Every time I talk about evolution, I feel like I'm a hard-nosed gumshoe from a 60's police TV drama looking over a dead body in a dark and dank back alley. After looking at the evidence, at some point I shake my head and shout out to all within hearing distance, "Confound it, this was no accident!"

If any subject puts people's panties in a bunch, this is it! So much ink and paper have been wasted on this subject, it's absurd. We'd have most of our rain forests intact if we could only get along here.

I'm not pointing the finger at just one side. From my perspective, both PiLCs and the faith-based crowd are guilty. This subject's worse than politics. Both sides tend to stomp their feet and demand they're right and everyone else is wrong.

And for good reason.

Because the outcome of this particular subject either reinforces or destroys a particular worldview. As such, everyone needs to take a deep breath, because frankly, this subject has less to do with science than it does with presuppositions.

As a gentle reminder, physics demands that we go where the evidence leads, regardless of the final conclusion.

Okay, let's do that.

While most of this debate is a matter of perspective, I believe it all comes down to semantics and one very important fact: the evidence suggests, whether you like it or not, that we were a product of design, not of chance. That being said, there's still room for evolutionary thought.

Way to straddle that philosophical fence, huh!

Evolutionary biologist Richard Dawkins says, "If you meet somebody who claims not to believe in evolution, that person is either ignorant, stupid or insane." So, yeah, lots of room there for differing opinions.

Let's address the most famous smoking gun: Charles Darwin. He originally studied to become a cleric in the Church of England, but over time became a naturalist.

Today that would mean he studied nature in the nude. I don't think that's the case here. If it were, then the pictures in his book, *The Origin of Species,* would be a lot different.

At any rate, he went to the Galapagos Islands in South America between 1831 and 1836, observed nature, and published his world changing book about 20 years later, in 1859.

His big theory was an idea he called 'natural selection.' This is where the survival or extinction of each organism depends on its ability to adapt to the environment.

If you need to see this in action, you no longer need to travel to South America. Any Junior High or Middle School will do just fine.

I believe Darwin was on to something. I also believe his apostles often cherry pick the sections of his book that shove a Creator off to the side.

That being the case, I'll pull out this quote of Darwin's to level the playing field. He was struck by, "the extreme difficulty, or rather impossibility, of conceiving this immense and wonderful universe, including man with his capacity for looking backwards and far into futurity, as the result of blind chance or necessity. When thus reflecting I feel compelled to look to a First Cause having an intelligent mind in some degree analogous to that of man; and I deserve to be called a Theist."

Okay, it's a long quote, and he uses words like 'futurity' and 'thus,' but even Mr. Darwin acknowledges that his theory of evolution most likely has an Intelligent Designer behind it.

Even Darwin threw chance out the window.

At this point in the game, I toss the ball over to Michael Behe's book *Darwin's Black Box* and his observation of 'irreducible complexity.' The phrase comes from Darwin himself.

Charles D. said that if an organism can be found that is more complex than the cell (which was as small as the PiLCs could see in the 1800s), then his theory of 'natural selection' should be tossed out.

The bottom line here is that Darwin understood that extremely complex designs could not have possibly been formed by numerous, successive, slight modifications.

To begin, they need a designer. That's why Behe and his crew coined the phrase 'Intelligent Design.' They're actually taking Darwin at his word.

Some PiLCs do their best to sidestep and look down at Behe, but to do so puts their own intellectual integrity in peril. Which, naturally, brings me back to the pre-supposition argument. As humans, we gravitate to the argument that best fits our belief system.

That's what makes Darwin such a firecracker. Non-theists latch on to the idea that *everything* happened by chance. They love to talk about natural selection.

In the other camp, Christians hate Darwin because they believe he's taken God out of the equation.

If everyone could step back and look at the big picture, I really don't think we're that far apart.

Maybe, just maybe, it's a little of both!

Take a Deep Breath

Let's look at micro and macro-evolution. Some Christians stand on top of the micro-only mountaintop and claim victory.

Granted, at present, there don't appear to be any interstitial species to get us from one group of animals to the other, which would be called *macro-evolution*.

Looking at the fossil record, we can see tons of *micro-evolution*; that is, changes within species. You can't deny it. Museums are built upon this fact.

But regardless of how many variations of dogs there are, at the end of the day, they're all still dogs (with the possible exception of the Chihuahua, which is basically a rat with fur).

Not to be the bearer of bad news, but the record and simple common-sense defeats macro-evolution every time. The evidence simply isn't there to support it.

According to the facts that we have on hand, the idea that even the most basic species evolved into a more complex species over the course of billions of years falls into the category of scientific fantasy.

Niles Eldredge, the curator at the American Museum of Natural History in New York city, says, "The fossil record we were told to find in the past 120 years (since Darwin) does not exist."

Time and time again the fossil records show fully intact species appearing as if out of nowhere. Evolutionists have been looking for *any* kind of transitional species for decades now and they just haven't found it.

The science section of the New York Times referred to our fossil record as something closer to revolution than evolution.

Time magazine accurately calls the explosion of fully evolved animals as 'Evolution's Big Bang!'

The fact of the matter is that fully formed life exploded onto the scene 530 million years ago and no one can explain it.

The amount of faith evolutionists exhibit in this regard is amazing. To avoid admitting a Creator made the universe and our world, evolutionists created the idea that every living thing was created from total random selection. That over billions of years, eventually, life would mindlessly find a way and that's how we got to where we are today.

But unfortunately, they've painted themselves into a corner. The theory that time and chance would somehow get us to our modern world is built on little more than but false hope.

Like a lot of theories, this idea was fine before we knew as much as we do now. But just like the flawed ideas that the earth is not only flat, but also the center or the universe, must go away, so must the idea of mindless, totally random macro-evolution.

The Cambrian era should be reason enough. Fossils of totally intact animals appear overnight. Wings appear with no developmental origins.

The search for transitional species is a dead end. Life simply exploded for no apparent reason and against the bedrock theory of evolution.

Not to beat a dead horse, but if you'll indulge me, I'd like to present what I believe are the best arguments we have to date against macro-evolution: eyeballs and sex.

My go-to atheist, biologist Richard Dawkins, says that "it is vanishingly improbable that exactly the same evolutionary pathway should ever be traveled twice."

That being the case, then how is it that something like 99% of all animals have eyes? We didn't all come from the same evolutionary pod. If evolution is totally random, then why do we see nothing but exceedingly detailed uniformity?

The eye is a miracle of engineering. Objects in the heads of countless animals around the world take in information, move it through nerves to the animal's brain, be it huge or teenie-tiny, and convert those images into something the animal comprehends as 'sight.'

The animal then reacts accordingly to those images and either has lunch or is someone else's lunch.

If evolution is based on random chance, then 1) how did something as complex as sight evolve over such a relatively miniscule period of time, and 2) how does every single animal on the planet have it? (Excepting bats for the moment, who evidently didn't get the sight memo. They were hanging upside down in a cave when the meeting happened, but they should have at least *heard* about it, for goodness sake!)

I hope you see my point. There wasn't a meeting of all the evolving species where they doled out things like fangs and wings and eyeballs.

According to the theory of evolution, every single thing on this planet was created by pure chance. That means each individual species had to evolve sight on its own. Unless we all evolved from the same original cell, and the probability of that is astronomical!

Hundreds of thousands of species gained the gift of sight virtually overnight. How did that happen? The evidence suggests these animals somehow appeared fully intact, all at once.

I say all of this knowing full well that love is blind. Animals could well have groped their way around for millions of years looking for the right mate. "Hey, you're not a Llama! Get off of me!"

Which brings me to my second point: sex. The wonderful and amazing and infuriating reproductive system. How did that happen?

If it takes billions of years for a species to evolve, how did the male and female parts work themselves out? Was every single species asexual until they could finally get their act together?

Humans are the most laughable example. PiLCs have actually suggested, with straight faces, mind you, that because of the complexity of the female reproductive system, it would have taken about five million years longer to evolve than the male reproductive system.

Seriously?

Let me state here for the record that as a man I cannot fully comprehend what women go through. I cannot begin to grasp what the other half of our species has to endure in order to propagate humanity.

Women have a full reproductive system. Men only have a starter set.

But how did the evolving thing work? Did the men just sort of hang around for five million years? Did they say, "You done yet? No pressure. You evolve, we'll be out hunting. Call us when you're done."

Are you getting this? You can tell that claim makes absolutely no sense, right? It's not just me.

I feel as if I'm the smart aleck in the back of the class with my hand in the air and a dumbfounded look on my face. "Excuse me, two questions. First, you do know what you're saying is impossible, right? And secondly, is this going to be on the test?"

Common sense shouts out that you can't have any one gender of any species take longer than a few months to get their reproductive organs in order or that particular species would die out, never to be heard from again!

The evidence is clear. Just like the universe came from a sudden explosion, so did all the species on this planet. For any species to creative their offspring, our planet had to have male and female components of each and every species (except for asexual frogs, evidently) here at the same time! This is 8th grade health class stuff, folks!

The eventual conclusion of what *caused* that explosion is where the debate has to move, not whether or not it happened. There's simply not enough time or chance to come to any other conclusion.

Before you think I'm falling too far over onto the side of religion, let me state for the record that biblical literalists can be just as far off of first base as the die-hard evolutionists. Both camps are somewhere out in either left or right field.

Here's my bottom line: it all comes down to semantics. Don't think of evolution as 'survival of the fittest,' or 'natural selection.' Think of it as Intelligent Design. Think of each species as a building block on the way to a grander plan.

When the Designer created the universe, He did so in stages. Our sun didn't just materialize out of thin air; it took two huge stars exploding their guts out into the universe before we got our third generation radiation friendly bachelor star.

I'm not upset that it took two steps to get to our sun. I can clearly see the Intelligent Design behind it.

The Creator had the same pattern with life. He created various species, wiped them out, built on those, and eventually brought humanity to the forefront.

When I look at the total impossibility of how carbon was created, yet at how it's currently one of the most prevalent elements in our universe, I see the Creator's meticulous and miraculous hand behind it from day one.

I see the same thing when I look at all the species on our planet. When I see the commonality between our bones or our DNA, I don't see any conflict with my faith. I see the Intelligent Design behind the building blocks that got us to where we are today.

With that said, recognizing I have most likely not changed a single mind, I'd love to put a pin in this highly inflammable topic.

On to other amazing fun facts about the formation of our home.

Fun Fact: Charles Darwin was born on the very same day in 1809 as Abraham Lincoln. He set out to be a doctor, but since he couldn't stand the sight of blood, he switched his major over to the study of theology. After taking a five-year voyage on the HMS Beagle, he came home, married his cousin and they promptly had 10 children. This led to his observations of 'survival of the fittest' which he eventually included in his world-changing book, *On the Origin of Species.*

Do the Continental

Around 2.5 million years ago in the Neogene period, the earth's continents started to slow their drifting and settled in to what we now recognize on our current maps.

This was after earth had been pelted repeatedly by a barrage of comets and meteors. No matter how many minerals and elements they brought with them, the destruction they left behind was unprecedented.

But that was nothing compared to the movement of our land masses. India pushed up into Asia, causing the Himalayan mountains to jump to attention. Australia cited irreconcilable differences with Antarctica and left for good, moving north east.

Grasses and deciduous plants sprang up around the world, gradually cooling the earth's temperatures.

And North and South America lightly touched at Panama, guaranteeing both a future canal and that the currents from the Pacific Ocean would never touch the Atlantic.

After eons of tumultuous and sometimes exceedingly violent change, the earth finally relaxed. It appeared we were ready to get on with it. But before anything could happen, we took a little breather to accommodate a brief ice age.

By 'brief,' I mean to say the ice age started around 21,000 years ago and lasted for about 10,000 years. That is one long winter. I don't know how the House Targaryen or anyone from Westeros survived their game of thrones!

The gigantic glaciers traversing our continents picked up and deposited the aforementioned precious dirt and helped to stabilize global temperatures. That is, if by 'stable,' you mean colder than a witch's mammary gland.

Technically, currently we're at the tail end of the last ice age. The melting glaciers fed rivers and waters around the world which, in turn, currently provides liquid refreshment to our population of close to eight billion thirsty souls.

In Canada alone glaciers scooped out and then filled some 32,000 lakes.

All of these benefits are wonderful. But as you can well imagine, it can't last forever.

If you lean toward pessimism, you should know that the odds of another cataclysmic disaster happening to our earth are pretty good.

And here I was worried about the hole in the ozone layer!

To make you feel a bit better about where we live, let's look at two randomly selected planets from our solar system...

Venus & Mars

If you are looking to make a move, do not even consider our closest neighbors!

Mars is way beyond being a fixer upper. It's a complete disaster! For starters, its south polar ice cap is pretty much entirely composed of dry ice. And if the northern one ever managed to melt, it would cover the entire planet in a red sea 10 to 20 feet deep.

Which might not be such a bad thing, considering everything else on the planet is ruined because of the relentless dusty winds that seem to be a daily occurrence.

Being a Weather Person on Mars must be so boring! "Our forecast for tonight? The same as it was yesterday and the day before that: Wind. No rain. Just dry, dusty wind. Back to you, Sally!"

I believe this is the reason Marvin the Martian is always so "Very, very angry." He has good reason to be!

Despite these downsides, the mountain ranges on Mars are fantastic! Compared to our petite 29,000-foot-tall Mount Everest, Olympus Mons on Mars is 65,000 feet high and nearly 300 miles wide. There's a rock-climbing experience for you!

It's all because of the weaker gravitational force on Mars. If we had a mountain that tall here, it would collapse under its own weight.

By comparison, Venus has a surface temperature of 900 degrees. I turn on the A.C. when the thermometer hits 75! I can't imagine 900 degrees! Life on Venus would be unbelievably hard!

"I'm sorry, son, we just can't make it to your baseball game. Why? Well, the last time we went, your mother burst into flame the second she stepped out of the car. I'm sorry if your team never got any orange slices, but we had a few more pressing issues! Not to mention a day here lasts an entire year, so your games are never called on account of darkness. Lastly, because of our weak gravitational pull, I put your sister down on the ground for one second and she floated off. We have no idea where she landed! And that's why we won't be supporting you in your dream of becoming a baseball player!"

Still, Nature's Out to Kill You

After everything I've written about our amazing planet, one would be forgiven if they conclude that I love nothing better than living the outdoors life. They would be mistaken.

I'm well aware that some people love nature. My wife is one of those people. She lives for the beach, and a day just isn't complete until she's either walked outside, watered her flowers or stood outside in a thunderstorm.

Whereas I believe that, as wonderful as it is, pretty much everything in nature is trying to kill you.

Here's a partial list of our current dangers: snakes, bears, jellyfish, boulders, tornadoes, hurricanes, heat, cold, oceans, cliffs and 98% of Australia.

If you survive being outdoors, it's just because nature had an off day. It'll try to kill you again tomorrow.

"What a beautiful sunset—scorpion!"

"Isn't the water warm this time of year—shark!"

"I love relaxing on the grass—deer tick!"

"Listen to the waves crash on the shore—tsunami!"

"Feel the warmth of the sun on your skin—cancer!"

As humans, we're *designed* to be *indoors*. We have no fur, claws or wings. We're the laughingstock of the animal kingdom!

Every animal but humans can see in the dark. After sunset we're nothing but blind snacks on sticks!

That's why, throughout history, man's main goal has been to find shelter.

My ancestors died giving me the right to have air conditioning. I will not disrespect their sacrifices.

Despite this overwhelming evidence, my wife is part of a cult of people who want to get back to nature. You can almost hear the ancestors from thousands of years calling out, "What are you, stupid?"

People go to Yosemite and think they're at Disneyland. "What a cute waterfall. Let's take a selfie—Ahhhhh!"

I have lots of friends who absolutely love to go camping. My question is: why? People spend thousands of dollars to go camping with all the comforts of home. Here's an idea: stay home!

Being indoors is a gift from God! For me, roughing it is a hotel room without Internet. When I catch a fish, it already has cellophane over it.

What's the worst danger you're going to face indoors? Black mold, but that takes years. If you can't escape that, you deserve to die.

My wife claims she can't live without fresh air. So, whenever we stay at a hotel I make her sleep on the balcony. I say, put your money where your mouth is!

Resources in Our Toy Chest

To close out this section, I'd like to pose a question that might seem blatantly obvious: don't you find it a little curious that almost everything the eye can see was provided for our benefit as a natural resource?

Trees and stone are wonderful for building shelters as well as shaping into musical instruments and art. Metal from the ground can be forged into both weapons and jewelry. Until we learn to harness the sun's power, coal and gas are indispensable for heat and fuel.

Water can be used for power, to quench thirst, to steam out wrinkles, add ice to a drink, or to cover us up from the waist down when we relieve ourselves in the ocean.

Animals can be used for companionship and transportation, not to mention helping in plowing, put on display in zoos and (sorry, vegans) to be served up as the daily special in about 10 million restaurants.

Feathers are great for stuffing pillows. Wool is ideal for making sweaters and scratchy suits! Fruit is utilized as food, garnishes and squeezed out for profit from Jamba Juice. Various plants can be eaten, smoked, broiled, fermented or used as medicine! Honey is pretty much bee barf, for goodness sake!

However, it should be noted that throughout history, snakes, cockroaches, rats and Brussel sprouts have uniformly been despised by every rational creature on the planet (with the rare exception of medical research and Pixar's 'Ratatouille').

It's as if the entire earth is one big toy chest provided for us to use however we see fit. Granted, a lot of people take what the earth has provided and don't put things back the way they found it, and whoever invented plastic needs to go back to the drawing board and make it biodegradable, but despite the drawbacks usually related to human error, our planet is off the charts amazing!

Once we discovered fire, all bets were off. Consider eggs, pasta, gold, meat and sand; if something wasn't useful in its natural state, our endless curiosity wondered what would happen if we heated it up?

The toasted Marshmallow when paired with chocolate on a graham cracker being the primary example. Glass and spaghetti are tied for a close second.

For some reason people in Japan were fire-averse and were so desperate for food they started eating their fish raw! I'm from Indiana. We like our food cooked! Our state bird is a cardinal skewered on a BBQ.

I give huge props to the person who looked at the alligator and thought, "That would make a great wallet."

His brother was standing nearby and shouted, "I'll BBQ whatever's left over!"

Their sister said, "I'll make a necklace out of the teeth!"

And their cousin 'Lefty' said, "See if my arm is still down in his gut somewhere!"

Comedian David Brenner told a great joke years ago about the bravest man who ever lived. He said it was the first Caveman who looked at a cow and said, "See that animal over there with the dangly things underneath? I'm going to pull on those and whatever comes out, I'm drinking it!"

I'm sure the first couple of thousand years of humanity were peppered with mass experimentation.

"That look good. Me eat it!"

"No! Remember Zog?"

"Yes."

"Him eat that. Now Zog no more."

"Me find something else."

How did we get wine? Did someone store some grapes, forget about it, the fruit fermented in the dark, and then when they drank it they got all giggly? After that the race was on to see what else would give us a good buzz when we smoked it or drank it. Corn, potatoes, grass, you name it.

Human ingenuity combined with our natural resources are a formidable combination that can sometimes result in a massive hangover.

Looking at our privileged planet, it seems as if there are a thousand conditions that must be met for any life to exist at all, and either we hit the coincidence lottery or there's something behind all of our good luck!

As I close this chapter, I ask you to consider the following: a grand Designer took 14 billion years of incredible invention and innovation to get to the point where this particular planet is filled with relational, fairly rational, spiritual beings living in the comparative lap of luxury at the top of the food chain. Maybe there's a reason for that.

The bottom line here is that we have been given an absolutely miraculous treasure trove of resources to help us live a better life.

File this under 'Things Needed to Cultivate an Attitude of Gratitude."

Recipe—One Earth

1. Form planet from molten lava. Set aside to cool.
2. Cover with water and plants. Let sit for four billion years to raise oxygen level.
3. Drizzle with asteroids and comets.
4. Add clouds to taste.
5. Add dollop of Dinosaurs.
6. Shape continents via tectonic shifts and volcanoes.
7. Destroy Dinosaurs. Bury to ferment.
8. Add thousands of species of animals. Snakes are optional.
9. Add humans.
10. It is good.

Fun Fact: The odds of being attacked and killed by a shark are one in 3,748,067. Even less if you don't go in the ocean. In fact, you are 10 times more likely to be killed by a falling coconut than being eaten by a shark. Who knew coconuts were so deadly? Where's "Coconut Week" on Animal Planet when you need it?

Fun Fact: There is an island off the coast of Brazil called Ilha de Queimada Grande that has the highest concentration of venomous snakes in the world. It is estimated there's one deadly golden lance-head viper for every square meter of land! Which could possibly be the reason tourism has had a tough go of it there!

The Tireless Factory

I am in awe of the human body. Not any particular one, mind you, although when the Olympics roll around, I tend to stand slack jawed in stark admiration of the Designer's creation.

Think for a moment what the factory you're living in is doing this very moment. Your heart is beating, your lungs are breathing, your eyes blinking and seeing, your brain translating black lines on a white page into comprehensible thoughts.

At this very moment, your skin is making new cells, old ones are dying off, your kidneys, stomach, liver and pancreas are all doing their individual jobs without you having to supervise a thing.

It's truly stunning. If I were to give any critique at all, it's that personally I could do with a lot less phlegm in the morning, but besides that, my body's aces!

What factory on earth do you know of that not only runs without supervision, but constantly replaces old machinery and, as much as possible, fixes parts that are broken down?

Not only that, but this amazing factory turns pretty much anything you stuff into its pie hole into fuel. It also lets you know when it's time to eat again (hunger pains), sleep (yawns), and how often you need to remove stored up waste (gotta go potty, gotta go potty now!)

I know, there are limits! You can't camouflage yourself to blend into the background (super shy teens being the notable exception).

We're not starfish, so if we lose a toe, that little piggy's never going to market again. On top of which, you can't fly (a personal dream of mine since I saw Mary Martin in the classic B&W perennial favorite, *Peter Pan*). Bummer.

Despite these considerably minor limitations, your body's a gift! You get to walk around on a floating rock in space in something you didn't make. Yes, you're responsible for the upkeep, but you've been given the keys to a precision machine that you totally take for granted. You know you do.

How many of you wake up shouting, "Thank you, bladder, for not exploding during the night! My pajamas and bedding appreciate you! Say, hair follicles, a big thank you for not jumping ship with those other rogue hairs on my pillow. Oh, and last but not least, liver, without you and your fine ability to flush toxins out of my body, I'd have to do a juice cleanse every two weeks, and I'm not sure my bladder could take it!"

The list of body benefits is close to endless. Your heart started beating before you were born, and up to this point, it has yet to take even a single minute off! Thank you for your service!

Then there's the human body's ability to create a seemingly endless supply of various gasses, fluids and solids. The majority of which are gross. From blood, to ear wax, to pus, to sweat, to snot, to milk, for goodness sake, how do all these things come out of the same body?

How do my eyes know to make tears to keep my peepers moist? How do my white blood cells know to attack any outside invaders? The marrow in my bones makes hemoglobin, which is pumped through miles of veins and arteries, which brings oxygen and nutrients to my cells.

Isn't that just flat out amazing?

The food I eat is broken down by acid and reduced to slime that is absorbed and used as energy. And whatever I don't need is broken down into waste that is stored in various parts of my body until I can find a convenient time to expel it.

I am living in the most multi-faceted factory on the planet that apparently works around the clock without anyone at the helm.

I feel a need to give my body a raise after so many years of unbroken dedicated service; I just don't know who to write the check to.

Just the amount of engineering it takes to get your blood to clot is staggering in and of itself. By all rights, you should be able to wipe out entire civilizations with something as lethal as a paper cut, but that's not the case.

You have a brain and a conscience that helps you determine right from wrong. You also have the ability to shut down Jiminy Cricket any time your inner id screams louder than your need to obey social rules and conventions.

Sharks don't have any of that. Sharks don't have a moral dilemma as to whether to eat a seal or a human. They just go for it! When a great white loses a baby tooth, they don't put it under a shell and wait for the shark fairy to come by. It's just us.

Humans have dreams and visions and memories. We watch images flicker on a screen and we feel emotions.

Just by having opposable thumbs, you are the envy of every animal on this planet. Jellyfish would kill to be you!

When you take just a moment to think about it, the whole thing is mind boggling! Regardless, most days I ignore the miracle of my surroundings and am only worried about making my rent!

Come On, Organs, Let's Work Together

Your factory is, in fact, several factories working together. When one breaks down, everything falls apart.

In no particular order, you've got…

1. A Central Nervous system
2. A Respiratory system
3. An Endocrine system (this is for your hormones. It's the one that goes crazy at puberty and totally rebels during menopause)

4. A Urinary System
    And bringing up the rear, literally,
5. A Digestive System

The Central Nervous system is the brains of the outfit, with the spinal cord conveying most of the instructions. But by and large, each of your systems works independently.

Which makes perfect sense. The lungs have their work cut out for them. They don't need to weigh in on which substances the kidneys remove, nor do I want my intestines telling my heart what to do. For everyone's good, let's keep the bowels and every other area separated!

The body sets a great example for the typical work environment or family structure. The brain is in charge. Deal with it. Just because the foot feels it knows in which direction it should go, the eyes are better suited for that task. And when the nose smells something like fire or a skunk, the legs need to obey instantly and ask questions later.

This is how the body would work if it were run in today's overly sensitive work environment…

Brain: "Legs, turn left immediately."

Right Leg: "Excuse me?"

Brain: "Turn left, please."

Left Leg: "Why should we turn left? I believe we have earned the right to weigh in as to which direction we should turn."

Right Leg: "I second that! How many years have we borne the brunt of supporting this entire body without even being asked for our opinions?"

Eye: "For once, could you just do what the Brain asks!"

Brain: "Turn left! Now!"

Right Leg: "You may be our boss, but if we're not treated better, we'll request a transfer."

Brain: "Just do what I've asked! I'll fill you in later."

Nose: "Ow! What did I just run into?"

Eyes: "A wall."

Nose: "Why didn't somebody tell the Legs to turn? Am I bleeding?"

Brain: "Hands, would you kindly reach up, touch the Nose and determine whether or not it's bleeding?"

Right Hand: "Certainly."
Left Hand: "Next time maybe we could get a little advance warning? We could have reached out to cushion the impact."
Left Eye: "Don't blame the Brain! It was dealing with the Legs!"
Right Hand: "Those two again? When are they going to get on board?"
Left Leg: "Organ Resources is going to hear about this!"
Right Hand: "No blood this time."
Nose: "Thank goodness!"
Left Ear: "No thanks to our Legs."
Left and Right Legs: "We heard that!"

The Largest Organ

The human body is an amazing piece of machinery that, thankfully, has a great covering. We have our bones, muscles, organs, veins and intestines which are all covered by our largest organ, our magical, stretchy epidermis.

Beyond all the amazing properties of our skin (sweat, regrowth, warmth, cheeks for Grandmas to pinch), I'm constantly amazed at how gross we'd be without it.

Skin on—the glory of Gina Lollobrigida and Chris Hemsworth (when he's in shape, not when he let himself go in Avengers 4). Skin off—Every horror movie nightmare you've ever seen.

Your skin is your first line of defense against the elements. It cools you down in the heat and does its best to keep you warm when you're freezing. That's right, goose bumps serve a purpose! They close up the skin around your hair follicles to retain your body heat.

These so-called 'goosies' also help heroines in slasher films know killers are hiding behind the door, so they come in handy in a multitude of ways.

When you cut or scrape your skin, it scabs over and heals as good as new. You can tattoo it, hang jewelry from it, and, when necessary, peel it back to get a better look at what's underneath.

Skin: it's your most loyal friend.

That dust in your place that never seems to go away? It's your skin, flaking off.

"Don't dust the old piano! It's all we have left of your Great Aunt Martha!"

As to the color, pigment or tone of your skin? Blame your parents. They passed their code down to you as you will do to your kids (assuming anyone in this generation ever has kids again).

Speaking purely for myself, I think one of the best things to happen to the human race is our growth in the area of intermarriage. It won't happen overnight, but the more we mix and mingle our colors, the more racism will fade into the background like a bad memory.

If our blending continues, what will the slogans be? "White with subtle accents of Brown, Black and Yellow is all right!"

Skin Types

While I certainly appreciate my skin covering, I can't help but wish I inherited skin from my dad's side of the family rather than my mother's ultra-sensitive, disease prone, pasty white epidermis.

Next week I'll go in for my six-month check-up at my dermatologist. He thoroughly goes over every inch of my body, giggling with delight at every anomaly he finds. Overall, it's a good thing he's so passionate about his job. I just think he finds a bit too much joy in it!

Near the end of my maternal grandfather's life, the man had to wear a full-length T-shirt and a wide-brimmed hat every time he stepped outside. Ultimately, it was his skin that did him in. Great. Something else I have to look forward to!

I've had so many bumps and spots frozen and cut off I'm losing track.

I came from the Coppertone generation that believed in a good old healthy tan. Turns out we needed warning labels on our tanning lotion: "WARNING: user is trading short term superficial appearance for eventual need to iron wrinkled skin."

My wife has olive skin. The type that absorbs the sun and turns brown in about two minutes. Because I tend to burn in the shade, I have learned to accept my vampire-like appearance.

That being said, because of my love of the water, I love to spend a day at the beach. I'm easy to pick out. I'm the one wearing the burka.

Dem Bones

More than half of your bones are in your hands and feet. Your bones are also very strong. A good-sized bone is just as strong as a comparable bar of steel. It's also a great deal more brittle, so don't bring a femur to a steel bar fight.

Somehow your bones know to grow at a steady pace until you hit puberty. At which point they grow like crazy until they slow down and stop when you hit 18.

They stay pretty much the same until you become an old codger, which is when they turn brittle and you can break a hip just by wearing tight underwear.

The only way to stem this relentless tide of decay is to regularly exercise and to stop drinking and smoking. Which is why so many old people break their hips; they've determined good health just isn't worth it.

Muscles

Between your skin and bones are, of course, your muscles. Or, in my mother's case, tiny wisps of tissue that could be convicted in a court of law for attempting to impersonate a muscle.

As far as muscle trivia goes, you should know muscles can only pull, they cannot push. Our muscles have been arranged in pairs, facing in opposite directions in strategic places.

Think of your muscles as AA batteries. One has to go one way, the other is put in upside down. Without it, your body would be useless.

Biceps and triceps are perfect examples. The biceps pull your arms up into an impressive flex, then, when you're done showing off for your girlfriend, the triceps can pull your massive arms back down to your side.

The downside of muscles would be cramps. They never announce themselves; they just cause immense amounts of pain when you're busy doing something else, like sleeping, or running.

The root cause of cramps is a build-up of lactic acid due to low oxygen levels. The only time-honored cure is to do what coach always said, and that's to, "Walk it off!"

Organs and Cells

The best estimate is that you've got a grand total of 78 organs sequestered in your body, although, like everything else in life, opinions on that number vary.

Which make no sense. Either we have 78 or we don't. Is there something in our body that's not sure if it's an organ or not? I can understand a PiLC losing count of cells somewhere after 30 trillion and rounding up, but c'mon, this is under 100!

We recently demoted Pluto from planet status to 'orbiting rock.' Did the same thing happen to some bile duct somewhere?

Regardless, all of your organs, voted into the club or not, are made up of tissues and cells. There are approximately 200 different types of cells in your body, each with their own very specific job.

Red blood cells are the flashy ones here. Everybody wants these particular cells. They're so popular the Red Cross will give you a bag of Cheez-It crackers every time you volunteer to bleed out some of yours.

The Adipose cells store fat, so they've fallen out of favor. They were in big demand in the Renaissance, but not so much today.

Your hard-to-get cells are the reproductive and hair cells. There are other worker bee cells, that we must respect, but we don't have either the time or the inclination to list them all here.

The amazing fact about your cells is that you have *trillions* of them! That's right, you and your body are teaming with cell action!

Somehow these trillions of cells all manage to communicate and do their work without stepping on the toes of every other cell around them. It's like a miniature version of Tokyo.

Fun Fact: If you pulled all of your veins, arteries and capillaries out and laid them end to end—which I wouldn't suggest because it would totally ruin your day—they would measure out to 100,000 miles! That's 12 times around the earth! You'd be dead, but it could be done!

Fun Fact: Every human body is made up of up to 50 trillion cells, which are constantly regenerating. You get all new skin every two to four weeks. (Mine's coming in all saggy now. I may be out of warranty.)

If I Only Had a...

This is where it gets fun. We can see the heart pumping blood. We can see lungs expand and contract to take in and expel air. We can even see liquids flow into the kidneys and watch liquid flow out of it (an activity for which males have a distinct advantage).

But the brain is a stealth organ. It's probably an insult to call it an organ at all. It's a grey-ish object that can be considered our command center. It runs the show. A bad case of food poisoning can lead to abdicating that position to the stomach for a few hours, but in general, you can always count on the brain to take charge.

Your brain contains 86 *billion* nerve cells known as neurons, joined by 100 *trillion* connections. Habitually smoking pot throughout high school shrinks that pool of working cells down to an even baker's dozen.

Compared to other animals, we're pretty far up on the neuron scale. Elephants have 23 billion neurons, Chimpanzees have seven billion and cats have an even billion. (500 million of those neurons are for stretching, 450 for sleeping and the final 50 million are set on 'ignore.')

The most basic explanation for how the brain works is this: the lower layer, or the brain stem (sometimes called the primitive brain), controls the automatic bodily functions such as breathing and the heartbeat.

The layer above the lower layer goes by the technical term:

r-complex. You'd think it could simply be called 'the middle layer,' but no! Even the brain can try to make you feel inferior.

Finally, we get to the uppermost layer, which is called the cerebral cortex, or the higher brain. This is where language and analytical thought occurs. That is, until the primitive brain figures out that the first part of the word, 'analytical,' is 'anal.' Then all bets are off and second grade humor ensues.

The brain is also divided into hemispheres. The left side of your brain controls the right side of your body and is mainly responsible for speech and language. If you're flunking French, blame your left hemisphere.

The right side controls the left part of your body and takes credit for sensory information and all creativity. When you have to write a paper or write a poem, make sure the right side of your head has had plenty of sleep.

How the brain sends out its information is what's mind-blowing. It's done through electrical impulses. That's right, you're a walking-talking electric machine! Some signals are so fast they travel through your body at 265 mph.

That is, until one of your impulses gets pulled over…

"Whoa, there, buddy, where's the fire?"

"On our finger! Our human just stuck his finger over an open flame. We need him to pull away!"

"Why didn't you say so? Follow me!"

Your reaction times should be noted here. If you see something visually, you usually react in 0.25 seconds. If you hear it, it takes 0.17 seconds to register. But touching something is the fastest of them all. When you touch something sharp or hot, you react in 0.005 seconds.

My suggestion here is to lose the starter gun in all Olympic races and replace them with very sharp pins aimed directly at the racer's rumps. False starts will be a thing of the past, and all the races will start so much faster!

Your body is also uniquely designed to either ramp up or cool down, depending on the circumstances at hand.

When life is good, the day is done and all you want to do is curl up with a good book or catch up on your latest shows, the body cooperates. Your heart rate decreases, your blood vessels narrow, your pupils constrict. Be careful here, as the bladder also relaxes, and that can lead to accidents.

But when faced with danger, such as a bully or your most recent crush approaching you, your body goes into fight/flight mode. Here your pupils dilate, your heart rate increases, your liver releases sugars to give you a boost of energy and, if you're a teenager, your voice goes up about 10 octaves.

My point in all of this should, by now, be obnoxiously obvious: we need to be soooooo grateful for everything we tend to ignore on a daily basis.

Up to this point, most everything I've talked about could be considered a 'worker bee.' Those other organs were not the big cheese. They didn't give the orders. With the brain, the buck stops... there!

While the brain is certainly busy running your body, it is also, at the very same time, capable of thoughts, actions and emotions simultaneously. Your brain is the ultimate multi-tasker.

You don't hear it complain, "Please! I can't organize your blood flow and help you do your homework at the same time!" No, it can handle it. Go ahead, put your brain to work.

It appears to house what we call the conscious self. It has the ability to create thought. That's truly stunning.

Somehow, we have acquired the ability to discern what is known as 'the moral code.' This is remarkable. We all know it's wrong to gossip, yet love to do it as long as we're not on the receiving end. The list of things that are right and things that are wrong is, surprisingly, fairly standard in all of our brains.

I doubt if you can fly anywhere in the world today and declare you intend on eating your host without getting at least a little pushback.

Some things are just not done! Murder, theft, violence against those who can't defend themselves and loud belching or armpit farts in church—these are the given no-nos.

I find it fascinating that, despite our differences in nurturing, most humans have more in common than we care to admit. Surely there's more to this than just random chance.

Ya Gotta Have Heart!

Let me get this out of the way: laughter really is the best medicine! Laughing can increase your blood flow and relax your blood vessel walls. So, for your own good, get out there and laugh! It also increases your pain threshold!

Ladies, the next time you're in labor, stop by a comedy club on the way to the hospital. "Ma'am, you're at 10 centimeters." "*Tell me a joke!*"

The heart is an amazing organ. If it stops, nothing else works. All of your cells are anxiously waiting for your blood to make its deliveries, but without the heart, ain't nobody getting nuthin' no how.

The average heart is about the size of a fist and weighs about 12 ounces, while the heart of a blue whale can weigh up to 1,500 pounds!

Your heart beats a little more than 36 million times every year. That's a little under 3 billion beats over an average lifetime. (I fully acknowledge that no life is average, we're all super special.)

It pumps out about 2,000 gallons of blood each and every day and beats over 100,000 during that period (significantly less if you're a politician).

If your heart stops, the brain notices very quickly. Within seconds, it registers a distinct lack of oxygen and promptly faints. If the heart does not start pumping again, in a matter of minutes your faint will turn lethal.

My friend, comedienne Christy Conder, says that she became convinced of a grand Designer in college when she studied the heart in her anatomy & physiology class. There she discovered all four chambers of the heart (aka ventricles and atriums) have to open and close in a specifically timed order with the exact same volume of blood entering and exiting each chamber in a specific rhythm for life to exist.

If any one of the chambers gets out of rhythm or stops working... *it's over*! How does it just keep going? It dumfounded her, as it does me.

Along those lines, heart disease is the #1 killer of *everyone* in this country! Not cancer, not any virus-of-the-month: heart disease. Someone, somewhere, keels over every 37 seconds from heart failure. That person needs to start exercising!

Lungs!

You gotta love your lungs! They draw in oxygenated air, then expel carbon dioxide. If you had dyslexic lungs, you'd be dead within minutes!

At rest, you breathe about 12 times a minute. While exercising, you could hit 20 times in 60 seconds. All told, you breathe roughly 8.5 million times every single year. When you add in exercise for the average adult, that goes up to 8.51 million times.

You would think your lungs would be in charge of how much air you need. You'd be wrong. Your blood is in charge here. The chemical receptors in your blood determine changes in oxygen, carbon dioxide and acidity levels. They then send that info up to the brain, and your noggin tells your lungs whether or not to speed up or slow down your air intake.

The amazing fun fact here is the sheer number of airways you have. There are about 1,500 miles worth of air passages laid out in your lungs.

At the end of every passageway are little sacs called alveoli. You have 300 million of these. Capillaries wrap around every single alveoli, take in the oxygen and send it out to your blood, which, in turn, delivers it to the 50 trillion cells in your body.

Did you get that? 50 trillion deliveries after every single breath!

Then the blood takes the carbon dioxide given off by your cells and sends it back to the prearranged drop offs and your lungs exhale.

Think of the organization this entails! Every second of the day, when you're awake, when you're asleep, when you're not paying attention in class, or on the road, you have 50 trillion cells shouting, "Please, sir, may I have some more?"

And your blood knows how to stay on the correct side of the body; oxygen bringers on the right, carbon dioxide recyclers on the left. It's like the most complicated kitchen in the universe; food goes out through one door and the leftovers come back in through the other.

For this system to work, once the carbon dioxide has been expelled from your lungs into the atmosphere, it has to go somewhere to be converted back into oxygen. Think of the foresight that's needed just for humanity to be able to breathe. We know the answer: I'll take trees for 200, please!

But those carbon dioxide inhaling, oxygen exhaling trees had to be in place well before humanity arrived on the scene. If the Designer had waited until mankind was here and they started breathing up a storm, the Creator would have had to start all over again by nightfall.

New York City owes a huge debt of gratitude to the city's founders who insisted on building Central Park. With so many skyscrapers in Manhattan, think how much harder it would be to breathe without all of their nearby trees!

A recent post on Facebook made me laugh. It said, "Quit trying to fly to Mars and just go plant a tree, for goodness sake!" From your lung's perspective, truer words have not been spoken.

Use 'Em or Lose 'Em!

I would be remiss leaving the subject of your heart and lungs without including the following plug—get off your hairy heinie and exercise!

People who exercise not only strengthen their all-important heart and lungs, but they also are at a lower risk for depression and have higher cognitive function as they grow older. It also lowers the risk for a whole slew of diseases, like diabetes. Not to mention you fit in your clothes better and don't get winded opening up the fridge.

As I stated earlier, your body is a factory. If you're feeling sluggish, examine what fuel you're putting into the factory and run a diagnostic test. It doesn't take a genius to figure out that if you're tired all the time, maybe you need to do more, not less.

At one point my ankle started giving out at inopportune times (not that there are many opportune times). My doctor said it was anti-intuitive, but I needed to use my ankles more, not less. Because my main exercise was swimming, my ankles weren't getting the workout they needed. So, I switched things up, took up walking a couple of miles on my off days, and I haven't had any problems in that area for a while.

I am the first person to rejoice at our culture's sedentary lifestyle. I wake up every day grateful I don't have to go out and hoe the back forty. But the fact that our jobs no longer demand any physical labor has taken its toll on our health.

I am also quite aware of my own hypocrisy. I am, down to my very core, inherently lazy. I love spending time in front of my computer, either writing or whiling away the hours looking at Facebook and YouTube. My idea of a great night is watching a movie, then bingeing on any number of Amazon, Disney+ or Netflix series. While I snack on a cupcake.

Of late, I have fallen into the habit of taking so many naps that I've reverted to sucking my thumb.

In short, I am not a triathlete in training!

For those reasons, I've joined a gym and force myself to go at least three times a week. When I can. If I feel like it. Assuming the weather's good. And I'm not traveling. Or sick.

If I'm really quiet, I can almost hear my arteries clogging.

Fun Fact: Our bones completely replicate themselves over a 10-year period. Which is so much better than doing it all at once. That'd be awkward. For no apparent reason, people would suddenly start staggering around like the Scarecrow from *The Wizard* of Oz. "Sorry, can't help it! New bones!"

The Eyes Have It

Your eyes were among your first organs to form. Within four weeks of fertilization, an unborn infant's eyes are beginning to develop. Interestingly enough, many newborns can move their eyes independently of each other, which can be a shock to unsuspecting parents.

During any 24-hour period, our eyes will move about 100,000 times. That's the equivalent of walking 50 miles! It's actually more if you're at the beach and are pretending to not look over at the girl in the bikini on the towel next to you.

You have 100 million light receptors in your eyes. These receptors are like pixels on a digital camera's sensor. Only there are 100 million of them!

The various images you see are converted into nerve signals in the optic nerve, which sends it back to the brain. All before you can even blink.

Studies have shown that people with dark eyes generally have faster reaction times than people with light-colored eyes. Brown-eyed people generally are better at tennis, while blue-eyed people pretty much get anything they want in life!

There are, naturally, several ways for your eyes to go wrong: from near and far vision, to cataracts, to color blindness, to glaucoma, to what I have: astigmatism. This is where your eyes don't line up correctly and either vertical or horizontal lines appear to be blurry.

As a kid in grade school, whenever I looked at an object up close, it had a 'shadow' above or below it, so I logically concluded I had X-ray vision. Imagine my surprise when, instead of being trained on how to use heat vision, I was fitted for a pair of Clark Kent bifocals.

Author Daniel J. Levitin makes a fascinating observation in his book, *This is Your Brain on Music*. He says that since light is colorless, the color we see is actually coming from our brain, which registers every particular light wave to a corresponding color.

If you extrapolate this to its logical end, we come to a *Matrix*-y conclusion: this world could well be entirely void of color. It could either be all white or shades of grey. We only *think* we see color because of how our brains are made and have come to accept our perceptions as fact.

This means life is not unlike a 3D film, where the images don't really pop out at you; you only think they do because of the lens through which you are looking.

To quote Spock, "Fascinating!"

Ears

Ears evolved over time in order to hold up our glasses as well as to give frustrated nuns something to grab on to as they pull young smart alecks out of their seats. In other cases, they also help us hear the world around us.

How ears do this is ingenious. While the eyes take in light and convert it into electrical signals for the brain to interpret, our ears convert sound waves into nerve signals.

Specifically, sound travels through your ear canal until it gets to the middle ear. This connects with the eustachian tube, which connects to the nose and mouth, which sometimes gets clogged up when you fly.

That's why yawning helps when descending and why babies tend to cry on landings. Parents need to get them to chew or suck on something to help relieve the pressure. Whenever I hear a baby cry on a plane, it's all I can do to not yell out, "Oh, for goodness sake, give 'em the boob!"

After the sound waves go through the middle ear, they pass through the fluid of the cochlea, or the inner ear. From there, the sound goes straight to your brain so that moments later you can shout out, "Turn that crap down!"

As the signals pass into your head, your brain determines where the sound is coming from and how we feel about it. Music can somehow touch our emotions, bring both sorrow and elation, while your parents stating you can't go to the party until you finish your chores can elicit feelings of dread and death.

Ears also help you keep your balance. When crystals form in the fluid filled canals, you can get vertigo. When it happened to our mom, it just confirmed what we'd all suspected for years: that our mother had rocks in her head.

Music, Sweet Music

While we can examine how our ears work, no amount of scientific explanation about the pitch of the sound, or how it causes our eardrums to wiggle, thus sending signals to our brain to translate, can explain why I love music so much!

Since I was young I have loved music with a passion. I can't play an instrument, I know nothing about music theory, but I know what I like! In high school I was horribly insecure, so many was the night I sat alone in my room listening to my albums and reading the liner notes.

To this day I can pick out Eric Gale's guitar on pretty much any album, or a Stanley Clarke bass line, or tell you how Gary Richrath started R.E.O. Speedwagon until lead singer Kevin Cronin came in and eventually edged him out.

What I can't explain is why I respond to music with so much emotion. There are a handful of singers that strike a chord in my very soul. Kenny Loggins, Michael McDonald and James Taylor are three men that just know how to sing a feeling, not just the notes on a page.

Besides the Beatles, who I will love until the day I die, I am a diehard Bruce Springsteen fan.

I can even tell you how it happened. I was in college, and Bruce was all the rage. I just didn't get the hype, so a friend loaned me a copy of his *Born to Run* album. The first pass through was fine, but by the second listen, I was hooked.

When Bruce came to town with the East Street Band and I witnessed his three-hour jaw-dropping, pedal-to-the-metal concert, I was converted into a fan for life.

I just listened to the entire *Born to Run* album again this morning, and I can't express how moved I was. The lyrics, the story-telling, the poetic imagery, the hopes, the dashed dreams, Clarence Clemons' saxophone, the tight band and Bruce himself. To me, that album is sheer perfection. If it doesn't move you, I worry for your soul.

We all have songs that affect us one way or the other. My dad loved Neil Diamond and Eddy Arnold. I can remember him relaxing late at night with all lights off and listening to Neil's *Hot August Nights* and Eddy's *I Want Some Red Roses for a Blue Lady*.

When I purchased the Apple HomePod (which can play up to 4 *million* songs!), the very first song I called up was Eddy Arnold's *Cattle Call*. Before Eddy even got to his first yodel, there were tears in my eyes. Just hearing that song brought back memories of my dad, and I couldn't hold back the emotion.

Music does that. Somehow sounds filtering into our heads can cause us to feel certain things, either good or bad. I find that more than a little miraculous.

Moses Supposes Our Noses Are Roses

Your nose has up to 12 million receptor cells and can detect 10,000 different odors!

Think of the smells you associate with pleasure (mine would be cinnamon rolls in the oven, freshly mimeographed paper, roses and babies), and then mull over the smells you just can't stand (if my wife orders brussels sprouts at a restaurant, I have to rotate our table until I sit upwind).

Smell is an amazing addition to the world around us. Anything that has a 'smell' is actually releasing scent molecules into the air. You (and your crazy dog) pick up those molecules by sniffing and then determining whether or not you're smelling pizza, a skunk, or any one of a thousand other scents.

I always assumed smelling was just something that naturally happened, but it's a two-way street. Our world has been designed so that everything gives off a smell. Some are pleasant, others not so much.

Those smells often translate into different emotions, be they pleasure, disgust or fear. The entire movie of 'Ratatouie' was based on this premise (along with the previously unknown culinary skill of rats).

Smoke can elicit a fight response. Tommy Bahama has perfected the smells of Hawaii and the accompanying mellow, "Hey, Brah!" feeling in their candles. Companies exist whose sole purpose is to add smells to food to make it more appetizing. Pumpkins and Peppermint would be minor-league players without these companies annually foisting them onto the public.

Noses may not make the all-star sensory team, but without one you'd just make a nuisance of yourself.

"How do I smell? Are my pits fresh? Am I totally rank or possibly passable?"

The body plays a cruel trick on teenagers. One day you're just a kid bopping around the playground taking a bath once a week, the very next you're shoved into the shower and told you're not allowed to get out until you've scrubbed every inch of your skin with a loofa and bathed in a vat of Axl.

I don't know why male teenager nostrils are impervious to odors that range from things that cause involuntary gag reactions to "seriously, open a window! How do you live like this!?" but they do.

Tongue Lashing

We use our tongues to wet our lips, help form words, lick ice cream, taste food, and to get in the way when the Dental Hygienist tries to scrape our teeth clean.

They also come in handy when you want to show your displeasure to the tattle tale who sits across from you in class as well as years later when she finally lets you kiss her.

Hands down the best movie line about this particular append-age is from *Young Frankenstein*, when Gene Wilder goes in to kiss Madeline Kahn and she pulls back as she exclaims, "No tongue!"

The tongue is not only used to taste food and move it around, it's also very important to help us form words. If someone has a 'lazy' tongue, they have a difficult time saying certain sounds, such as 'l's' or 'r's' as evidenced by Gilda Radner from SNL imitating a famous newscaster saying, "Hewwo, I'm Bawbwa Wawa."

As to flavors, the tongue can pick up and discern between sour, bitter, salty, sweet and the newest flavor added to our original top four—umami. We have burger places in LA called Umami. The only thing I can figure out is that the new additional flavor taster helps parse out tasty hamburgers.

The tongue can also be used as a lie detector test. In more barbaric times, several countries in the Middle East would heat a spoon until it was red hot and place it against the tongues of suspected liars. If the tongue was wet, the spoon would not stick. But as liar's tongues were assumed to be dry and saliva free, the spoon would stick!

I much prefer the modern lie detector test. Regardless of the outcome, one doesn't leave with blisters on one's tongue!

Fun Fact: The average human has over 10,000 taste buds, while chickens only have 30. It is the ultimate irony that if you fed a chicken to a chicken, it probably wouldn't taste like chicken!

Fun Fact: The next time you take a big whiff of perfume, know that it is mostly likely made of Ambergris, a waxy secretion belched out by Sperm whales. Regardless of its pleasant smell, it's still made from whale puke!

The Blood!

Guess how many red blood cells are in a single drop of blood? One thousand? 100,000 thousand? Nope. You have *five million* red blood cells in every drop of your blood. It must get crowded in there!

When you hear the phrase, "the life is in the blood," it is absolutely accurate. The blood not only carries oxygen to your several trillion cells and then returns the carbon dioxide waste, but, along for the ride are several other necessities of life. Both red and white cells are in the blood, as well as platelets (handy to have on hand in case you need a blood clot). But your blood also contains wastes, nutrients, cholesterol and antibodies.

The trip from the lungs to the heart to your tissues and then back to the heart and lungs again takes about a minute. That's right. This amazing fluid circulates through 100,000 miles of very tiny tunnels at a very high speed and then rushes back again, ready to take another trip.

To successfully do its work, blood needs to be constantly replenished. That's where your bone marrow comes in. Those blood making factories produce millions of blood cells every single second.

Please try and take all of this in. While you are staring off in space, wondering about your place in the universe, your body is working overtime to insure nothing interferes with your existential crisis.

Your lungs suck in air, which is transferred to your blood, which circulates around your body, which feeds every inch of you, which then goes back to the lungs, which then exhales the air it no longer needs.

Oh, and by the way, the blood needs to be filtered by the kidneys some 20 to 25 times a day!

If you had to be aware and responsible for all the things your blood does on a minute by minute basis, from feeding to filtering to replenishing, you'd be dead in a matter of minutes, plain and simple.

Even if you remembered to circulate the blood, you'd probably forget to continue manufacturing new blood cells. Then, when you're distracted by a small shaving cut that needed to clot, you'd probably forget to send the carbon dioxide back out through the lungs.

Fun Things to do While on the Road

Here's an interesting point: what do you think the body naturally does when one starts to bleed internally? Your instinct would be to double up on production of new blood cells, right?

Wrong!

For some reason, on an internal bleed, the body decides to stop all production, and in doing so, causes a myriad of symptoms designed to catch the attention of the owner.

This is what happened to me several years ago. I was in Tampa, Florida, when my body decided to shut down.

I thought I had a mild case of the flu. Turns out I was at death's door, knocking quite vigorously. Which was quite surprising considering I couldn't muster the energy to tie my own shoelaces.

For about a week I ignored all the signs that my body was shutting down. I had a gig that weekend and I wasn't about to slow down just because I felt a little under the weather.

One fact that I was ignorant of is that, because of the internal bleed, my body was absorbing the blood, digesting it, and sending it out as waste.

To quote my emergency room doctor, "When you crap black, go the ER." File this under, 'good to know!'

When you are a few quarts low on blood, certain tell-tale signs emerge. One is that you look like death warmed over. If you think 'Casper the Friendly Ghost' is a hot look, then I heartily suggest bleeding internally!

The other indicator is that you have all the get-up-and-go of a slug. A dead slug. A dead slug that has been run over repeatedly by a steam roller. Yeah, that pretty much describes it.

The people at my gig were great. Naturally I insisted that I was fine and that "the show must go on!" But after about a minute on stage, I accepted their offer of a stool. I did a two hour show of 'sit down' comedy.

After the show and some research online in my hotel room, I finally figured out what was happening to me. I called and scheduled an appointment with my doctor back home in Los Angeles.

I never got there.

The next morning, I managed to drive my car back to the rental agency at the airport. The problem was, making that short drive took every last bit of energy I had. I sat in that car and couldn't get out for the longest time. Still determined to make my flight, I struggled out of the rental car garage and shuffled off to the terminal.

That's as far as I got. Completely out of juice, I sat on a bench outside the airline check-in for at least half an hour. It was as if I had left this world and was living in the land of Jell-O. Everything moved in slow motion. I looked at my watch, saw the time of my flight come and go, but I couldn't do anything about it. I've never felt like this before and I hope I never feel this way again. I didn't have the energy to even stand up. All I could do was pray for help—but nothing came.

After a good long rest, I teetered into the terminal and walked over to the helpful attendants at Delta (who deserve many kudos for all they did both then and after my ordeal).

I simply said, "Hi, I think you need to call an ambulance for me." Then I staggered over to the closest seat and collapsed.

The ambulance arrived shortly thereafter and I became 'that guy' in the airport. The one that everybody walks by, stares at and thanks the Lord it isn't them.

The emergency responders put me on the rolling gurney, shoved me in the back of their ambulance and took off. A new guy did his best to take a blood sample, but after several sticking attempts, gave up. How could he know I had no blood? I told him my son was an EMT and absolved him from all guilt.

The hospital is where the true adventure began. They determined that I was, indeed, several quarts low and immediately started a transfusion. For your information, most people have a blood level of 12 to 14. I was at 7. I was told much later that anyone who has 6.9 or below is resting comfortably in the morgue.

Over the next few days we began a fun pattern: they'd fill me up with blood while they went looking for the leak.

They tried gamma ray technology, an endoscope and finally had me swallow a camera the size of New Jersey to see if they could locate the leak (if you want to look this one up on YouTube, I go into a bit more detail about the size of the camera and my inability to swallow pills).

Ultimately, they announced that wherever the leak was, it had healed itself.

When I was ready to check out some five days later, the doctor gave me my prognosis: "It was a freaky thing."

That's it. There was nothing I could have done to prevent it. Nothing I can do in the future to stop it from ever happening again.

Something in my guts had ruptured and, after some R&R, had healed itself.

I certainly know the symptoms now, so it won't ever get that far along before I seek help, but that particular experience left me with several ambivalent feelings concerning our current medical system.

To be sure, I am filled with awe at what we can do with our knowledge and expertise. Though my own personal scavenger hunt ultimately turned out to be unsuccessful, they were able to look in my insides with several different machines without disemboweling me. For which I shall ever be grateful.

The nurses and doctors were all fantastic. People who dedicate their lives to healthcare have my undying respect and admiration. I will, however, make a possible exception of one particular nurse. I believe her name was 'Ratchet.'

This sadist woke me every single morning at 4:30 am to take my blood so the doctors could have it by their 9 am rounds. Her, I didn't like.

You read that right. In order to determine why I was losing blood, one crazy nurse kept taking more of my blood.

Despite that one bad apple, with their help (and several transfusions) I was able to leave the hospital and make it home and have never had another episode.

Freaky thing, huh?

In hindsight, evidently, I was an idiot. If I had managed to get on that plane ride home, a nurse later told me that I probably would have died.

We'll never know if the nurse was right or not, but the point here is to listen to your body! When you feel as if you're walking through Jell-O, go get your fine self checked out!

My last statement is to encourage everyone of age to become a blood donor. It truly is the stuff of life, and when you need it, nothing else satisfies quite like some good, fresh blood.

But nothing happens without volunteers like you and me going in every eight to 10 weeks to replenish an ever-dwindling supply.

Just know up front that the questions they ask you are intensely personal. I have a Rapid Pass, where I fill out all the questions before I go in to give blood later that day. But for safety reasons, they have to ask you the very same questions again when you check in, to make doubly sure you didn't have sex with a needle-using homosexual from a third world country from the time you filled out the questionnaire to the time you come in to give blood.

"Well, gee, it's only been half an hour. I think you have way over-estimated my sexual prowess, so no."

Even with such ridiculous questions, it's still well worth it.

Your Digestive System

To get your body to operate at full capacity, you need fuel. Without it, everything else goes to pot.

I believe most of us know how this works. You take in food at one end, use what you need and discard the rest as waste from the other end which can then be used as compost to help plants grow.

Which is why I'll never be a Vegan! Yech! "Do you know where that asparagus has been?"

To be more specific, the human body passes food from one end of the factory to the other in a number of very specific and ingenious steps.

Step 1) The mouth. Here's where your food is broken down, both by chewing and adding saliva. After that, it's swallowed and dropped down the esophagus. If you've ever heard your mother scold you for not properly chewing your food, you may now officially forgive her. She was only looking out for your stomach.

Step 2) The stomach. This organ (which is sometimes larger, sometimes smaller than your eyes) douses your meal in gastric juices. If you really want to aid your digestion, marinate your steak in this stuff to get a head start. Once it's been broken down, you now have a product called chyme. Your stomach takes about two and a half to five hours to finish its job. When you are super full after dinner and you feel disgusting, this is why. Your stomach's taking its sweet time in turning your meal into something useful.

Step 3) The small intestine. The chyme is pushed down into your small intestine to be broken down further by enzymes sent over from your pancreas and bile supplied by your liver. This is where most of the food's nutrients are absorbed. Food stays another three hours in this area. Unless, of course, your food decides to 'go straight through you' and this is just a quick fifteen-minute stop on the way to the exit.

Step 4) The large intestine. Most of the water from your food is absorbed here, along with whatever nutrients the small intestines missed. If your body can't use a particular food, it's pressed into feces and stamped ready for removal. Corn seems to be of particular interest here. Sometimes corn moves through the entire system and hasn't even been touched. I often wonder why we even bother eating the stuff.

Step 5) Evacuate. Go number 2. Sit on the squatty potty. Pick your own disgusting 'you're so mature!' euphemism here.

I will admit I don't care for this last step. I never have. That being said, I am so grateful I live in a time of history that has both toilets and toilet paper. To imagine living at a time or place where one cannot relax and read either the paper or a book of jokes is, to my mind, the height of uncivilization.

This is also the reason I don't camp. If nature came equipped with toilets, I might reconsider. Until then, for me, roughing it is staying at a Motel 6.

6) Repeat steps 1—5.

Fun Fact: The largest and strongest muscle in your body is the gluteus maximus. Consider taking advantage of this the next time someone asks you to loosen a stubborn jar lid!

Not So Fun Fact: George Washington was essentially killed by his attending doctor when the quack leeched out several liters of our first President's 'bad' blood. It's only been in the last 200 years or so that PiLCs have determined we need *more* blood to fight disease, not *less*!

DNA and Friends

Let's look at how your cells communicate—because nothing we've been able to invent even comes close to the sophistication of your body's high-tech system.

Each and every cell in your body has a double helix library of three billion base pairs providing 50,000 genes and covering 24 chromosomes.

You may be crammed into your jeans, but it's nothing compared to what is crammed into your genes! Thank you, ladies and gentlemen, I'm here all week!

Those three billion base pairs and 50,000 genes somehow manage to engineer *100 trillion* neural connections in the brain. With 100 trillion connections, it's only natural that eventually some of them would get crossed. Especially at the speed at which they're flying!

"We need to tell the kidneys they've got some toxins coming their way!"

"Ahh! I just missed the exit! I'll have to take the next turn off and come around again!"

If you consider yourself an overly sensitive type, it's for good reason! You have 10 million nerve endings for smell alone!

I know a woman who had no sense of smell. I also know people whose sense of smell is so keen they can discern flavors of particular wines just by swirling it around in a glass. I fall directly in the middle. I'm acutely aware when someone 'dealt it,' but fall flat when it comes to wine pretension. "Ah, yes, this bouquet gives off the distinct impression of being made from…grapes."

The above functions happen because of the information contained in your DNA code.

Specifically, the DNA molecule is shaped in the form of a double helix (picture a twisted, circular staircase), and its information- carrying capacity is determined by the series of chemical compounds that comprise the steps of that stairway (or rungs of a step ladder, if you prefer).

I like a stairway, because I can picture it going up and up forever. A ladder has to lean against something or you'll get fined by OSHA.

As you look at your DNA molecule, picture each step as a different piece of coding consisting of exactly two letters. The letters in this mix are either A, T, C or G.

It's unclear why these letters were chosen, except the obvious answer: if X, Y, Z were used, scientists all over the world would constantly be examining their zippers.

As our computers use 0s and 1s, your DNA uses countless combinations of these four letters in its software to spell out very specific instructions for each cell.

Here's where it gets fun. The DNA spells out a very specific code. But what good is a code sitting alone in its room? It needs to get to the Cabaret! (If you don't understand that reference, go watch some Bob Fosse musicals, for goodness sake!)

To get the DNA's information to where it needs to be, we have our RNA. That's the messenger molecule! It's the combo Uber driver and cellular service of the nano world.

The RNA takes the DNA's information over to the proteins, where they put the information into action.

Think of DNA as Upper Management. They determine who does what and when in their factory. The RNA is middle management. They deliver the DNA's orders to the factory floor. Proteins are the workers. They carry out DNA's wishes with no allowance for deviations.

The good thing about proteins is that they know their place. Rare is the protein who yearns for a better life.

Imagine some upstart protein getting its assignment from the RNA...

"But I want to work in the heart!"

"Sorry, bub, your code says you're a toenail."

"But I've been working on my ventricle flash cards. I've memorized the blood flow charts! I'm ready!"

"Nothing I can do about it. Take it or leave it."

Finally, the wonderous recombinant DNA you hear so much about doesn't exist in nature. It's the product of brilliant splicers with very steady hands.

PiLCs have figured out how to manipulate DNA and RNA and turn out augmented molecules.

"Think those proteins are real?"

"Please! They're so fake!"

Our Genomes

If you're a child of the sixties, you might remember a Disney movie called *The Genome Mobile*. If memory serves, it had very little to do with science and, for some reason, centered around children and their budding friendship with a wacky crew of dwarves.

Still, Disney was ahead of its time, as it took science years to catch up.

I was given a Fitbit watch for Father's Day, and while the device itself is wonderful, the instructions were written by someone who had only the most tentative grasp of grammar. It said, "To program, device must in hands be. Try not to program. Do." It appears my Fitbit was designed by Yoda.

Fortunately, our bodies do not have that problem. With their handy genome instruction book on hand, communication is clear and concise.

In the text of the human genome, it consists of all the DNA of our species. It is the heredity code of life. Each cell of your body carries this code. Don't worry about it being stolen. The DNA sequence of the entire human genome is estimated to be about three billion base pairs in length.

It is so long that to read it out loud would take something like 31 *years*. If Robin Williams were alive, he could do it in 10 minutes, but then he'd sweat all over it and it would be rendered useless.

To give you an idea of how difficult it is to isolate a problem in the DNA code, if *just one letter is off*, out of three billion base pairs, then you've got yourself a problem.

This is why your teachers in elementary school kept drilling it into your head that 'spelling counts!' One little mistake in your DNA and there's hades to pay!

In Francis Collins book, *The Language of God*, he recounts the amazing story of narrowing down the search for the 'one wrong letter' that causes cystic fibrosis to a small stretch of two million base pairs on chromosome seven.

Narrowing the search down to two million choices out of three billion base pairs sounds great! But then the reality of going through two million steps on the double helix ladder sunk in. It was a Herculean task that took years to accomplish.

It was like individually testing out two million Christmas lights until the bad one was found.

After years of chipping away, Francis and his team actually found the culprit, and now PiLCs are on their way, hopefully, to helping eradicate a horrible disease.

Proteins and Amino Acids

Proteins are another fascinating part of your body. PiLCs have accurately ascertained all the building blocks of a basic protein, but for some reason, they can't seem to put one together. It's like all proteins were manufactured at Ikea, the directions are in Swedish and we're missing the screwdriver do-hickey thing.

PiLCs unlocked the secret to proteins over 40 years ago and they're still flummoxed as to how they go together.

Here's a math problem.

We humans have in the neighborhood of 70,000 genes.

Those 70,000 genes house the same number of proteins.

Proteins are strings and/or coils totaling between 200 and 1,000 amino acids.

That means the 70,000 genes need to organize up to 70 million amino acids into very specific structures.

Those genes make up the 30 to 50 trillion cells in our bodies.

You ever look in the mirror in the morning and think to yourself, "I just lost over 500 billion cells and you can't even tell the difference!"?

Our genetic package, known by the PiLCs as the genome, is made up of about three billion nucleotide base pairs per cell. That's right, *per cell*.

If you've ever wondered exactly what information is stored in the double helix-shaped strands of our DNA, that's it!

All the connections between the genomes and proteins and amino acids is beyond the comprehension of the brightest person who ever lived. Because we're talking trillions and trillions of connections. No wonder I'm tired all the time! My body is in a constant state of hooking up! Give it a rest, everybody!

Ever meet someone who's really good at working the Rubik's cube? I can do my best for about a decade and get nowhere. But the pros can take that multi-colored cube, twist it six times and, voila! puzzle solved!

It's like that with our Designer and proteins. All the puzzle pieces are laid out on the table, but no matter how hard we try, we can't fit them together. The Creator comes in and says, "No, see, it's simple!" He waves His hand over them and, well, you can guess the result.

DNA is another example. A friend of mine explained to me that while the DNA code is amazing, it's still just the delivery system, much like the hard drive in your computer or a DVD player. It's complex, but it's only the player.

The program inside the DNA is what makes you who and what you are. That part of the program is still a mystery to us. We can see what the DNA player is playing; we just can't figure out how the information got in there.

What I'm saying is, if you were thinking of building your own human from scratch, you'll be much better off focusing on the old-fashioned way of impregnating a human egg, because we're not even near the point of knowing how all of our parts came to be.

We know what they do and how they work together, but when it comes to creating genomes and amino acids and proteins, we're way behind the 8 ball. If you're really interested in becoming the next Dr. Frankenstein, check back in a millennium or so. By then preschoolers will be creating their own pets.

Pain

To close, we move from things we can't see or feel to quite the opposite: *pain*!

Face it, you hate pain. Be it physical or emotional, you do your best to side step both it and the consequences that come with it. And you're in good company; entire pharmaceutical companies and parental strategies are built on pain-avoidance.

It wouldn't be too off base to say most of our lives are built around avoiding the p-word. We even exercise (causing short-term pain) in order to avoid long-term pain.

Paying our taxes hurts, but not as much as the fines that come later or, worse yet, being put in prison for trying to avoid them altogether.

The fact of the matter is, pain can be a good thing. It alerts us to small problems before they become big problems.

How many times have we heard of someone who put off going to the doctor, only to arrive too late. "I'm sorry about your leg falling off. Maybe you should have come to us six months ago when you tried to glue it back on."

We have different kinds of pain. There's the dull, general ache, then the sharp, localized pain and finally, the pain that comes when a friend or loved one won't stop pressing on your last nerve.

Even though most of us believe we could live without it, where would we be without pain? Think of how many stupid things humanity does right now with our pain receptacles fully in place! If we couldn't feel pain, our idiocy would be off the charts!

Granted, baby deliveries would improve exponentially, but every stupid sport in existence would explode overnight! Free form rock climbing, motocross racing, asking girls out on dates; all of these dangerous activities need to be approached with extreme caution.

If you want to thank anyone for their help in this area, the man who invented anesthesia is to forever be praised. The only reason I can tolerate the dentist is because of Novocain.

The man who invented this wonder drug was a German chemist named Alford Einhorn. Why we don't have an annual parade in this guy's honor is beyond me.

Before Novocain and anesthesia were invented, people relied on copious amounts of alcohol and biting down on shoe leather. Which, I'm sure you can see, was entirely counter-productive in the field of dentistry.

Now, if someone could just invent a *silent drill*, my visits to the dentist would improve exponentially.

The point here may not be obvious, but is very important. Pain is a gift. We need it. Pain gives us very strict boundaries. Our bodies have pain receptacles for a very good reason: they keep us alive.

The innumerable nerve endings woven throughout our body are invaluable. They are flashing red lights put in place in order to warn us to stop doing whatever it is we're doing!

Dull aches turn into big aches unless we deal with them. Twinges, cramps, stabs, spasms and stitches are our body's way of cautioning us to stay on the straight and narrow.

Fear often does the same thing. When the bells go off in your head, they're ringing for a reason! They're telling you to not do whatever idiotic thing you're planning!

I'm deathly afraid of heights for a very good reason. If you fall off a tall precipice, you will probably die. People who have no fear when they stand on the edge of cliffs are idiots because they are one stiff breeze away from being a corpse.

I'm of the opinion that our culture is the first one in history that has made the world so safe that we have trained ourselves to ignore our pain and fear sensors.

That is why we now have both adrenaline junkies and the most fragile generation ever. In the past, people dealt with pain every single day. Today we don't know what it feels like to hurt, so we either seek it out through adventure or run to a safe space at the slightest provocation.

Just my two cents.

The Cumulative Total

For the universe to have been miraculously formed over billions of years, apparently for our benefit, for our planet to sit so safely and sustain us on the edge of a deadly galaxy, for our bodies to operate so seamlessly without even a minute's down time, well, for me, it all adds up to one huge inescapable conclusion.

I hope the first third of this book has filled you with a sense of awe over the amazing multitude of miracles that have led to our existence.

Any one fact or figure may not be enough to sway you, but my hope is that the cumulative total of unexplainable phenomenon about our universe, our planet and our bodies is enough to convince you that something greater than mere chance is behind the sometimes-unexplainable creative curtain.

That being the case, the next section of the book begins my audacious attempt to properly introduce you to the One who created everything you see and most everything you experience.

Don't give up yet!

Recipe—One Human

1. Mix dust thoroughly.
2. Create bones. The shoulder bone should be connected to the back bone. The back bone should be connected to the hip bone. The hip bone should be connected to the leg bone. The leg bone should be connected to the foot bone. Continue until fully formed.
3. Add one heart. Circulate blood.
4. Add conscience (aka as Jiminy Cricket)
5. Create lungs. Breathe into them.
6. Make them male and female.
7. Add sense of sight, smell and touch.
8. When they ask for noses, have them think you said 'roses' and give them big red ones!
9. Add instinct to female. Add dumbfounded look to male.
10. If needed, add brain.
11. Pour in sense of humor.
12. Important! Do let humans overbake. They will believe they have made themselves!

Fun Fact: The human eye is made up of over two *million* working parts. It blinks, on average, over four million times a year. More if you're guilty of something. Thankfully, once our eyes reach their maximum size, they stop growing, whereas our nose and ears never stop (list this under Reasons-You-Should-Be-Glad-We-Don't-Live-To-Be-1,000-Years-Old!).

Section II
The Explanation

A Proper Introduction

After reading the previous chapters I hope you are as amazed as I am about the absolutely miraculous series of events that got you here.

In this section my intent is to give credit where credit is due. Only one character is bold enough to step up to this marvelous creation and say, "Yeah, I did that."

Why He did it and what we are supposed to do about it are different matters that I will attempt to unpack in subsequent chapters.

'Attempt' being the operative word here. While I think I understand a few things about God's character, I could easily be barking up several wrong trees. That said, please take what I say with an entire lick of salt and compare it to your own experience. Hopefully, between the two of us, we'll end up pointed in the right direction.

A Knee Jerk Reaction

The elephant in the room here is the poor reputation that is now firmly attached to the word *Christian*.

The average parishioner is thought to be an ultra-right wing, racist, ignorant goose-stepping fool. And that's on a good day!

I will attempt to persuade you over the following pages that the majority of the faithful are not *that* kind of Christian. Regardless, from your perspective I could well turn out to be even more offensive!

Like it or not, the God of the Bible lays out a series of rules and suggestions that He states rather matter-of-factly will make our lives better. I suspect this is where a great deal of our disagreement originates.

Secondly, even if they don't follow them, everybody on the planet seems to know the guidelines Christians are supposed to live by. The fact that we so often fall unbelievably short of our own code of behavior prompts the rest of humanity to label us as hypocrites.

Every time a self-professed Christian is caught with his or her hand in the metaphorical cookie jar, the cries of "hypocrite" rise up across the land.

No argument.

We're also liars, perverts, cheaters, cowards, racists and way too often turn a blind eye to our hurting brothers and sisters.

In other words, we're no better than anyone else on this rock.

Ouch.

My point in starting off here is that I don't want what I have to say to be measured up against a holy writ of perfection. I am nothing if not imperfect.

One of my best traits is an overwhelming sense of guilt. I know my faith states quite emphatically that I'm forgiven, but the old tapes of my life-long litany of mistakes and missteps seem to play on a constant loop in my brain.

All that being said, my intent here is to go forward with one main purpose in mind: namely, to explain, diffuse and shed light on the methods behind the madness of a God whom I believe has been massively misunderstood and, quite frankly, found guilty by association with His frequently faulty flock.

If, in the telling, I tend to lean more on my go-to of sarcasm rather than Hallmark soliloquies of love, please forgive me. That book will have to be written by someone else.

May I Have the Pleasure...

I love a well-constructed story. In my line of work the artistry of a joke comes down to how well the author can deliver a laugh. I can be fooled by exaggeration or a twist, but regardless of how we get there, by the end of the journey I love to express my surprise and wonder with a gut-wrenching laugh.

Mystery writers can somehow string you along with misdirection and suspense until they finally reveal that the innocent looking guy from the first act did it.

Musicians play with sounds and lyrics to evoke emotions. Painters, dancers, poets and sculptors all use their talents to, hopefully, make us look at the world in a new way.

God is the original artist. He created an immense art project from His imagination leading up to one surprising punchline: us.

I have no idea why anyone, deity or not, would go to so much trouble, but apparently that's exactly what He did.

As we begin to lay out who this grand Designer is, let's start with a classic TV game show, *What's My Line?*

For those of you who were born after the wonderful era of black and white TV, I'll set the stage for you.

A mystery guest signed in, then sat behind a table across from four cocktail-party witty semi-celebrities who, while blindfolded, would ask the contestant pointed questions until the foursome either ascertained the contestant's identity or hilariously failed.

If victorious, the contestant would go home with a grand total of 25 dollars and a lifetime supply of Rice-A-Roni.

It was TV at its best!

In this scenario, the show would go something like this…

Kitty: "Are you paid well for what you do?"
God: "No."
Kitty: "Are you famous?"
God: "In some circles, yes."
Kitty: "Have you ever dabbled in politics?"
God: "Only behind the scenes."
Kitty: "Are you in the movies?
God: "Not anymore."

Kitty: "Are you known for doing miracles?"
God: "Yes."
Kitty: "Are you the maker of Playtex Cross-Your-Heart bras?"
At Kitty's ribald question, everyone shares a boisterous laugh. The studio audience takes quite a while to calm down. When they do, Bill Cummings comes in for the kill.
Bill: "Then, are you... God?
When God admits Bill has guessed correctly, everyone takes off their blindfolds and has a good laugh.

Pleased to Meet You!

Up to this point, I've been calling the One who made everything either 'the Designer' or 'the Creator.'

While those are both accurate descriptions, it is well past time to introduce the Entity who takes credit for everything you see, touch, taste and experience.

His name, not that it's any surprise at this point, is God. He has other names, of course, from Yahweh to Jehovah to He-Who-Shall-Not-Be-Named, but for clarity's sake, here we'll call Him God.

That being said, those three simple letters pack a punch with just about everyone. Some see G-o-d and react with anger. Others with love. A lot of it boils down to how you were raised and how many positive or negative religious experiences you've had over your lifetime.

Allow me say two things: 1) If you're mad at God, the odds are you're really mad at His church and not Him (and, I suspect, for good reason!) and 2) The God I want to introduce you to is probably not the God you want, but He is the God you need.

Because the Bible is the book where God introduces Himself, I will be mainly talking about Christians and Jews. Those are the two groups who claim to adhere to the thoughts and precepts laid out in the pages of God's instruction book.

You certainly may hold on to any other random religion of your choice, but know that the bulk of this book will not be focusing on a comparison/contrast but rather a deep dive into one particular deity's character and modus operandi.

Slightly More Accurate Attributes

When Moses asked to see God way-back-when in the Old Testament, God told him that request would be impossible. Not because He didn't want Moses to see Him, but because of the very real fact that any man who looks on the face of God will die.

Remember that climactic scene at the end of *Indiana Jones* when the box containing the 10 commandments was opened and the spirits flew around melting the faces off of the Nazis? Yeah, it would be like that.

God arranged to hide Moses in the cleft of a mountain as He 'walked' past. After the mountains rumbled and rocks came tumbling down, Moses saw His back and got a hint of how big God is.

Later, when Moses went in for his daily communion with the Spirit of God in the tabernacle tent, he came out every time with glowing skin. If you need to wear SPF 50 just to be in the same room with God's Spirit, you can rest assured He's fairly glorious.

I find it interesting that the Bible doesn't bother itself with trying to describe what God looks like, nor does it try to prove His existence. It matter-of-factly assumes He is who He says He is. I guess it's up to us to prove that He's not.

Despite the lack of physical highlights, we are given clues as to His nature. Here are a few highlights from His resume…
- God is all powerful and creative (Genesis 1:1)
- God is faithful (1st Corinthians 10:13)
- God is light (1st John 1:5)
- God is patient (2nd Peter 3:9)
- God rightly judges our thoughts and attitudes (Hebrews 4:12)
- God is spirit (John 4:24)
- God is perfect (Psalm 18:30)

- God is a righteous dispenser of justice (Psalm 50:6)
- God gives the gift of eternal life (Romans 6:23)
- God shows mercy and compassion (Micah 7:18, 19)
- God is love (1st John 4: 7-9)
- God's plans are unchanging (Psalm 33: 11-13)
- God is slow to anger but punishes the guilty (Exodus 34: 5-7)
- God is an all-consuming fire (Deuteronomy 4:24)

From this we have absolutely no idea if He likes long walks on the beach, prefers dogs over cats, or if He's a DC or Marvel man, but those are things I suspect we'll learn the more time we spend with Him.

I think the purpose of stating these attributes is so that we can compare ourselves to them. Speaking for myself, I fall short in every single category. This is God's definitive list of "I'm Holy and you are not."

This is the list we need to look at whenever we're mad at God or think we know better than Him as to how to run our lives or the world.

God's People Don't Always Follow God

Now let's address the downside. We need to place the blame for pretty much every idiotic, stupid, mean, intolerant thing that's ever been done in the name of God squarely at the feet of the church.

In other words, the long list of hurtful deeds we see splashed across our newspapers and history books are usually committed by people who claim to follow God, not by God Himself.

He did not endorse them. They are not on His side. They are hiding behind God's robes to perpetrate unholy acts. Unfortunately, He's not willing to come down here and defend Himself. He gives us enough credit to differentiate between what He endorses and what He does not.

The number one rule for God is to, say it with me, class, "Love the Lord your God with all your heart, soul and mind and to (emphasis added) *love your neighbor as yourself.*"

That's your litmus test. When you look at any event, be it the opening or the bombing of a hospital, ask yourself a very simple question: was it loving?

If the event was orchestrated by people who love their neighbors as themselves, it will be evident very quickly. People will be blessed by the actions of the people acting in the name of God.

In fact, the single greatest sign of any group acting in the name of God is that their actions are altruistic. They are unselfish. They put others' needs above their own. Those are people who are trying to do the right thing in a world that often doesn't give a rip.

Undoubtedly, as you look over the long list of mistakes that have been made over the centuries, from the crusades to the Spanish Inquisition to the KKK, it's a common mistake to blame God for these abominations. Mainly because a lot of these lower forms of humanity cherry pick a Bible verse or two in order to rationalize their behavior.

Even if you don't know God or His book, it should be pretty simple to look at the hatred being spewed by various fringe groups and determine that, hey, those people are not following the first rule of the book they claim to follow! They're using the name of God to get away with murder! Now I get it!

So, if possible, don't blame God for the actions of a few heinous people. While He loves them as He loves all of His (often idiotic) children, in no way does He approve of their choices.

I wish every time some shyster fleeced the flock, or a greedy hypocrite conned their congregation, the clouds would part, God would stick His head out and say, "I'm Yahweh and I do not approve this message."

Fun Fact: Christianity is still the most adhered to religion in the United States, with 65% of polled American adults identifying themselves as Christian in 2019. This is down from 85% in 1990 and 1,000% in the Fifties.

The God of the Bible Is Probably Not the God You Want

The above heading is undoubtedly true, but, to clarify, He's the God you most desperately need.

Which begs the question, what exactly are you looking for in a God?

Yes, it would be great to have a deity on hand to give you that job you've always wanted, or, better yet, to help you win the lottery so that you never have to work again. Then after you add on a better love life and an endless supply of chocolate that will never make you fat, what are you left with?

If I'm being honest, I'd want my God to be all powerful. Really, really powerful. Like, strong enough to make a rock even He can't lift!

The kind of power I'm talking about isn't about a magic genie who can provide my favorite three wishes. I'm talking about someone or something who isn't restricted by the things that bind me, like time, decay and a sluggish metabolism.

He should also be off-the-charts smart. Wise is probably the better term. And loving. I'm looking for a God so smart, wise and loving that He'll know which of my endless requests to ignore because He not only knows what's best for me, but actually cares about my well-being.

To fill out the rest of the list, being creative is a plus. Should be organized. Can't abide a scattered God. ("Now, where did I put

166

those blessings?") Even though it's messy, should offer free will. Oh, and willing to die for me is the clincher.

If God has all those attributes, I'll look the other way when confronted with a few of the more confusing parts, like being washed in the blood and allowing so much pain and suffering down here. More on all that later.

For My Next Three Wishes...

When most people look for God, what they really want is a concierge. A magical genie. A Santa Claus for every season.

But that's not who God is. The God of the Bible is the Dad who wakes you up in the morning to go run so that you'll be in shape for the upcoming track meet.

He's a Dad who knows what's good for you so He'll actually prevent you from getting a promotion or the recognition you feel you deserve because He knows you'll get a big head if you get too much too soon.

He's the Dad who gives you only as much as you need, almost never as much as you want.

Take a moment and look at your life from God's perspective.

God is your parent. He created you for a purpose. He loves you beyond anything you can even comprehend. He wants nothing but the very best for you.

Understand this: if you need discipline, then that's what you're going to get. When you spend every day screaming and demanding a new pony (metaphor alert!), but God knows you're not mature enough to muck out the stall every morning, then guess what, your barn's going to be empty!

God's probably going to give you a gerbil or a goldfish or a pet rock. If you can manage to take care of the first small piece of responsibility, He may well bump you up to the next level. But if your goldfish is sleeping upside down after a week, God, in His infinite wisdom, may conclude that you're not quite ready for something that has to be fed every day.

God wants you to reach your highest potential so that you, in turn, can help other people reach theirs. That's the system He has set up. It's not about you, it's about your tribe.

God wants you to trust Him, and frankly, that takes a lifetime of trial and error to achieve.

You can't see what's coming around the corner, but He can. He knows what you need to do to be prepared for whatever disaster's barreling down the mountain. Often that means He will put you in uncomfortable situations.

Life is one big athletic contest, and every day is another day of practice to get ready for the big event.

You should also know God is more concerned about your character than your comfort. Every time you whine about how hard it is, just remember that you probably have running water, a toilet and a grocery store within a five-minute Uber drive from your house.

For the first several thousand years of humanity's existence, when we woke up in the morning, we had to go catch breakfast!

If we wanted a nice glass of wine, we had to go plant a vineyard first!

Being overweight was considered a status symbol! "Ooh, they've got enough to eat! I wish I had their life!"

Sometimes when you're crying out to the heavens, "Where are you, God?" He's thinking, "Perfect. You're right where I want you."

In my own experience, I have seen God come through (usually at the very last second) time and time again. He has a perfect track record. I've also noticed that He rarely comes through with an overabundance. It's usually just enough to get me through until the next crisis.

This is something I do my best to remember every time I'm in a jam, because I believe my attitude has a lot to do with how quickly I pass or fail a test.

One lesson I've learned is that Christianity is a hindsight religion. I am almost always nearly blind when faced with any crisis de jour, but I can usually reflect in most situations with 20/20 vision.

As I look back I can see that God has always come through for me, often saving me from myself.

God can be a coach, a mentor, a mother, or a shoulder to cry on. Sometimes he's Mr. Miyagi from 'The Karate Kid'; other times He's Obi-Wan Kenobi.

What He's not is a magician, an errand boy, a genie, or a servant who's there to serve you. To make this relationship work, you have to put yourself in the right position; namely, acknowledge that He is the universe MVP and you're not even in the same league.

While it's frustrating that we don't get a sugar daddy for a deity, we do get someone who loves us more than life itself. He loves us so much, in fact, that He will go to any lengths to save you.

He even calls Himself the bridegroom and says that we are his non-gender specific bride. Which, if you take literally, when it takes place, will be the biggest case of polygamy ever! "Do you, several billion people, take Jesus to be your lawfully wedded husband?"

And the elect said, "*We Do!*"

The Formal Claims

If God does take credit for creating our current living arrangements, one would hope He declares the same more than once in his book. It just so happens, He obliges and then some.

Hebrews 11:3 states…

"The universe was formed at God's command, so that what is seen was not made out of what was visible."

Somehow God spoke the universe into existence. He didn't go into his toolshed and find some old 2X4s to slap together a rickety swing set for us to play on.

Nor did he swing by Ikea and spend an afternoon trying to figure out how to put the cosmos together only to discover when He tried to stand it up that He left out a shelf and had to start all over.

No, according to Him, He merely spoke and, shazam, we got the Big Bang. Fairly impressive.

In Psalms 90:4, He says,

"A thousand years in your sight are as a day that passes, as a watch in the night."

See, God's telling us right up front that His time and our time are entirely different. If a thousand years is like a day to Him, what's 14 billion? Something around, I don't know, six days?

He also made a similar statement in Romans 1: 20...

"For since the creation of the world God's invisible qualities—his eternal power and divine nature—have been clearly seen, being understood from what has been made, so that people are without excuse."

Between you and me, it's the 'without excuse' part that gets me every time. I usually imagine most end-of-life face-to-face exchanges going something like this...

Us: "You're right, I didn't believe in you. But how was I supposed to know?"

God: "At some point in your life, you looked up at the stars in the heavens, right?"

Us: "Still, that doesn't prove your existence..."

God: "You observed nature and how the seasons and cycles of life all lived in harmony?"

Us: "Of course, but that's not definitive proof..."

God: "You experienced the miracle of birth with your own kids."

Us: "You're taking credit for that? My wife —"

God: "I cured your mother, saved your father and remember when you thought you lost your son?"

Us: "Those could all be coincidences..."

God: "Remember all the times I nudged you to talk to that person or to take that job?"

Us: "That was you?"

God: "I blessed you with good health, intelligence, good fortune and a wonderful family."

Us: "And I appreciate all that, but…"

God: "Remember when you hit that patch of black ice and slid across four lanes of traffic and didn't get a scratch?"

Us: "Yes…"

God: "Do you really think the day you met your wife was just dumb luck?"

Us: "Oh…"

God: "Now that you can see clearly, why don't you take a minute to think back on everything I did for you."

Us: "…Fine! But the least you could have done was send me some kind of sign!"

In Isaiah 45:6,7 He says,

"I am the Lord, and there is no other. I form the light and create darkness, I bring prosperity and create disaster; I, the Lord, do all these things."

We have some major unpacking to do surrounding the 'create disaster' claim, but putting that aside for the moment, it's pretty clear that the God of the Bible states time and time again that He's the one responsible for our current living situation.

We may not totally understand how we got here, but the Creative Designer isn't shy about taking credit. Granted, He doesn't take out billboards touting His most recent sunset ("Every time you 'Ooh' and 'Ahh,' it's like you're saying 'Way to go, God!'"), nor does he come in and take a bow when a rose blooms.

He's stated very clearly what He's done and He's content to stand on His record without the help of a P.R. firm.

The majority of you reading this are most likely too young to remember 'Have Gun, Will Travel.'

It was a popular Western on network television back in the sixties when no one in the country had anything to do after eight o'clock at night, so once a week about 50 million people watched a guy named Paladin ride his horse from fake back studio lot to fake back studio lot in search of a plot.

My point in describing that is to give you his catch phrase. He was a cocky guy who liked to say, "No brag, just fact."

That's how I see Yahweh's following claims. They're not there to puff up God in any way. They're there to show us the One who claims to have made all that we see and experience.

To add to the above claims, here are few more statements that more or less the complete list...

- God created everything (Genesis 1 & 2)
- To reiterate, God made everything (John 1:3)
- God created heaven and earth and is before all things and holds all things together (Colossians 1:16-17)
- God created earth and man and commands the heavens (Isaiah 45:12)
- His grace was given to us (with Jesus) before the beginning of time (2 Timothy 1:9)
- His hope was promised before the beginning of time (Titus 1:2)
- He loved us before the creation of the world (John 17:24)
- He chose us before the creation of the world (Ephesians 1:4)
- The heavens declare the glory of God, the sky proclaims His handiwork (Psalms 19:1)
- Jesus is His son, through whom He created the world (Hebrews 1:2)

Hopefully, these are enough to support the argument that God isn't reticent about claiming to be the force behind all of creation.

And while some creationists like to push the idea that believing in anything other than a strict six-day creation is to deny God's involvement, and is tantamount to blasphemy, I respectfully disagree.

I happen to think all of the above verses and science coincide perfectly. Science has done an amazing job proving beyond a reasonable doubt how the universe began. God just happens to be the one taking credit for it. To my mind, the two align very nicely, thank you.

Please bear with me if I'm over emphasizing this point, but I believe that both sides of the debate have truths on their side. It's the long list of debatable particulars that I find tiresome and, if I may be so bold, more than a bit irrelevant.

Even though I'm writing a book on the subject, my whole intent is to show the miracle of the creation, not to stake my claim on how exactly He did it. The fact that He did is enough for me.

Suffice to say, I believe we will all know with unfailing certainty how all this came to be—someday. And probably not on this side of heaven. But our curiosity will be sated.

Speaking for myself, I plan to be first in line for the 'Creation Explained!' lecture in heaven. If I may make a prediction, I suspect there will be many more people saying, "Oh, I get it now…" rather than, "See! I told you!"

But you never know…

Fun Fact: The center of Christianity has moved to the global south. While North America and Europe used to be top dogs in the Christian world, today they pale next to South America, China and Africa. In a stroke of irony, many so-called Third World countries are currently sending missionaries to the U.S. and Europe.

Beautiful Proof

One of the proofs that God is, indeed, God, is the world around us. To put it bluntly: beauty.

God's creation is one that exhibits both form and function. Beyond merely serving a purpose, there is an aesthetic quality to His immense art project.

The universe, our world and the nature that surrounds us didn't have to be beautiful. But because they are, I believe they draw us to their Creator.

As I drove home the other day, it struck me that the sky is blue. Why? It certainly doesn't have to be. It could be any number of colors, but blue is so peaceful and calming and sets off the greens and browns of the earth perfectly. It's an artistic choice that goes unnoticed because we see it every day.

I'm sure there are a dozen reasons why blue works so much better than orange, but I'm content that God did it for a reason.

Have you ever seen mankind try to create or improve on beauty? Usually, at best, it's a swing and a miss. Think of Las Vegas or Times Square. They've got lots of glitz and glamour, but the soft beauty of a beach at sunset beats everything we've ever come up with by a mile.

If communist Russia designed the world, everything would be efficient, but made of grey cement with the occasional ornament. I also would not be keen on praying, "Our comrade, who art in heaven..."

Humans do their level best to create beauty but we are limited in our scope and ability. It seems the very best we can come up with, compared to God's works, could be considered kindergarten finger paintings. They're cute, but they don't measure up.

Just look at the human body. Yes, when we let ourselves go, we tend to look like sideshow carnival acts, but in our purest form, we're works of art.

Look at the wide variety of sizes and colors God has given us. We are all variations on a theme. The next time you're at an airport or at a mall, just stop and watch the human parade pass you by. Tall, short, fat, thin, old, young; it's endlessly entertaining.

Humans are God's walking, talking snowflakes. We are all made of the same stuff, but each of us is molded and decorated slightly differently.

Color me overly optimistic, but I pray for the day when we can all drop our fear of everyone who doesn't look like us and accept the very real fact that 1) *Everyone* is different and 2) Underneath our decorative covering, we're all exactly the same!

Sorry, had to get that off my chest.

His Name

It may not need to be pointed out, but God is off-the-charts smart. He's said things that we can't even begin to comprehend. Which has got to be frustrating for Him. Why He didn't make us smarter is anybody's guess. We'll find out one day. Until then, just know that no matter how many degrees you have, you'll never be the smartest one in the room.

His name is a perfect example. The biblical name of God has four letters. All consonants, no vowels. This is designed for our benefit. It's a safety feature ensuring no one oversteps their bounds and calls out to the God of the universe without a real good reason. His name is one that literally cannot be pronounced.

Modern culture has graciously given His son the middle initial,

'H,' but I can't find that in any of my Bible translations, so I'm going to put that one in the 'disregard' pile.

Back to my point. Each of the four letters in God's name has a corresponding number in the Jewish alphabet. In this case, those letters add up to the number 26.

Faith-based PiLCs have pointed out that we have 26 dimensions; which is total news to me, as, on a good day, I can only observe three to four. I don't know what I'd do if I had to deal with 22 additional dimensions, so maybe it's a good thing they're off limits at this time.

Regardless, even His name has a hidden message behind the obvious meaning.

That's the thing about having an alphabet that assigns letters both a sound as well as a numerical value: it can be very confusing.

"I know she said she loved me, but after I added up her declaration of love, it came out to 666. I think she may be evil!"

Let's Deal with the Negativity

There is, admittedly, a lot of baggage that comes with the title 'God.' His name and His followers have been smeared in the press of late, so a little explanation is in order.

First and foremost, is He a jealous God?

The answer to that is yes. But not in the context in which you understand jealousy. He doesn't sit around up in heaven pouting, "I can't believe they fell for *that* god! What does he have that I don't?"

God desires a relationship with you. Apparently, that's why He went to all this trouble. Because of that, He wants to be your number one BFF. He wants to be your lover. He wants to be your all-in-all.

While a lot of people consider this petty, to be honest, I don't think God cares a whole lot about anyone else's opinion. In this case, I'm pretty sure He feels as if He deserves to be in your #1 position.

If you look at everything He created just for you, everything He sacrificed, you might get an inkling of His sense of entitlement.

Understand, God is not shy about stating His desires. If you need further clarification, He put it in His top 10 commandments; "Thou shalt have no other Gods before me."

If you're thinking you're safe now, as petty gods went out of vogue with the Roman empire, you'd be sadly mistaken. Anything you value more than God is considered an idol. That means wealth, pleasure, fame, your dog, anything! If you love it more than God, you've got yourself a little monkey on your back that the Bible would describe as an idol.

Admittedly, this is hard. God wants you to check pretty much everything in your life to make sure you have the right perspective.

While you may think this is rather a lot to ask, it can best be compared to a marriage relationship. When one side 'cheats' on the other, it's not just that the rules have been broken, but rather, the heart of the spurned lover.

In the past, to get right with God, we'd burn a sacrifice, cover ourselves with sackcloth and ashes and beg for forgiveness. Today most of us would schedule a session with our therapist putting most of the blame on God.

"How do you think I feel? He expects me to stay a relationship with Him, but I never even see Him! I mean never! Oh, sure, I feel His presence now and then, and occasionally I'll get a peace that passes understanding, but after the week I had I need a hug and someone to rub my feet!"

Fun Fact: (To be read like Casey Kasem from the American Top 40) All told there are 955 names and titles of God in the Bible, but here are the top five. Coming in at number five, it's El Roi which means 'the God who sees.' Number four is El Elyon, or 'God most high.' Debuting in our number three spot this week is Abba, which means 'daddy.' The number two most requested name for God means 'The Lord,' and we translate that as 'Yahweh.' And finally, the most popular name is Elohim which simply means 'God.'

Really? Fear? That's What You're Going For?

There are sections in the Bible where it says we must fear God. That phrase is one that needs some serious unpacking. If this rubs you the wrong way, the reason is purely a matter of semantics.

Here, 'fear' does not mean the shake-in-your-boots or wet-your-pants kind of fear. That kind of fear is what the Cowardly Lion experienced in *The Wizard of Oz* when he ran off down the hall and crashed through the window.

What we consider fear is nothing at all what God requires. He definitely wants us to respect Him and all that He has done for us, but, as He puts it, "Perfect love casts out fear."

So, which is it, then? Do we fear Him or do we not?

A better translation would actually be 'awe.' We are told to hold the Creator of all things in a position of awe. Be amazed at what He has done and you'll find yourself in the correct posture of humility. He doesn't care for haughty. He totally digs humility.

C.S. Lewis found the right balance when he talked about Aslan, the God character in The Chronicles of Narnia. When Lucy found out he was a lion, she asked if he was safe, to which Mr. Beaver replied, "Who said anything about safe? 'Course he isn't safe. But he's good. He's the King, I tell you."

Ultimately, the bottom line is all about respect. Hopefully you wouldn't greet the Queen of England in a T-shirt and cut offs eating a pastrami sandwich. Entering the throne room of heaven to greet your Father should also come with a large dose of reverence.

Aw, Hell No!

Admittedly, this particular category is a doozy! I bring up the subject of hell with a great deal of trepidation. But in the interest of full disclosure, I don't think this hot potato can be tossed aside without dealing with it.

One of the great excuses to 'swipe left' on God has been, and will always be, the subject of H-E-double hockey sticks. As in, "I refuse to believe in a God who is so cruel He would send the people He claims He loves to eternal damnation!"

Yup, on the surface, it sure looks bad. But, as with everything else, let's parse this out a little, because I believe some perspective is in order.

I come at this not as a fire and brimstone preacher. In no way am I frothing at the mouth, shaking my finger at a room full of sinners and claiming every man, woman and dog are doomed to burn in the lake of fire! I understand that style of preaching was popular in its day, but it has, thankfully, gone the way of the dodo.

That being acknowledged, in order for you to make an informed decision, I figured it was important to lay out *everything* about God, warts and all.

Here's how I understand it.

God is holy.

We are not.

And never shall the twain meet.

Frankly, this shoves most of humanity out. Maybe not a few of the pure-as-the-driven-snow girls I dated in high school, but most everyone else you know fall into the 'holy-adjacent' category. Which, according to the rules, just doesn't cut it.

In and of itself, this creates a very interesting dilemma. It certainly appears that God went to an awful lot of trouble to create a race of people He can't be with.

"Excuse me, Lord, but according to the schedule, it's time to create earth." "Aw, what's the point? Mankind's going to fall anyway!"

It shouldn't come as too much of a surprise (knowing who He is), that God managed to work something out.

He said, "Okay, how about this? People are never going to be perfect. I love 'em, but most of them are going to be one big hot mess. I don't want them to be punished for their mistakes, so... I'll take that on! All they have to do is agree to let me be punished for what they've done and we'll be good. Deal?"

I'll be the first to admit that this, on the surface, makes absolutely no sense. Why set up such a crazy system? Why not just make a world where there is no sin and therefore, no need for any kind of clemency exchange program?

Not to mention no need for a heinous punishment if the deal isn't accepted! Right? (This is where free will enters the picture. Be patient, I'll tackle this one a bit later.)

For now, all we can do is look at the game God is playing and try to make sense of the rules. To reiterate...

God is holy.

We are not.

If we accept God's terms, we can be forgiven and adopted into His family. Otherwise, we're back to "never the twain shall meet."

So, what does that mean, exactly? What if we don't want to accept His grand gesture? What's Option B?

In order to be completely fair, for those who choose to reject Him, God set up another path.

He respects you that much.

But He's also very clear that there will be consequences for that choice. He will graciously allow you to hem and haw and waver up to a certain point, but after you cross the finish line, all bets are off. After death, your choice is set in stone.

Either He pays for your mistakes or you do.

Dr. Mark Brewer, my old pastor from Bel Air Presbyterian

Church, explained hell better than anyone I've ever heard. He said that we have to literally climb over God to get into hell.

Understand this: God has done everything in His power to keep you from making a particularly bad choice.

The facts are these: if you want to reject God, He allows that. Unfortunately, because the soul never dies, it's a permanent consequence of what is most likely a very prideful decision.

I believe the main problem people have with God is the fact that He insists on judging the world. The way we've been taught, God is love, and love never judges.

That's where the problem begins. We have a modern society's definition of love. More often than not, it's merely the passive hope that if I treat you as you want to be treated, you'll love me back.

God's love is much different. He says love without boundaries is not love.

His love is the kind that demands the best from us and will not stand for anything less than our best. And our best sometimes means we need to be corrected and often (cover your ears!) disciplined!

Real love is sacrificial.

Real love is altruistic.

Real love gives me the last bite of chocolate cake—thus speaketh the Lord!

The end result of love is God begrudgingly accepting our total rejection of Him, if that's what you ultimately choose to do.

While I totally concur that it looks bad from our perspective, I have no idea of the pain this arrangement must cause Him.

I know what He did to insure no one would have to be separated from Him, but I have no idea how it must feel to be rejected after literally laying down your own life to save your child.

I'm of the opinion we are entirely too cavalier about what God did in order to save us from an eternity of damnation. I could certainly soft soap this, but the possible reality of it all is much too big to down play it.

Because we don't understand the magnitude of God's sacrifice, I believe our reaction to the crucifixion is muted at best.

I don't know what hell is like. No one does. But it appears to be the only option open to every person who doesn't want to be with their Creator.

I'm not saying I like this! Nor do I endorse it! I wish it were different! But I didn't make up these rules. I'm just trying my best to make sense of them.

I seriously wish there were a third option. Maybe not purgatory, but a nice spot between heaven and hell where you can explore your options before you make your final decision.

Oh, wait, that's called life on earth! Okay, I seriously wish there were a *fourth* option!

To be honest, every description of hell sounds unspeakably horrible. One that demands we do everything in our power to guarantee we don't end up there.

We joke about it quite a lot and put our collective heads in the sand, but if it is a real place, we would be fools to not immediately act in order to miss that gruesome door prize.

I know rock stars love to say they'd rather party in hell with their friends than spend eternity in heaven with a bunch of stuck up pious people. Were that word picture true, then frankly, so would most of us. But that's only because an incorrect picture of eternity has been painted.

A few hints of what heaven is going to be like are listed in the first few chapters of the book of Revelation.

Jesus already said we each get our own mansion, but here He lays out a few more choice gifts: a new body, a new name, a crown, an outfit of white, authority over the nations, and allowed to sit with God on His throne. (I can only imagine how long that line's going to be! It'll be like Disneyland without a FastPass.)

It all comes down to who you want to rule over your life.

The natural part of you would love to be king or queen over every facet of your existence. But, seriously, you've lived with you for quite a while. Do you really think you're the best judge of what is and what isn't good for you?

Before we die, every human is allowed to make one irreversible choice. Choose away. But, please, for your sake, choose wisely!

But Why?

Every discussion of heaven and hell eventually leads to the ultimate question: why?

The answer is blatantly obvious—the majority of humans refuse to do anything without either the possibility of reward or the threat of punishment.

In other words, after every offer we instinctively ask, "What's in it for me?"

Heaven is the ultimate positive reinforcement, while hell is quite the opposite.

Be honest, would you still go to work without the threat of losing your home? Would you still knock yourself out on a presentation without the promise of praise from your friends? Would you still pay your taxes if there weren't the threat of jail time?

Positive and negative reinforcements are helpful tools in every parent, politician and employer's toolbox.

We learn early on that there are consequences for lying, cheating and gossiping. If there weren't, we'd keep doing them!

We all know stealing is wrong, yet we still do it from time to time. But if I lived in a culture that cut off your hand for a first offense, I'd never even *think* about taking something that wasn't mine, even if I thought I deserved those paperclips from the office!

Separation from God isn't intended to be a surprise. In the interest of full disclosure, God spent quite a lot of time discussing both heaven and hell. In each case He describes one in glowing terms and the other in frightening word pictures.

If you're the rare bird that chafes against both positive and negative reinforcement, you'll undoubtedly have a tougher time deciding what to do.

You'll have to decide to either accept or reject God based on the simple, somewhat unsatisfying line, "Because I said so!"

Sometimes cowardice and/or fear can be a valuable asset!

Fun Fact: 72% of people who say they're religious believe in heaven, but only 58% of those folks believe in hell. Of those who say religion is *not* important, 32% still believe in heaven and 22% believe in hell. Pulling up the rear in the stats battle are atheists. Not surprisingly, only 5% of that crowd believe in heaven and another 3% believe in hell. In all three cases, regardless of affinity or enmity toward religion, hell just can't catch a break!

A Final Thought

Imagine, if you will, God as a painter. He created a stupendous work of art that everyone agrees is beyond amazing.

The point I need to underline here is that God is still *outside* of the painting.

He didn't somehow imbue His art with His consciousness. If you pray to the painting to give you something, you're just praying to oils on canvas. If you want to pray to the artist, He'll hear you, but not if you pray to His creation. We're to see God's creativity as reflections of His personality in our surroundings, not believe that's where He has taken up residence.

I write this because I often hear people say that God is in that flower, or that sunset, or that baby's laugh. I may be a spoilsport, but I disagree. I believe He's the creative force behind all those things, but He doesn't exist in them.

Bottom line, the universe, as big as it is, can't contain the essence of God. He's too big for that. His creation is His sandbox. He can build or destroy whatever He chooses, but He doesn't live in any trees or random waterfalls or stars, for that matter.

If you truly want to find God, He's not playing Waldo; He's very easy to find. He says it Himself; He's in heaven. Go ring on that doorbell. At least you're likely to get an answer.

And once you do that, He'll gladly take up residence in you. More on that later, but to me, that's one of this world's biggest jokes. God is, truly, all around us, all the time. The twist is that His nature lives not in His creation, but in His children.

As of this writing, we currently seem to be in very short supply of people who act as if they are children of the King.

There's Got to be a Loophole!

One other major sticking point of Christianity is the question about exclusivity.

Is there really only *one* way to heaven? Surely no one today is able to swallow that!

Since Jesus claims to be the only way to God, we can reject both Him and His claims if nothing else just for sheer arrogance, can we not?

Our society is all about tolerance, and this is the number one example of intolerance.

Except that it's actually exactly the opposite. This is such an example of extreme tolerance that it must catch people off guard.

It is open to absolutely everyone.

No exceptions.

Come one, come all!

Hurry, hurry, hurry!

All right, Christianity's not going to get off the hook that easily. While it is *an absolutely free offer while supplies last*, it does make the rather grandiose claim that implies other faiths out there just might be ever-so-slightly…missing the mark.

That's certainly insulting and worthy of an angry meme, isn't it?

Despite what often happens in schools, life is not graded on a curve. When the rubber meets the road, either you get this particular answer right or you don't.

Just take a look at all the differing views there are in the world today concerning God. Every faith, from Buddhists to Muslims to atheists, each offer up their own version of the universe and have their own answers to the grand and mighty questions of 'Who am I?' 'How did we get here?' and finally, 'Where do I go when I die?'

I totally concede that it's in our nature to wish that every single road will eventually lead to God. Unfortunately, that's not where the evidence leads us.

If all roads lead to God, then it really shouldn't matter what we do or how we live our lives, because He knows we're all idiots. In that scenario everyone should get in regardless of their belief or behavior.

This is where common sense and reason step up to the podium to respectfully disagree. Just because you want everyone's answer on their tests to be graded as 'right' doesn't make it so. It's not racist or hateful to accept the rationale that there could actually be *one* right answer. It's actually quite logical.

Where we come from, or how we were raised, or how many tats or piercings we have is irrelevant to this issue.

The bottom line is really quite simple: which choice is true?

And the pleasing line "There is truth in all religions," while comforting, doesn't pass muster. There may well be various truths scattered throughout all the faiths. There is undoubtedly wisdom that can be gleaned from many different worldviews.

That's not the issue.

The God of the Bible is quite explicit in His point of view in all this. He claims He is responsible for everything we hold dear and, as such, as the owner and original Creator of the entire cosmos, He says He has every right to determine who, and who does not, get to be with Him for the rest of eternity.

It's not unfair. It actually makes perfect sense. What doesn't make sense is the alternative version where chaos is the order of the day and everyone is accepted by their own god, regardless of their beliefs or lack thereof.

A Multi-Faith Heaven

Imagine for a moment what the afterlife would be like if everyone's view was correct.

You'd have a bunch of Hindus in one area, waiting to go back to earth to live another life, either as a reward or a punishment for what they did the last time.

No Buddhists would be there because the good ones reached Nirvana and ceased to exist.

Mormons would show up just long enough to drop off their bikes before they jettisoned off to their own personal planets.

I don't even want to describe what the Muslims are doing, but suffice it to say you'd better hope there's plenty of housing; otherwise the place will be overrun with women previously known as vestal virgins.

I can only imagine the atheists will organize a peaceful protest outside the holy city, insisting it doesn't exist and filing paperwork to sue God for having the unmitigated gall of forgiving their sins without written permission.

Personally, I like to imagine the heaven described in the Bible; a place where we spend our days alternating between eating at lavish banquets and either worshipping or working for God.

I don't know where the idea of harps and clouds came from, but those are nowhere to be found in the ad brochure that I read.

The difficulty here is that if you stumble over this issue and reject God because of it, you are actually guilty of what's known as 'Anthropomorphism,' a big word that means your pride has led you to believe you know more than God.

In practice, it goes like this, "I don't understand this, nor do I like it. Therefore, it is wrong!"

And that, my friend, regardless of how good it might feel to express those thoughts, is a dangerous place to be.

Forget about heaven for a moment. Just imagine what life would be like here on earth if our society totally embraced the "live your truth" mantra. It would be complete anarchy!

People who believe in survival of the fittest would be able to kill, steal and lie with absolute impunity!

You wouldn't be able to say what anyone was doing was in any way wrong, because that opinion would be based on your truth. Everyone else's truth would be that they're allowed to do whatever it takes to stay alive and/or to get ahead.

To give a more pragmatic example, it's currently the government's job to protect the populace. Without a single system of rules and regulations in place, no one would know what they are and what they are not allowed to do!

In that system, the cops wouldn't know who to arrest!

"Do you have any idea how fast you were going?"

"It doesn't matter, because in my truth, it was under the legal speed limit!"

"Move along!"

His Personality Traits

While God certainly has tons of points in the plus column, He's also got some baggage (not the least of which are some of His children!) that could take some time to digest.

I think one of the most amazing things God created is not our world (although a sunny beach with a cold strawberry margarita is in the top 10), but a little thing called free will.

God is big enough to let us make our own choices, even though He knows most of us are complete morons. But without it, our love for Him would always be suspect.

It's as if He's placed us smack dab in the middle of a candy store and said, "If you love me, you'll only have a single Nestle's Crunch bar and then give away the rest of the goodies to your friends." I'm sorry, but are you nuts?

My cousin Chris says, "Life is one long test to see if you're paying attention." I totally agree with him.

I think maybe that's why we are surrounded by so many temptations. And it seems that when you pass one test, God smiles and then sends along another. Only harder. Apparently, life is one long high school algebra class.

Recipe—A God

1. Heaping tbsp of all knowing.
2. Heaping tbsp of all powerful.
3. Heaping tbsp of ever present.
4. Mix three versions into one, yet keep separate.
5. One dash of all loving.
6. Salt with holy.
7. Mix in incredibly creative nature.
8. Mix in unselfish giving and let rise.
9. Let simmer. Must be patient to a fault.

Fun Fact: If the world's religions could be represented by 100 people in a room, here's how it would break down… 31 people would be Christians (and by 2050, a little under half of those Christians will be living in Sub-Saharan Africa). Sixteen people would be agnostic and/or atheists and 24 people would be Muslim (however, several of those Muslims would be pregnant, so get ready for the numbers to dramatically shift). Fifteen people would be Hindu, seven are Buddhists, six people follow other religions and one person in the room would be about 20% Jewish on their mother's side.

Let's Start Thumping!

As we dive into the best-selling book of all time, a clarifying statement needs to be made.

Most people reject God and the Bible not for what it says, but for what they think it says. Granted, a lot of what it says is hard to swallow, but that's where context and interpretation come in handy.

We really need to take a good look at this book and do our best to figure out what it's trying to tell us and why.

An Overview

Not to oversell the Bible, but it's not just one, but four, that's right, four books in one!

It's:

1. An introduction of God and His Son.
2. An instruction book for humans.
3. The story of God's pursuit of those stubborn humans.
4. An accurate predictor of the future!

Now, if I were God and I wanted to give my children an explanation of who they are and who I am, I'd try to cram everything into one easy to find source.

Stone is too difficult to carve and it's a pain to turn 200-pound pages. Writing in the sand only lasts until the tide comes in. Looking at all my options, I'd have someone invent a book!

The Bible is a treasure trove of information and entertainment. It's got action, sex, sacrificial love, important people doing really dumb stuff and a great ending where evil is vanquished.

It's also a literary masterpiece. It's written in poetic form, straightforward historical drama, allegory, parable and an advice column in the middle.

I believe a lot of our current problems with the Bible come from the fact that we often don't know in which context to read it. For example, Pastor Tim Keller explains the discrepancies between the first two chapters in Genesis very simply: Genesis 1 is a song, while Genesis 2 is a literary account of the same creation event. If you try to read them without understanding the genre they were written in, you'll come away more than a little confused.

All that to say, the Bible's not to be read as just one form of literature. When you look over the rather saucy Song of Solomon, you're not supposed to take it literally. It's a poem for lovers.

God created sex and He's given us a Cinemax cable special explaining how it's supposed to be done. But if you think Solomon's making love to a woman with the breasts of a fawn or that he's literally an ivory tower, you're missing the point.

That particular book was written in code so that adults would get it, but it would go over the heads of all the kids who managed to get their hands on it.

It's the biblical version of how I understood rock & roll as a pre-teen. I had no idea what the Beatle's *Lovely Rita, Meter Maid* was all about until I was much older. I had a similar Ah-ha moment when I listened to *Happiness Is A Warm Gun* many years later.

King David wrote a lot of songs. We get a wonderful selection of his greatest hits in Psalms. Now, did he really want God to destroy all of his enemies in the most sadistic way possible? Perhaps. The point here is not what God did or didn't do after David's endless lamenting. Rather that God allowed David to vent.

God loved His child David's honesty. That's why God said David was a man after His own heart. The songs are given as an example for us. We are to come to God no matter how we feel. David didn't hide his feelings. High or low, angry or melancholy, David came to his Father with his whole self. We are to follow his example.

The night before Jesus was crucified, He sat His disciples down for their last lecture at what we now call the Last Supper. This is one of those events that should be highlighted in yellow in every Bible. He said and did a lot of very important stuff before and after this particular event, but on that fateful night, He laid it all out one last time.

Go look at John 14 and 15 with that in mind, but even if you do, you can't take all of it literally. The disciples weren't trying to eat His body or drink His blood. Jesus claims to be a metaphorical vine. We are not real branches. But when you read it, unless you're especially dim, the point is understood.

If Jesus had His last supper in my high school, some dweeb in the back of the class would probably raise his hand and ask, "So, what kind of wine are we going to be? Put me down for Boone's Farm!"

Another point brought up repeatedly is that the four gospels do not line up exactly. That was done for a very good reason. They are four different perspectives of the most amazing jaw-dropping historical event ever.

If they all matched up perfectly, we'd be suspicious of collusion. As it stands, we know each eye witness did his best to recount his perspective of the events of the day.

Each book was also written for a different audience. Matthew was written for the Jews; that's why it's heavy with Old Testament references. Mark was recounting Peter's testimony. That one is for the working man. Luke was a gentile doctor. Ultimately his historical statements have been found to be extremely accurate, but as with most doctors, his handwriting was so bad that no one could decipher it until pharmacists were invented. Finally, John's book was written to tie the previous gospels together in one big fat spiritual bow. Think of him as the clean-up batter.

After Paul's gospels, where he spends most of his letters berating various churches for getting pretty much everything wrong, we find ourselves dropped off in the land of Revelations.

This book is wild! It's loaded with fantastic imagery. A lot of it we can understand, but a lot of it we can't. This book was written in apocalyptic language to hide the true meaning not from the kids this time, but from Israel's enemies.

Context, People!

I say all this to help you understand what you're diving into. If you live in the world today, the odds are you're heavily influenced by Greek thinking. You're most likely linear in your thoughts. You want a beginning, middle and end.

That's perfectly fine. But understand that the Jews didn't operate that way. Theirs was an overwhelmingly oral history. They took care to repeat the stories so that no details were either left out or added. If the majority of our population couldn't read or write, we'd probably do the very same thing.

The best way to describe their way of talking is circular. They tell the story once with just the headlines. Then they tell the story again with a few more details filled in. Then, if there's still more to unpack, they'll tell it again.

If you're Jewish, this doesn't come as a shock. But if you're a gentile and you read the Bible, it can be very confusing.

Regardless, all non-Jews need to know this if they're going to give the Bible a fair shake.

The majority of the scriptures were written by Jews and we need to understand a few things about their culture before we drop the publisher a strongly worded letter about sloppy editing.

The Hebrews were also big on dreams and the interpretation of those dreams. God didn't have TV or the press to get His ideas out. He had to use what was on hand, so a lot of the time He sent along dreams and visions along with the occasional flannel graph.

I love reading the old stories and more often than not have

come to the realization that humans haven't changed one iota over thousands of years. We started off small and petty and we've not risen above our original set of operating instructions.

The nineteen sixties were a wonderful time of change and hope, but Gene Rodenberry and others in his Optimists Club actually believed that mankind was evolving into a better race.

Somehow, they managed to see no evil, hear no evil and speak no evil and pretend civil rights violations and the Vietnam War weren't a pair of festering boils.

The entire *Star Trek* series is based on the idea that in the very near future humanity actually gets its act together! So much so that they feel obligated to go spread the gospel of love and peace out in the universe using phasers and photon torpedoes.

To be blunt, Gene and his fellow cock-eyed optimists didn't follow the evidence. Like it or not, we are who we are.

Samson never seemed to think with his head, Moses was a murderer, Jonah wanted to see his enemies destroyed and threw a hissy fit when God decided to spare them.

With all that said, it stands to reason that the best way to understand the Creator is to simply read His communication to us.

Duh!

But as you do, my advice would be to take a step back now and again in order to see the forest for the trees.

Accuracy?

Some people love to put down the Bible and say that it was cobbled together from various unsubstantiated manuscripts that someone with Machiavellian political motivations decided to put together into a book in order to subjugate the masses into doing their evil bidding.

The truth of the matter is that the Bible has been proven right time and time again by something as simple as history.

The Roman historian Josephus was not in any way a Christian, but his writings not only call out the historical person of Jesus, but he even notes that Jesus was declared to have risen from the grave in the small Roman province of Jerusalem.

Luke, the gentile doctor, was the most noted historian of that time, and nothing he wrote in either the Book of Luke or its companion, the Book of Acts, has ever been refuted.

In fact, Josh McDowell claims in his *book Evidence That Demands A Verdict* that there is more corroborated historical evidence that proves Jesus was born, died and was raised from the dead than there is that Napoleon invaded Russia.

Hebrew 101

Culturally speaking, the ancient Jews are about as understandable as the Amish are to the average Beverly Hills High School student.

"What do you mean you don't post your selfies on Instagram?"

"What be a selfie?"

First off, the Hebrews were a race of people who believed what a person said was ironclad. The spoken word was considered sacred. I would hate to be a teenager living in that kind of world…

"But thee said thou didst love me!"

"I believe-ist I said I didst love thy brisket!"

"Close enough. This be my father, entire family and a Rabbi to marry us."

Any promise between two people was considered a solemn covenant that could *never* be broken. That's when people knew it was really, really serious.

To fully explain, this is what you had to go through to enter into a covenant…

1. You take off your coat or robe and pledge yourself to the other person.
2. You take off your belt, symbolically exposing yourself.
3. You split an animal in half.
4. You cut yourself and mix your blood with the one you're

making the covenant with. (This tradition has lived on, although sometimes spit is seen as an acceptable substitute for blood.)

5. You exchange names. (In the Jewish scriptures, Abram became Abraham and Yahweh became known as the God of Abraham.)
6. In order to remember the covenant, you make a scar, usually on your arm. (This tradition is still practiced by certain tribes in Africa.)
7. You give the covenant terms, such as, "If you're attacked, my tribe will fight alongside you."
8. You eat a meal together.
9. You both plant a memorial, such as a tree or a bush, to commemorate the covenant. (I love that the tradition of planting trees in Israel continues to this day.)

As you can see, a covenant was a deadly serious agreement, usually made between two tribes. It said, in essence, "If you get attacked, we've got your back. And, more importantly, the reverse is also true!"

If you think the above ritual demanded quite a lot of hoops to jump through, you're right. Everybody knew what a covenant was, and if you had the evidence of a scar on your arm, or perhaps several, a random attacker coming after you knew that he was not only threatening to fight you, but everyone you had made a covenant with. This cut down on tribal raids considerably.

Other cultural highlights include the constant blood sacrifices sprinkled throughout the Old Testament, the never-ending fighting with their neighbors and let's not forget the circumcisions.

On the bright side, as a race, they're extremely funny, smart, talented and totally rule the annual Nobel peace prize, so it all evens out.

My daughter pointed out how their habit of studying the Torah from an early age helped their lineage form literary brains. If you want to know why there are so many Jewish lawyers, it's simple: "The bar exam? Please! I passed my bar mitzvah at 13!"

Like it or not, the Hebrews are God's chosen people. The fact that they managed to survive almost 2,000 years without a homeland and unrelenting persecution is a miraculous feat no other group of people can even come close to. If survival were an Olympic sport, the Jews would take the gold every year and everybody else would be fighting for either silver or bronze.

There's a verse in the Bible that states anyone who stands with the Israelites 'will be blessed.' That's just *one* of the reasons why I will stand by the Jews until the day I die. (The fact that the Christian Messiah came out of their bloodline is just icing on the cake.) It also helps that some of my earliest friends were from that tribe.

I'm sorry if this unwavering allegiance offends your sensibilities. They're the ones God chose through which to explain life.

If it helps, they not only brought us bagels and the deli, but after Vaudeville and the Catskills, even their detractors have to admit they practically invented stand-up comedy! Granted, I'm at best Jewish adjacent, but it's safe to say I'm a lifelong fan.

Fun Fact: In 1900, over half of the world's population had never heard the gospel. By 2019, that number had shrunk to 28.4%. That leaves over 2.2 billion people who are considered 'unevangelized' or, more accurately, 'people who have never seen *Veggie Tales*.'

Fun Fact: William Tyndale was the first person to translate the New Testament into English. As a thank you, he was later burned at the stake.

The Bible II

A Few Instructions

A fairly famous acronym for the Bible is 'Basic Instructions Before Leaving Earth.' It's not a bad way to look at it.

From this book we learn how to train up our children, what a good marriage should look like and how to gird up our loins. Personally, until I read the Bible, I was not a loin girder. Now I rarely leave the house without first double checking my girding.

Part of the proof of the Bible, to my mind, is that in some cases, it doesn't even try to make sense. At least not to us mere mortals. It lays out some information that just needs to be accepted, whether we understand it or not.

It's a very delicate balance, holding on to what we can observe as truth and what we have to take on faith.

My favorite two example are the Trinity and predestination.

God claims to be one entity and yet, at the very same time, is somehow divided into three persons. That's a task that would be impossible in our 3-dimensional space, but, PiLCs theorize, not so hard in another dimension.

Who knows, it may even be commonplace! Everyone in heaven, if they're *anybody*, just has to have three bodies! It's just what's done, darling!

Still, if you try to figure it out, your head may well explode. You have total equality between the three parts of the Trinity, yet a definite hierarchy. God is the Father, Jesus is the son and the

Holy Spirit is sort of a motherly comforter minus the hot cocoa late at night.

Jesus and the Holy Spirit do God's bidding, but they say they're all on equal footing. The point I think we're to be left with is that somehow, the Triune God is in community with itself and has made an offer for all of us to join in that holy co-op.

I don't get it and I don't think I'm supposed to. There are some things God lays out for us that are, I believe, deliberately confusing. Next to the Trinity, the rabid popularity of a few vacuous pop stars comes to mind, but there are a host of others.

The other head scratcher is predestination. Somehow God can hold in perfect tension our own free will and His divine cannot-be-thwarted plans.

Does God draw us to Him, or do we accept Him out of our own need? The answer is 'yes.'

Throughout, the Bible is literally filled with paradoxes and dichotomies. The Jews expected (and still do, I might add) their Messiah to be a great king, a great warrior. They got a carpenter. You generally don't expect the guy doing your kitchen cabinets to save the world.

Have a trial? Be joyful! Someone slaps you? Turn the other cheek. If someone asks for your jacket, give them your shirt. See a pretty girl? Look the other way.

These are the easy ones!

You've got to believe in something you can't see, touch, smell or hear. You get to heaven not by works, but by faith. But if you don't do the works, that's proof you don't have the faith!

Love your enemy, leave your mother and father. The meek shall inherit the earth. The dead shall bury the dead. The sheep will make it, the goats are out of luck.

You try and teach this to preschoolers using finger puppets! It's very hard!

The point here is a hard but good truth: the Bible doesn't tell us what we *want* to hear. It tells us what we *need* to hear.

When it comes to things like forgiveness and having faith when times are hard, I wish it were a bit more lenient.

I wish it said, "And lo, if thy enemy doth irritate or besmirch thee, the Lord thy God shalt smite them. Seriously, just sayeth the word and the hand of Jehovah shalt fly out of the sky and smacketh any and all who have displeased thee into next week. Thus, shalt all the heathens of the world learn their place, and ye shalt be feared and given various unearned promotions because of it."

Instead, the Bible bends over backwards to be trustworthy, proven by its never-ending advice that usually isn't even close to what we would come up with.

To quote Tom Hanks' character from *A League of Our Own*, "The hard is what makes it good."

Worry

One strong example in this category is that the Bible says we're not supposed to worry because the birds of the field don't worry and our Father in heaven takes care of them.

Most people hear that and are greatly comforted that God is in charge. When I hear things like that, I get depressed and think, "Man, I wouldn't even be a good bird!"

I'd be that one sparrow thinking…

"Aw man, look at the worm that guy scored! I got up early for nothing! Probably all the good worms are taken!

"I'm out here, working my beak to the bone but does my family appreciate it? The wife's squawking for a bigger nest, and every time I try to feed my kids they say I don't regurgitate it right.

"Most of 'em are good eggs, but I didn't ask for all those mouths to feed. I was happy flying solo. But I got a thing for red breasts and when she came bob, bob, bobbin' along, I was done for.

"I'm not as young as I used to be; I've got male pattern molting, bird legs and crow's feet. And lately she's been flocking together with her birds of a feather and I'm worried.

"I suppose I should be happy. At least I'm not a lily in the field!"

What NOT to Do!

The Bible is filled with stories of heroes and the like, but it also has story after story of people that seem to continually do the wrong thing.

I find stories about people who do exactly what they shouldn't do to be extremely helpful. Yes, the hero story is all well and good over the long haul, but it's the failures of life that seem to stick with me.

Why the Bible features these stories of our less-than-perfect ancestors is obvious to anyone who's been alive more than a decade: we learn our lessons both from both good and bad examples.

The Bible offers up tons of stories from each column. Sometimes you get a bonus and have both the good and the bad on display in one deliciously complex character! When you read the story of Samson, for example, you see the story of a man who fights for the cause of God, but whenever he was off duty, he became one who clearly operated out of a position of lust.

Delilah came to him three times and asked him for the secret to his strength. To get her off his back, each time he told her a little white lie. After each white lie, when he was asleep, the Philistines would run in and try to kill him by doing exactly what he had just told Delilah.

Somehow this meathead never put it together that his girlfriend might not be as pure as the driven snow!

"Boy, the wildest thing happened last night! I told Delilah the only way to defeat me was to tie me up with ropes. Which is totally not true, 'cause I'm not an idiot. Anyway, the strangest thing: when I was asleep, these Philistines soldiers ran in, tied me up with ropes and tried to kill me! I woke up and totally killed them, of course, but isn't that so weird? The next night I told Delilah the ropes had to be WET! Which is totally not true, 'cause I'm not an idiot. But, wouldn't you know it, later that night another bunch of Philistines came in and tied me up with wet ropes! I killed them, of course, but what are the odds? Anyway, now Delilah's mad at me 'cause I lied to her. I wonder if there's a connection?"

The Top Ten

There seems to be a lot of confusion surrounding the 10 commandments. Like so many other things in the Bible, they serve more than one purpose.

The 10 commandments are most certainly a strong foundation for a fair and equitable society, but they are, ultimately, given to us not as a set of standards for us to aspire to, but rather, as a perfect picture of a target we will never hit.

Say what?

While people seem to love to moan and groan about how prohibitive the 10 C's are, they're certainly not the worst set of rules that have ever been handed down. Those first set of 10 rules are the basics. They're entry level commandments. They're Algebra I. You have to pass that test to move on to Algebra II.

In the New Testament Jesus drills down even further and says if we even call our brother a fool, we're guilty of murder. You might as well open up a suite for me on death row, because I'm guilty!

Jimmy Carter became famous in the seventies by admitting that because he lusted after women in his heart, he was guilty of the sin of adultery! Even though he was dead right, he was mocked mercilessly for it.

In summary, God gave us just 10 short rules to show us 1) who He is and 2) how we can never measure up on our own.

Confusing? Of course it is; it's from the Bible!

Word to the Wise

If nothing else, the Bible is chock full of helpful hints on how to live. Over time I've gathered a few verses I find to be extremely helpful. I've also found that different sections speak differently to me at different stages of my life.

Wisdom is the hallmark of this book. Even a cursory look will often yield a nugget or two.

I'd be hard pressed to name my favorite, but the most helpful is an easy choice.

A few decades ago, my marriage was in trouble because I happen to have an anger problem. I could give excuses and blame ineffective lessons and communication from my formative years, but the bottom line is I've got a short fuse.

To get a handle on my problem my wife and I started counseling together. On the side I had my own guy I saw for extra credit.

He was very old, very wise, short and wrinkled with pointy ears. I was seeing Yoda.

"Love her you must. Think not of yourself you will!"

He crammed one particular verse down my throat every time we met. It's a tidbit of wisdom Solomon recorded in Proverbs 4:23: "Above all else, guard your heart, for it is the wellspring of life."

Yoda broke down that verse into three parts.

This is important! Not many verses start out waving a flag suggesting you give it priority.

- Do this! It is an action. It is not passive. Be proactive.
- Here's why! What you store up in your heart affects your whole being.
- I don't know about you, but I like to stew over problems. I tend to rehearse what I should have said in an argument in my car, or bathroom, or any old place. Frankly, it's fun. No one ever interrupts me, and it's the only time I can win.

Imagine a grand Shakespearian production where I played all the parts, slayed everyone who opposed me and ended up victorious standing on a heap of my defeated enemies. Each sequel repeated the same plot beat for beat.

What a moron! I was polluting my heart, and those murky and dark waters flowed out and took over my persona. I was spending my days trying to drown myself in self-justified negativity.

The solution was simple. I became of aware of my feelings. Whenever I moved from disappointment over to anger, the inevitable outcome was that my emotions got the better of me. The best way to nip that in the bud was to guard my own heart and to stop rehearsing my anger.

Have I forgotten that rule more times than I care to admit? Unfortunately, yes. But every time I remember it, my life is just that much better.

Need I remind you that's just one example! The Bible is literally filled with "a-ha" moments like that just waiting to be discovered and applied to your life.

Come on in, the water's fine!

Fun Fact: In the Old Testament, a large group of boys mocked the prophet Elisha for being bald. Elisha cursed them and two bears came down from the mountains and killed 42 of the boys. Apparently one for each of the hairs left on Elisha's head. I can't say for sure what the deep life lesson here is other than the obvious: mock God's bald prophets at your own peril!

The Theology of Story

It has been observed that humans are hard wired for certain things. We react to certain stories and songs because they seem to ring true. Why is that? Why do certain stories and songs resonate and others drop by the wayside without making any impact whatsoever?

The answer is that a good song, book or movie is an echo of a tale as old as time. Stories resonate with us because they reflect the 'big story' that somehow rings true. Like it or not, humans seem to react favorably to 'His-story,' if you will.

I love the idea that besides being a fine introduction to both God and His plans for us, the Bible is, at its core, one story.

It certainly takes its sweet time to get there (Tolkien and *The Lord of the Rings* saga has nothing on God), but when you step back, you can see the building blocks to an intricately designed tale.

One that we all, consciously or not, try to emulate when we tell our own stories.

For authors, the possibly very depressing fact is that if your sweat-of-your-brow piece of change-the-world creativity doesn't hit the basic beats of the Bible, it's probably going to fall flat. Sorry.

To fully unpack this, you'll have to read my friend Sean Gaffney's book, *Evaluating Story: A Christian Look at Film, TV and Theater.*

As Sean describes it, every story worth telling actually follows a pattern. It's a pattern every casual Judeo/Christian knows from their days sitting in Sunday school or listening to the Passover story.

If you think your drama teacher in high school invented the three-act structure of rising action, crisis, climax and denouement, you haven't been paying attention.

In case I've been too subtle up to this point, let me lay out an audacious claim: every single successful story you have ever heard reflects the story in the Bible.

Cue spit take. "Wha-? Every single story? How is that even possible?"

While the Bible is made up of dozens of different books and hundreds of individual stories, they are all part of one fabric that tells the compelling story of God chasing after His children.

Like every good novel, it's got action, adventure, intrigue, jealousy, death, betrayal and some good ol' fashioned humor. That's right, humor! The Bible is funny!

I don't have time to unpack all the jokes held within, but trust me on this, the Bible runs the full spectrum of comedy, from exaggeration to irony to sarcasm to downright crude jokes.

Back to my point. If the Bible does indeed tell God's story, then why on earth should every successful story need to reflect it?

That, my friend, is the genius of God! What better way to draw people to Him? He hard wired a sense of morality and story into our hearts so that when we hear or see something that reflects that story, we say, "Yes, that feels right. Now I will go out and love my fellow man."

But beyond that, after a lifetime of hearing reflections of the God-story, when we are introduced to the real thing, it shouldn't come as too big of a surprise when we take to that story as if we've been searching for it our entire lives.

It's the most basic set up and pay off ever created!

If you believe God made us, it's not too far of a stretch to believe that He put His imprint on our hearts.

If you have a favorite movie or book, from Star Wars to Harry Potter, I guarantee you, the plot follows the Bible beat for beat. If it didn't, you wouldn't love it.

It's almost as if you can't even help it. We are like the monster in *Frankenstein* when he hears the haunting violin music. We are drawn to it much like moths to the flame.

I will also point out that when a story starts off great and then fails to satisfy at the end, it's because the stubborn authors said to themselves, "Why follow convention? Let's shake things up and have the villain win!" Those authors are usually called failures.

That's the reason you feel so dissatisfied when you finish a story that doesn't follow the Bible's pattern. It's almost as if it betrayed you. The pull of what our hearts want is just that strong.

What, then, is this Theology of Story?

Tell Us A Tale!

I've never met anyone who doesn't like a good story. Some people who shun theater and TV are drawn to endless sporting events, which, I'm sure you can guess, are *stories*!

One team comes in as the underdog, the Gladiators battle it out as the clock winds down. One team leaves victorious, the other is eliminated from the competition. It's got all the elements! It's David and Goliath without the messy clean up after.

As my film teacher, Tony, from the American Film Institute, used to say, (with a very thick Italian accent) "It's a horse race, folks!"

Billy Wilder broke down the secret of good movie making into three simple steps. Act I: Send your hero up a tree. Act II: Set the tree on fire. Act III: Get your hero out of the tree.

It's as simple as that!

Even if you're not a student of drama, you know the ingredients of a good story. There's a beginning, a middle and an end. It's a no-brainer!

You hook the audience, bring in the action, make us squirm as we watch the characters stumble through the narrative, then eventually wrap everything up with a bow.

Writers call each step of the story a beat. There are five basic beats we all know and love...

1. Balance. Here's where the story establishes what is normal.
2. Unbalance. Wouldn't you know it! Something happens to upset the normal world.
3. Quest. Our hero does something to restore the balance.
4. Crisis. Something happens to prevent the hero's plan from working. All is lost!
   And finally,
5. The New Balance. Some sort of happy ending is established. The balance is restored.

I'm sure you recognize every story you've ever seen or heard in the above list. From *Jaws* to *Star Wars* to *The Wizard of Oz*, they all follow the sacred beats.

But do you also recognize the story of the Bible? Let me lay it out for you.

The Biggest Story Ever Told!

The Bible starts off with *balance.*

Big surprise, that's Eden. All was right with the world. It was, in a word: paradise. Personally, I don't know how any self-respecting paradise could exist without the occasional luau, but to each his own.

At this point, Adam and Eve are naked, having a grand time frolicking with the animals and lounging around in waterfalls. No worries, no danger, no tan lines.

It's important you remember the paradise from which we came, as the ultimate goal of this story is our never-ending desire to, as folk singer Joni Mitchell put it, "get back to the garden."

It seems nothing good can ever last, so we have a little thing called the *inciting incident.*

This is also known as the *catalyst.* We go from what we knew to a whole new ball game!

Satan enters the picture, is upset he's not in charge, separates Eve away from the herd and convinces her that paradise could be just a little more paradise-y if she'll only disregard the only rule God laid down.

The fall happens, Adam and Eve don't have a thing to wear and off we go from what was normal into the great unknown.

God has no choice but to kick His tenants out of His garden. He also lays a curse or three on them. In story terms, this is the *big event*.

Now the hero is forced to leave his old life and go on a journey. Note that the hero here isn't Adam. The first man eventually dies and is remembered to this day by such phrases as, "I don't know him from Adam," and "It's Adam shame."

No, the hero of the Bible is God. Even though He kicked humanity to the curb (He gave them fair warning!), He now starts a very long arduous journey to get back His true love.

God introduces Himself to Abraham, becomes His God, and begins weaving a lot of foreshadowing of His Son, the coming savior, throughout the Old Testament.

His *quest* is to restore His relationship with humanity. A knee jerk reaction could well be that His angry, judgmental attitude didn't help matters a whole lot, but that was for a purpose! He had to show mankind they couldn't reach Him on their own.

In Act II, God tries various ways to restore the balance, but He knows nothing will work until He goes down there Himself.

That leads us to the story's *midpoint pinch*.

This is where it gets personal. There's no going back after this. The hero doubles down in an all-or-nothing attempt to win.

This is the event we like to celebrate as Christmas. The Nativity is God breaking through into our time and space. The hero knows this is the only way to restore the broken relationship. But, as with all good stories, it's not going to happen the way we think it should.

After every midpoint pinch, there's always a *temptation*.

This is where Satan enters the picture again on cue and tries to con the hero into giving up, that's it's just not worth it, that there's got to be an easier way!

If the hero accepts the offer of second best, then the story is over. Here, before Jesus starts His ministry, He goes out into the desert. After some 40 days, the Son of God does what Adam and

Eve could never do; He rebuffs the lying tempter and we get ready for a final showdown.

It doesn't happen right away, of course. Good stories take their time. Jesus takes a few years in order to establish Himself as the Messiah. He certainly knows what's coming, but everyone around Him is totally clueless.

Eventually we arrive at what is known as the *crisis*.

In film school they asked us to identify the crisis of the Bible. Thinking it was a trick question, we all sat silent until a timid hand rose and correctly answered, "…the crucifixion?"

In classic terms, the crisis cannot go well for the hero. He must lose. He must die. In our movies and novels, the death can be metaphorical. It can be a near death. But in the big story, our hero dies. Dead as a doornail. There's no way back from this one!

And now we have to wait. We don't just say, "Don't worry! Here He is!" No, now we come to the *wafer beat*.

This is where all of the hero's friends experience a sense of loss. They fear for their lives. They wonder what they could have done to prevent it. Guilt and sorrow abound!

In other words, the weight of the crisis has to hit home. It was a long journey and we feel cheated because now it's all over! The good guys lost! I want my money back!

But wait! He's only mostly dead! Okay, in real life Jesus was most certainly really dead. But for story purposes, we know our hero must have something up his sleeve. We have hope!

In *the Princess Bride*, Wesley says true love never dies, it can only be delayed. I don't know if screenwriter William Goldman knew he was perfectly describing the resurrection, but he may have had an inkling.

Finally, after what feels like years, we come to the showdown of the story. The good guys face the bad guys in a winner-takes-all battle in the *climax*.

Surprisingly, the Bible's climax happens off screen. Jesus defeats death and all we get to see are people running to and fro shouting, "Dude! You're not going to believe this!"

Against all odds, the hero has come back from the dead! He wins! Jubilation! Parades! The talk show circuit!

 Because we're currently in this particular story, it's hard to see the next beat. In truth, we haven't come to it yet. We have to skip ahead. This is called the *new balance* or the *denouement*.

This is where a newer, better paradise is found. This is the new heaven, or what the Bible calls the new Jerusalem.

After all this time, the Hero and His loves (now numbering in the billions!) are reunited. All is forgiven. The old wounds are forgotten.

It's a new day. Our Hero enters the new, much improved paradise, sits back, puts His feet up, and tells His children the timeless story from the beginning.

The reason we want to believe in the ending is that we've seen everything else in the story. Why would the ending change? God's already won! He's just being His normal, patient, drag-out-the-ending-to-infuriating-lengths kind of guy. Paradise will be regained. It's a foregone conclusion. You can bet your life on it.

In a nutshell, that's the theology of story.

So, the next time you watch a great movie or read a great book, know that you are really enjoying a reflection, or echo, of God's original story. It's endlessly comforting to me. I hope it is to you as well.

Fun Fact: The Guinness Book of World Records estimates that more than five billion copies of the Bible have been printed. Half of which the Gideons International group claims are currently sitting in hotel nightstands. No other single book has sold over a billion copies, but the collected works of Shakespeare and Agatha Christie are in the billion copies club. The Harry Potter series has sales in the hundreds of millions and is the current leading contender vying for the top spot!

Our Past, Present and...

The fourth and final layer of the Bible is one that is truly amazing—it can predict the future!

Throughout both testaments, the Bible gives both subtle and blatant foreshadowing of Jesus, the future co-mingling with gentiles and the eventual end of the world. It also lays out a few other predictions that came true to the letter.

The biggest prediction is given right out of the gate. After the pivotal moment involving Adam, Eve and some kind of Apple product, the Bible states that the serpent will bruise the heel of man, but that 'He' will someday break the serpent's head. Clear as mud, right? This is where you need to realize that, sometimes, the Bible is just pure poetry.

The serpent represents Satan. No big surprise there. Man is none other than the Adam we've all come to love and resent. The second Adam is Jesus. He's called that because He represents the power that comes into the world specifically to defeat the rebel alliance once and for all.

While Satan will, in fact, 'bruise God's heel' (via the crucifixion), when Jesus comes back from the dead, Satan will be defeated forever, breaking his head. The symbolism is there if you're privy to a few basics.

It's like a good movie that pans past the gun resting over the fireplace mantle in the first act. You may not notice it, but be forewarned, in the third act, when all is lost, the hero will reach for that gun and defeat his enemy. It shouldn't be a surprise, but it was introduced so long ago that we totally forgot about it!

God's predictions are a lot like that. They've been hiding in plain sight for thousands of years. Some are big, others are so small they seem inconsequential. Still, they're in the story to prove a point: God is outside of time. He can see the future and He knows, beyond a shadow of a doubt, what's going to happen.

It's as if He's taunting us, "Can your god do that? Maybe it's time to trade up."

In his book, *Evidence That Demands A Verdict*, Josh McDowell trots out the case of the ancient city of Tyre. Not a big metropolis for us, but at the time, it was a semi-important fortress on a small land mass just off the coast of modern-day Lebanon. Because the city was surrounded by water, accessible only by one tiny ribbon of land, it was almost impervious to attack.

In Ezekiel 26, the Bible makes a few rather bold predictions. It says Nebuchadnezzar will lay waste to the city. So much so that the entire place will be wiped out, no one will ever build on it again and that someday fishermen will spread their nets over the once proud site in order to dry them.

On this side of history, it may not seem like much, but guess what modern fishermen do on the ancient city of Tyre now? It should come as no surprise that everything the Bible predicted came to pass and the once proud city is now little more than a flattened area used to dry out fishing nets!

How do you explain Ezekiel's 100% accurate prediction? One that is still true over 3,000 years later! If you ask me, that's pretty cool.

There are plenty of other predictions, of course. Rather than bore you with obscure biblical facts, let me point out that the accuracy rate for Hebrew prophets is 100%. If you didn't hit that mark, you were stoned for being a false prophet. As you can guess, this cut down on the number of part time neighborhood psychics considerably.

Foreshadowing

Despite what most people understand and/or believe, Jesus is not merely a New Testament creation. He is, in fact, all over the Old Testament.

God is the perfect story teller, so He spent an inordinate amount of time in the O.T. foreshadowing His Son's appearance. He did a rather extensive 'pre-introduction' of His Son so that humanity would not freak out when He finally showed up. A lot of good that did.

St. Augustine came up with a rap to help explain how the Bible works: "The new is in the old contained; the old is by the new explained."

One of the best books on this subject *is The Miracle of the Scarlet Thread.* Just like the science books I waded through, this book takes a deep dive into the minutiae of scripture and successfully lays out all the ways Jesus is woven throughout the tapestry of the Hebrew scriptures.

Here are a few of my favorites…

We have to start off with Abraham. He's the first human in recorded history to ever bargain with God. When Jehovah stated He was going to wipe out the twin cities of Sodom and Gomorrah if He couldn't find 50 good people there, Abraham managed to talk the Almighty down to 10.

How he did it was brilliant. He laid out 'successful bartering 101' with the Almighty. He said, "You are king of all. I am but dust. Would you destroy the city for the sake of, say…30?"

It's seriously like a Monty Python routine. By the end, God agrees to stay His hand if He can find just short of a dozen people who are good.

As the two cities were summarily wiped out anyway, it's a good bet they were rotten down to the core.

But the parallels to Jesus join the story when Abraham is instructed to kill his son, Isaac.

Let the record show that Abraham did not consult with his wife before he went on this potentially deadly journey with his son.

I can just imagine the discussion if he had let loose with that bombshell!

"You're what! You are aware I was 90 years old when I had Isaac! That's 9-0! My eggs were literally dust, but the Lord blessed us with a son. And now you want to go and kill him? Have you lost your mind? I thought pawning me off as your sister to the Pharaoh was bad enough, but this! This takes the humus!"

I'm sure it was just easier to ask for permission after the deed was done.

Note the similarities to the Messianic story: Abraham sets off to sacrifice his only son. The journey takes three days where he's sure his son is as good as dead. Still, Abraham has an unshakable faith that God will somehow restore his firstborn.

Remember God had previously made an unbreakable covenant that Abraham's offspring would be as numerous as the stars in the sky, and if Abraham didn't come back with Sarah's boy, he was as good as dead. So that couldn't happen.

Side Note: the mountain top Abraham traveled to is thought to be a hill just outside of Jerusalem. Many believe it's the very hill where Jesus was eventually sacrificed. File that one under, 'too cool.'

Just when Abraham was about to kill his innocent son, God saw His servant's faith and told him that He, Himself, would provide a substitutionary lamb in Isaac's place.

Note that God said He would provide a *lamb*, but when Abraham looked up, he saw a ram caught in the thicket, which he used instead of Isaac.

Don't let the salvation of Isaac distract you. The substitutionary lamb God promised was, in fact, not a simple slip of the tongue. It was a prophecy of another lamb who would be sacrificed many years later.

Before I move on, consider, for a moment, how freaked out Isaac must have been throughout this whole episode. I suspect he never went on another father and son camping trip ever again.

"Camping? With you? Uh, no thanks, I'm way behind on my dung shoveling."

I wonder what was going through his mind when his dad started tying him up and then laid him out on a bed of kindling?

"Hey, dad, these ropes are kind of tight. What's with the knife? I'll never stay out past curfew again, I mean it! It was one time! Okay, I took your best camel, but I washed him down after! He's as good as new!"

Passover This!

Then you've got the Passover. If you've ever been to a seder, the connections to Jesus are myriad. Whenever I celebrate with my Jewish friends, out of respect for their traditions, I tend to bite my tongue a lot.

It's no coincidence that Jesus was crucified on the Passover. It's yet another example of God's story-weaving skill, as two separate stories converged in astounding ways.

The first Passover happened when the 10th plague floated over Egypt and the first-born son of every family was killed by the angel of death—unless, that is, their house was covered by blood.

This blood had to be painted over the door of every Hebrew family using a hyssop brush. This brush, as fate would have it, has tiny bulbs filled with water that would break open as the blood was painted over the doors, mixing the blood with the water.

Not only were the Hebrews saved by the blood, but need I remind you of the spear thrust in Jesus' side years later, resulting in Him bleeding out blood and water?

When the Passover celebration was started, it was intended to remind the Hebrews of God's everlasting protection. It also sneaks in the story of the coming Messiah.

Traditionally, spotless Passover lambs are purchased and presented on the Sunday before the meal. (Parading through the street on Palm Sunday, anybody?)

Then they are slaughtered on Friday at 3:00, the exact time Jesus finally succumbed to His many wounds.

It's very important that when the Passover lamb is killed that no bones be broken, just like Jesus when He died.

Then you've got the matzo bread, which is pierced and scoured. It's like God's not even trying to hide the symbolism!

If that's not enough, one third of the bread is broken off, hidden in a bag and then broken. Hmm, which part of the trinity was separated from the others and eventually broken? Alex, I'll take Jesus' foreshadowing for $200!

The Tabernacle

The next introduction of the Messiah comes in the desert with Moses and the Hebrews after they had escaped the clutches of the Egyptian empire.

Wandering the desert for 40 years must have left them with some time on their hands. What better way to keep everyone focused than to build a home for God?

God instructed Moses to build a tabernacle in which He could dwell. Nothing too fancy, just a little tent with a place outside for the occasional BBQ.

This tabernacle is the forerunner of the temple Solomon eventually built. Both places are crude replicas of God's house in heaven.

Here's a really cool beat-your-neighbors-in-a-Bible-trivia-contest fact. The tent had two coverings. The first was badger's skin. This was a dull, grey covering that impressed nobody. Underneath that, unseen by anyone just passing by, was ram's skin that had been dyed red.

The tent was the physical foreshadowing of Jesus. He came in a humble human dwelling that covered up the sacrificial God He was underneath.

Oh, it gets better! There was only one entrance into the tabernacle courtyard, and that was through a gate facing east, where the sun rose and the tribe of Judah camped. Jesus came from the tribe of Judah and their flag displayed the figure of a lion. Nothing symbolic there!

Then you've got the High Priests. When Aaron and his sons were consecrated, their priestly garments were sprinkled with blood. God, being holy, could not receive them unless their sins were covered by blood.

Yes, it's the whole-weird blood thing God has going on, but as weird as it is to us, at least He's consistent. None of this, "Blood? Oh, no, that's so last millennium! This year it's all about gluten free bread!"

The illustrations above are just a few of the blatant examples of God doing His best to introduce His Son to His children well before He arrived on the scene.

One last thought on the blood and the seemingly endless sacrifices God demanded in the Old Testament.

Maybe the purpose behind them was to tire out the Jewish people so that when Jesus finally came, they'd say, "Wait, no more sacrifices? No more shopping for the spotless dove, lamb or goat? No more messy clean up? It's done, once and for all? Finally! Sign me up!"

I bring up all of these archaic facts because I believe they're just as fascinating as the creation of the universe. An unfathomable mind outside of time has been meticulously weaving a story over thousands of years that ultimately gives us meaning for our very existence. I stand in awe at the very brilliance of it all.

Fun Fact: The Old Testament contains over 300 Messianic prophecies Jesus managed to fulfill. The odds of one person fulfilling just eight of those predictions would be one in 100,000,000,000,000,000. For one person to fulfill 48 of those prophecies would be one chance in 10 to the 157th power. Thus ends the reading from the book of Immaculate Calculations.

And Now, the End is Near

As of this writing, unless I've missed the signs entirely, despite several near misses, the world has yet to end.

When I was a young man in college, I was fully convinced the end of the world was imminent. I came home full of excitement that I knew how and when the world was going to end and was very disappointed when my parents didn't seem to share my enthusiasm!

My dad said that when he was in college, he had learned the very same thing, and since nothing had happened up to that point, he was fairly confident it might not happen by the next weekend.

That was a tough lesson for me. Yes, I'm that sick individual who got mildly disappointed that the world didn't end on his watch!

Still, the Bible verses are there, warning mankind of the ever-looming eve of destruction.

Even though the timing is fuzzy and taking way longer than anyone ever expected, don't be deceived. If God cannot lie, and His reputation is built on His unfailing honesty and faithfulness in keeping His promises, I can promise you that without a doubt, some day in the not-too-distant-future, this world as we now know it will cease to exist.

When entropy and death are thrown out on their collective ears, the world will experience a new birth, and that's going to be pretty wild to see.

With all that said, if you're at all curious about the end times, there are approximately six trillion books on the subject. Most are impossible to wade through due to the endless "I've discovered the heretofore-hidden secret" diatribes laid out by very excited authors.

Without getting mired down in too many details, here's the gist of how the world's going to end…

Ever since Jesus defeated Satan and death at the cross, Beelzebub has been seriously ticked off. He laid low for a while, much like Sauron in *The Lord of the Rings* trilogy, but without the cool ring of invisibility.

The end of the world represents Satan's last gasp effort to defeat Jesus and claim control of this world for himself. Why he just won't give up and go away is beyond me! Satan is the poster child of sore losers everywhere.

The final battle is going to be in a place called Armageddon. Up to now you probably thought that was a really cool space movie with Bruce Willis and a loveable crew of roughnecks. It so happens it's a real place in Israel and the location of the epic final battle.

Just before all literal hell breaks loose, Satan sets up a puppet government through a minion called the Anti-Christ. I doubt very seriously if that's his real name, but it could well be.

"A vote for the Anti-Christ is a vote against baby Jesus!" Who knows, give it a few more years and that slogan could well be a winner!

At any rate, the Anti-Christ has some really cool powers that amaze everybody. That is, until he goes into the newly rebuilt temple in Jerusalem and claims to be God.

Spoiler alert! The Jewish temple has to be built on the original temple grounds, which just happens to be occupied at the moment by a very sacred Muslim site. Don't know how it's going to happen, but in the very near future, expect a transfer of ownership.

Oh, and lest I forget, this is where the whole mark-of-the-beast thing comes into play. This is a very nasty deal where Satan sets up a system of commerce that controls how everyone on earth buys and sells everything. At first blush, it sounds like Amazon, but it's even more insidious!

You will no longer have to worry about cash or credit cards or having your identity stolen! All you have to do is have a mark put on your right hand or forehead. That's it!

The downside is that everyone who takes the mark will be swearing allegiance to the real dark side, so it does come with considerable baggage.

After these things happen, you can kiss your fanny good-bye with extreme confidence. If you thought the 10 plagues in ancient Egypt in Moses' day or the Covid-19 pandemic were bad, just wait.

This time around literally billions of people are going to be wiped off the face of the earth by earthquakes, plagues, disease, tsunamis and just plain evil.

And while the desire will be to blame it on the Christians, by this time, they will have left the building via a very strange thing called the rapture.

The rapture is where Jesus comes back just before the final curtain and ushers his homeboys off stage. It's sort of a cosmic 'Edelweiss' moment.

To find out what happened to their Christian brothers and sisters, everyone who's left on earth has to read all the *Left Behind* books, and that will be hell for them.

Anyway, after all is said and done, Jesus comes back in the clouds on a white horse. For Jews, this will be the long-awaited coming of their cherished Messiah. For Christians, it will be their second coming. For everybody else, this will be their own personal come-to-Jesus moment.

A battle happens, blood rises up to the bridles of the horses in the valley of Armageddon (eww!), Satan and his minions are defeated, and Christ goes about setting up the kingdom He intended all along.

There are dozens of other details, but these are the big hunks. I say all this for one very good reason: pay attention to what God says in the Bible!

We may not understand it all, but when it comes to things like the end of the world, or losing your soul just to gain the world, it's well worth your time in seeing what must be done to be on the right side of grace when your time comes.

Warnings

I've noticed our current society seems to be obsessed with warnings. It seems every product now has to come with not only a life-time guarantee, but an endless list of warnings of what will happen if you attempt to use their manufactured item incorrectly.

I've seen plastic bags with, "Warning! Do not place bag over head!" I've even seen "Warning! Fire is hot! Do not throw irritating little brother onto coals."

I can't wait for knives to catch up with this trend, "Warning! Long edge and pointy end are sharp! Do not stick cooking utensil in another living thing as repeated stickings may cause injury and lead to excessive bleeding and eventual death."

Our whole society is based on warnings. If you drive too fast, you'll get a ticket. If you drink and drive, you could lose your license. If you don't use the right deodorant, toothpaste, make-up, hair color and drive the right car, you'll die an excruciating death alone surrounded by cats (who will eat you long before you're ever discovered).

The Bible is filled with warnings. A lot of them are basic, such as "bad company corrupts good morals." Some are mildly insulting to our modern anti-slut shaming culture: "A woman without discretion is like a pig with a gold ring in its snout."

But other warnings should be written out in bold print! Seriously, I don't understand why we can have the red-letter edition where we see everything Jesus said, but nobody's come up with the brilliant idea of highlighting everything humans need to avoid.

That way we could just flip through the Bible until we come to something that jumps out!

"Warning! Thinking you are hot stuff will lead to your eventual downfall and humiliating comeuppance!"

"Warning! While pursuing pleasure can be acceptable in

moderation between consulting adults, excessive pursuit can lead to a police line-up meth-head mug shot."

"Warning! Do not confuse God's patience with implicit agreement."

"Warning! Even if a close friend suggests it, never jump off the Empire State building."

"Warning! Accepting any kind of universal one-world chip or mark on your right hand or forehead is worse than jumping off the Empire State building!"

"Warning! While a bird in the hand may well be worth two in the bush, always wash your hands immediately after handling said foul."

"Warning! Do not die without first having a very serious conversation with your maker about the condition of your eternal soul."

Hey, it couldn't hurt!

Recipe—One Bible

1. 66 books.
2. Different styles contained within books.
3. Must be both direct and oblique, demanding a lifetime of study
4. Secrets to life contained within.
5. Lay out both future and past.
6. Explain who and what God is and why humans are here.
7. Map out long journey God has taken to win back humanity.
8. Show endless sacrifices of creator.
9. Give humanity hope.

†††

Fun Fact: The world's largest Bible weighs 1,094 pounds, is 43.5 inches tall and when laid open stretches to 98 inches wide. The world's smallest Bible can literally fit on the tip of a pen. PiLCs etched the 1.2 million letters of the Old Testament onto a tiny silicone disk, which they call the Nano Bible. Ant Man is currently waiting on the delivery of his order of the New Testament.

Fun Fact: The most expensive religious book in the world is not the Gutenberg Bible, which fetches a mere $5,000,000, but rather the Bay Psalm Book, which was sold for over $14,000,000! It's the first book printed in America and was the Puritan's attempt to make their own translation of the Old Testament book.

His Middle Name Doesn't Start With 'H'

I'm sure you've heard the phrase, 'Walk a mile in someone else's shoes.' Putting basic hygiene and potential toe cramps aside, it's a great reminder that everyone you meet comes with quite a lot of baggage and, as such, empathy should be our go-to. It rarely is, but it should be.

I would like to ask you, for just a moment, to pretend you're Jesus.

For those of you who already think you're god, this should come quite easily. The rest of you will have to tax your imaginations a bit.

Assuming the Bible is right, Jesus had been with the Father in heaven for, literally, forever. The plan for humanity's redemption was put in place, and He was the guy the other two outvoted to carry it out.

No doubt the Holy Spirit gave Him a bit of a pep talk: "Jesus, it's only logical! The Father can't look on anything unholy. He'd have to walk around with His eyes clamped shut the entire time! And I'm a spirit. Mary can't cuddle me. You can't be a carpenter if you can't hold the tools. Like it or not, you're the best one for the job!"

So off He went, down to earth, to fulfill His Father's wishes.

That's a First!

There's a long list of 'firsts' here you may not have considered. Jesus was the first person to enter our time and space who was fully man and yet, at the same time, fully God. Don't ask me how this worked, but it's what happened.

Jesus wasn't God from the waist up. He wasn't God on Tuesdays, Thursdays and Saturdays. He wasn't God on High Holy days. He didn't magically become God at His baptism. He was fully God and somehow, fully human living as a baby, a teenager and, eventually, as a man.

While it's hard to understand, it makes perfect sense. Jesus had to be a perfectly sinless sacrifice to accomplish His primary task. If He were a normal human up to some pre-determined moment of enlightenment, then what about all of His normal, every-day, made-a- lot-of-mistakes kind of life up until then?

No, He had to have a God-centered sinless soul from the get-go in order to side step the relentless tide of temptations that befall us all.

"Hey, Jesus, want to go get wasted tonight?"

"No, thank you, I'll be home praying to my Father in heaven."

"Dweeb!"

Another first is that the One who actually invented time now had to live in it.

God can see the past, present and future simultaneously. When you move through time like we mortals have to do, you have to wait for what sometimes feels like *forever* for most things.

Which is yet another bonus round point for Jesus that I don't see any other god stepping up and claiming: He came down to us. He walked around in our bag of bones for a few decades. Not for a star-studded weekend, but for the drudgery of a lifetime!

Can you imagine Jesus as a kid, out playing with His friends?

"Liar, liar, tunic on fire!"

"I don't want to play hide and seek! Jesus finds us every time!"

"Jacob, you should try to love and respect your parents a bit more. They've had a rough go of it."

"Mom, I don't need swimming lessons, I can walk on it!"

I suspect He also used the bathroom for the first time. I say "I suspect" because I'm hoping against hope that when we get our perfect bodies, we won't ever have to evacuate any waste ever again. If heaven has toilets, I'll be severely disappointed.

Other firsts: His body was decaying. He had gas. He got hungry. He felt everything humans feel. It had to be extremely odd. Not that any of it came as a surprise to Him, but it's one thing to create the human body; it's quite another to live in it.

All of that is the human side. Now, imagine Jesus from the God side.

He had to be off-the-charts smart, but He was stuck on a planet full of imbeciles. Imbeciles whom He loved, to be sure, but imbeciles all the same.

As God He knew every person He met before they were even born. He knew every detail of their lives as well as the condition of their hearts. The sheer knowledge of that experience is overwhelming to me.

When the guards ripped out His beard and beat Him with their fists, He loved them as children who went astray. He could also see the spiritual dimension around Him, so there was no doubt as to who was responsible for egging the guards on in that particular beating.

I believe this knowledge and a bottomless empathy for His children is what enabled Him, in His final moments, to utter, "Father, forgive them, for they know not what they do."

What's even more amazing to me is that He stared into the faces of people who betrayed, lied to and eventually killed Him with the full knowledge that He was going to the cross to pay for their sins.

A little part of me thinks that when He was being abused by the guards, He thought to Himself, "Man, I'm going to have to pay for that later!"

Don't just think of Him as someone who paid the debts of some far off, unseen debtors. He took the blame for every despicable thing people did right to His face!

As a person who tends to hold on to a few delicious grudges going as far back as kindergarten, no matter how hard I try to let them go, that one's difficult for me to comprehend.

Judas must have been the toughest. Peter suffered from incurable foot-in-mouth disease, but Judas was with Jesus for three years, pretended to be His friend, skimmed a little off the top from the paltry sums they had, and then eventually betrayed Him—all because Jesus wasn't sticking to the savior script Judas had in mind.

It's a scary thing when we think we know more than God. Especially since I do it pretty much every day.

I personally believe that Playboy publisher Hugh Hefner did irreparable damage to this culture pushing his relentless agenda of casual sex, but he did print one picture I find liberating. He published a picture of Jesus laughing. I was surprised when I found out where it came from, but despite the baggage it carries, I love that picture because it gives me hope that from time to time Jesus was able to let go of the immense burden that was placed on His shoulders and just let out a belly laugh.

Imagine for a moment if Jesus was a humorless rule-keeper. Or worse, the stereotypical Jewish mother...

"You want me to heal you? I'm carrying the burden of the entire human race and no one does anything but ask me to answer their prayers. What am I, chopped liver? Would it be so hard to ask me what I'd like once in a blue moon? But no, I'll just serve you day and night until they come and take me away. But will you miss me? The one who knit you together in your mother's womb? Mr. Big Shot is too busy to even pray! Would it kill you to call out to your Father every now and again? He misses you!"

Can you imagine what it must have been like to raise an absolutely perfect child? That had to freak out His first-time parents a little. As in, 'Is this normal?' We won't know until we get to the other side and watch the Hi-Def video presentation, but He had to be extraordinary.

The 'terrible twos?' Forget about it. Every time Mary talked to her relatives, I'm sure all she could say was, "No, He's been an angel. No trouble at all!"

Now try and imagine what it would be like to grow up with Jesus as your older brother! Comedian Michael Jr. has a great routine on this. Check it out on YouTube.

Make Up Your Own Jesus

One thing you can say about Jesus is that after 2,000 years, no one's forgotten his name! Whether people use it to finish their prayers or toss it off as a curse word, it certainly seems to be gaining in popularity.

I'm curious as to why no other gods' names are used as swear words. You never hear, "Krishna, that was a nice catch!" Or, "Oh, yeah, well, Vish*nu!*"

But for some reason everybody and their cousin thinks it's perfectly acceptable to drag Jesus' name through the mud.

One of the main problems of Christianity is that a great number of people just don't understand who Jesus was. Instead of seeking out the truth, it's very popular for people to paint Jesus in their own image.

I'm sure you've heard that Jesus was all love, all the time. That He was meek and mild. That He never condemned anybody! These are all partially true, but they only paint a fraction of the picture.

My favorite is that He was just a good and wise teacher. I'm sorry, but do we normally kill our good teachers?

"The award for Teacher-of-the-Year goes to Mrs. Mizrahi. String her up!"

To answer this charge, I would like to defer to C.S. Lewis in order to lay out, what I believe, is the quintessential statement about Jesus. It cuts through the myths and the mystery surrounding this historical figure.

He says, "A man who was merely a man and said the sort of things Jesus said would not be a great moral teacher. He would either be a lunatic—on a level with the man who says he is a poached egg—or else he would be the Devil of Hell. You must make your choice. Either this man was, and is, the Son of God; or else a madman or something worse."

Still, there's a lot to unpack about Jesus. There are misconstrued misconceptions surrounding Him that I think are caused mostly by wishful thinking.

It doesn't take a PhD in psychology to understand people want Jesus to be a God who fulfills their needs. If you want love, then poof, Jesus was a man of love. If you want hellfire and brimstone, you can find it in there. And if you want to totally ignore Him, you're allowed to do that as well.

My attempt here is to diffuse some of the myths, step back and introduce the Man who came to earth to introduce us to God.

Admittedly, a big part of the deluge of misinformation concerning the character of Jesus is that many people in the church don't have any idea who He is! Hey, if we don't know, then how can we expect the world to get it right?

Race

There's a bit of controversy about what Jesus looked like. After about a split second's worth of thought, it's not hard to realize that the white bread Jesus pinned up in a lot of churches couldn't be further from the truth.

He was born in the Middle East.

In Africa.

Of Jewish descent.

With no mirrors, tweezers or dental work.

I highly doubt he was crowned prom king.

Even the Bible says He was nothing special to look at. He was the definition of humble. Everything that made Jesus special was underneath the façade. If He was a chick magnet, it would have defeated the purpose of His visit.

While artists take extreme liberties with their depictions of the Son of God, I have no doubt that when I see Him, I won't have to ask for any I.D. (The permanent halo backlighting should give Him away.)

†††

Fun Facts: While Jesus managed to remain sinless throughout His life, His rogue's gallery of relatives did not. His ancestor Jacob was a schemer, Judah sold his youngest brother into slavery, David had a man killed to cover up his adulterous affair, Solomon had over 1,000 wives and concubines and Rahab was a prostitute. And you thought your family was screwed up!

Follow Who, Exactly? II

Jesus Was Funny!

I was working a big fundraiser one weekend when I was taken aside and summarily chastised for making 'Jesus' jokes. It seems I offended one of the big donors by talking about the Bible in a 'funny' way.

There was not any particular routine or joke that stood out, mind you; it was all of them! The exact line that was thrown at me (not by the old coot himself. He complained to the organizers instead—implying that if I didn't shut up, his money would dry up) was, "Show me in scripture where it says Jesus ever laughed."

That statement fills me with such sadness. Can you imagine living with such a person?

"You there! Stop with such frivolity! There will be no laughter in this house! The Lord Himself never laughed, so neither shall we! I have spoken!"

I was not allowed to throw any enlightenment towards the erroneous attendee that weekend. I was simply told to rein it in. Since I wanted to get paid for the event, I put a cork in it. Sadly, the love of money won out.

The truth of the matter is that Jesus was, indeed, funny. And if He made jokes, I suspect He occasionally laughed at them as well.

Although this does present quite a theological conundrum: if Jesus knows the future, can He ever be surprised? And if He knows every punchline ahead of time, does this mean He's spent an eternity doing the 'polite' laugh?

That aside, to even suggest that Jesus never laughed shows a great ignorance of the scriptures. One doesn't have to go very deep before a few telling phrases pop up. It says several times in Psalms that God laughs at us and our foolish plans.

Proverbs 17:22 says...

"A merry heart does good like medicine, but a broken spirit dries the bones."

My point is simple: if God is described as laughing, and His word then makes the very strong suggestion that a merry heart is the only way for us to live, then how can anyone think that, He, Himself, is a dour sourpuss all the time?

Humans only have a modicum of intelligence (a mere sliver of what God possesses), yet we are able to see incongruous situations which can cause us to laugh. Does anyone really dare to suggest that God is too dull-witted to catch the humor in any given circumstance?

The problem with laughter may well be at the root of what the old rich dude was secretly afraid of: comedy is dangerous.

Granted, we can put foul-mouthed mocking in the 'bad' category right alongside unabashed anger and unbridled lust. But there are versions of all three expressions of humanity that are actually good. God wants us to hate what is evil, desire our spouses and, for our own good, laugh to release our burdens.

Sure, do your best to only use and experience uplifting humor, but don't throw the baby out with the bathwater here!

To drive the nail in even further, let me perfectly clear: Jesus told jokes! He did! You don't get the attention of the throngs without throwing in a few jokes. Granted, the miracles helped, but Jesus was throwing out zingers!

The type of humor popular in Jesus' day was called 'Chinese exaggeration.' These are the type of jokes that stretch the joke to such an extent that everybody knows you're making a point.

Anybody remember the stories about the guy with a *log* in his eye complaining about a friend with a speck in his, or the one about the servant who was forgiven a billion-gazillion dollars from his master only to throw a fellow servant in debtors jail over a hundred bucks, or the big clincher, how it's easier for an entire camel to go through the eye of a needle than it is for a rich man to make it into heaven? (The last story seems to be tailor made for the uptight donor at my charity event, don't you think?)

Jesus also spent an inordinate amount of time insulting the ruling class. He called the Pharisees a brood of vipers! He said they were like whitewashed tombs!

He was playing to the crowd, folks! He was getting them riled up! That's why the Pharisees hated Him so much! He was publicly humiliating them! And nothing ferments hatred faster than wounded pride—inflicted by a mocker!

In all these cases Jesus knew exactly what He was doing. He was the master at using humor because (drum roll here, please) He invented it! We can laugh without fear of reprisals because if God created it, a joyful heart is, indeed, good!

Lastly, don't tell me that Jesus traveled around with an entourage of guys for three years without somebody cracking wise at every opportunity, or, at the very least, giggling over inopportune bodily noises. Most of the disciples were blue collar workers, not snooty high-brow intellectuals.

They laughed and they cried. And like every good leader and parent, Jesus encouraged both emotions.

Jesus Was Not Nice

While you may accept Jesus was funny, this category's even tougher to swallow. Though it's not PC to say it, I need to state for the record that Jesus was not nice. At least not in the way that we currently define that word.

By 'nice' I mean He wasn't a wimp. He wasn't insipid. He didn't just shrug things off and go with the flow.

Jesus was the very definition of strength. He called rich people hypocrites and bucked every social norm there was by hanging out with tax collectors and prostitutes.

He was the ultimate warrior. He had all the power in the world, but only used what His Father allowed Him to use.

To be clear, Jesus claimed to be God. That's not nice. That's not preaching non-violence. He came here with a job to do and He knew it. It doesn't take more than a cursory glance through the gospels to see quite clearly that Jesus had a Messianic complex. He really thought He was the Son of God.

You've got to deal with that fact. You can't pretend that Jesus was Floyd the Barber who went around telling people to love one another. If that were all that He did, then I don't think you'd find many people who would be willing to die for Him.

Jesus very clearly laid out who He was, who He thought God was and what each of us has to do to have a relationship with both Him and His Father.

He was bold, loving, humble, empathetic, wise, unselfish, courageous, radical, strong and possessed unflinching honesty. Please don't insult Him by saying he was merely *nice*.

A Resurrection? You Can't Be Serious!

And now we get to the crux of the matter. Did Jesus really come back from the dead? It's unbelievable, to be sure. But from all accounts, it actually happened and, as such, we're stuck with a very inconvenient truth.

Know upfront that if it's all a lie, Christianity can be thrown out on its ear. The great apostle Paul was quite emphatic on that point.

C.S. Lewis said, "Christianity, if false, is of no importance, and, if true, of infinite importance. The one thing it cannot be is moderately important."

I include that quote because I think Mr. Lewis, from my perspective, anyway, is a flipping genius. When it comes to confronting

and explaining this rather unwieldy faith, it should be noted that
my three heroes on this topic all have something in common. They
were all atheists who set out to prove, once and for all, that Christianity was and is a complete hoax.

To a person, after doing their best to disprove it, they all came
away totally convinced that there is so much overwhelming truth
to the Christian faith that they could no longer deny the facts. They
are, in order: C.S. Lewis, Josh McDowell and Lee Strobel.

While there are many, many good strong thinkers out there (Tim
Keller being my current favorite), these three resonate with the
cynic in me, and I would highly encourage you to get their books
to take a deep dive into the proofs of Christianity.

If it were not a religion that could stand up under scrutiny, believe
me, these three intellectual heavyweights would have found a crack
in its armor.

I'd suggest starting with Lewis' *Mere Christianity* to lay the
groundwork, then moving on to Strobel's *The Case for Christ* and
if you need even more proof, strap on your big boy & girl pants
and read McDowell's *Evidence That Demands a Verdict*.

Finally, to see how the other side operates, read Lewis' *The Screwtape Letters*. I could go on and on, but for now, commercial time
is now concluded.

The proofs I give here are from the books listed above. I will
reiterate a few, but if you want the full list, I'd encourage you to
dive into further study on your own.

First, there's the actual day of the resurrection. Make no mistake,
for the testosterone crowd, it's embarrassing. One of the proofs
of the resurrection of Jesus is that after the arrest and crucifixion,
the men were hiding from the authorities, and the women were
the only ones brave enough to go to the tomb. I say this is proof
because for the rest of their lives, the disciples had to repeat this
fact and be razzed for their cowardice.

Then there are the guards. Roman guards had a very strict set of
rules. If they fell asleep while on duty, they were killed. End of story.

Yet, somehow, after telling their superiors what happened, how a dead person of interest escaped from a grave, of all things, right under their noses, the guards were let off the hook. The powers that be made some flimsy excuses, and the Roman government let it slide. Unheard of!

Then there are the witnesses. When Jesus came back, He didn't do it in secret. He made the rounds. At one point He was seen by over 3,000 people. That's a lot of eyewitnesses! Surely someone in that group would have recanted if it were a prank.

Finally, the disciples never wavered on their insistence that Jesus actually rose from the dead.

You may remember the name Chuck Colson. He was known as the hatchet man back in Richard Nixon's administration. After he was arrested for his crimes surrounding the Watergate scandal, he held out for bit, but soon sang like a bird to the authorities, just like everybody else.

While in prison he became a Christian, and this was one of the reasons that tipped the scales for him; he said that his highly trained and well-paid group of politicians didn't last more than a few weeks under intense questioning.

But the disciples, an unruly group of amateurs, all went to their graves (many under torture) insisting that what they said was the absolute truth. Jesus rose from the grave and appeared to them and to His followers before He ascended up in to heaven.

Yes, we were not there, but there are mountains of historical fact surrounding this extra-ordinary event. It was not a rumor that grew over time. It was not wishful thinking. No one had an ulterior motive, here.

This was an event in human history, that, if true, is way more important than the latest stock market numbers and whether or not your favorite rock star is up for a People's Choice Award.

This deserves to be moved to the top of the list under Events That Changed the World (followed by Lincoln's Freeing of the Slaves, Gunpowder, The Discovery of the New World, and The Beatles).

Examine the Evidence!

If you're like me, you have several friends and acquaintances who love to gush over the latest program they're watching on the approximately five million subscription media platforms we now endure.

If you trust the recommendation, you may actually tune in to see for yourself. Once you do, you are either hooked or you turn the show off with an exclamation of, "What were they thinking!?"

Jesus is like that. You have tons of people telling you He's the best thing since sliced bread, others who say He's a myth and still others who walk around with signs stating that if Jesus ever comes back, we should kill him again.

This is one area you can't rely on hearsay. Your decision needs to be based on your own personal exploration. I will touch on this in a chapter or two, but suffice it to say, you owe it to yourself to take a deep dive into the life of this person who claims to be God.

Our lives are filled with tons of distractions, I'll give you that. Sometimes getting up in the morning takes all the energy I've allotted for the day. Then there's work, and working out, and relationships, and relaxation, and eating, and binging, and then it's time for bed!

That being said, if something is important, we all somehow find the time to squeeze it in. Trust me, Tik Tok and Instagram will be there tomorrow.

Especially if your life feels as if it's out of control! You need to look into Jesus! Let Him be your ultimate life coach!

Sad to say, this is one area you can't delegate. "Miss Jones, read the Bible and get back to me with your recommendation on this Jesus fellow. I want it on my desk first thing in the morning!"

Fun Fact: When the Bible refers to Jesus as a carpenter, the Greek word 'tekton' is used, which can mean any kind of craftsman. Since there were no trees near Nazareth, the town where Jesus grew up, and there was a huge stone quarry just outside of that town, it is now believed that the cornerstone of the Christian faith did not work with wood but was, in fact, a stonemason.

It's Not Fair!

One of the big bugaboos about Jesus is His rather unmoving stance that He is the only way to heaven and to the Father.

Regardless of the long list of positive things Jesus has done for humanity, the big black mark in the negative column refers to His insistence that it's His way or the highway.

I've already dealt with the "exclusive/inclusive" debate, so let's take a moment to look at the oh-so-common "It's not fair!" reaction.

On that point you are absolutely right. Christianity is in no way 'fair.'

It is not fair that one side of the relationship has to take on the lion's share of the work.

First, God had to make a universe. Including, of course, our home, planet earth, as well as our moon and our sun. Then He had to create an intricate timeline for humanity to start modern civilization.

Once that happened, He orchestrated it so that your mother caught your father's eye, then He knit you together in your mother's womb and watched over and protected you your whole life. So far, not fair at all!

But the final straw is that Jesus had to pay for all of your transgressions, even though, let me be clear here, they are *your transgressions*!

You don't have to pay a dime for His forgiveness. It's like Christmas and Hanukkah and your birthday combined to the 10th power.

It's patently obvious none of this could be considered *fair* by any stretch of the imagination.

Everything is decidedly lopsided in your favor. He prepares, makes, and takes care of everything. If His punishment for failure seems too harsh, that should be okay, since He's even offered to take the hit for you!

Be honest for a moment. Pretty much everyone breathing on this planet knows that the phrase "it's not fair!" is nothing but code for "this is not going the way I want it to!" It's selfishness, pure and simple.

I will never forget a comment I heard several decades ago. The Pope was giving a talk. Whether you like the current or any Pope is not the question. A certain amount of respect should probably be given to anyone who has achieved such a position. Anyway, the Pope was giving a declaration and said something politically incorrect that a certain relative of mine disagreed with. When she heard it, she immediately blurted out, "Just who does he think he is?"

I'm not even Catholic and I wanted to shout out, "He's the Pope!"

This is a perfect example of how we all react to Jesus and His demands.

Is any of this fair? Not for a second. He didn't ever intend for any of it to be fair. He intended it to be just. He intended it to be overflowing with grace.

Don't ever ask God for what's fair. You won't like the result.

Mind Blown!

As I read through and highlighted my way through a stack of physics and religious books, one very major point blew me away.

Jesus declared Himself to be many things, but He kept coming back to His main three...

He's the light of the world.

He's the bread of life.

He's the living water.

The obvious point He's making is that we all need food, water and light to survive, and He personifies all three. We need look no further for our sustenance. He's the great provider.

But let's dive a little bit deeper. When Jesus says "He's the light of the world," what does that mean, exactly? Sure, He brings illumination to a darkened world, we get it. But is there something more that we're just not seeing?

As I tried to explain in the first section, Einstein pointed out over 100 years ago that light is outside of time.

If light exists outside of time, it could well be the metaphysical link between the timeless eternity that existed before our universe was formed and the world of time, space and matter that we currently occupy.

Einstein theorized that light and matter are the same thing. What if Jesus' claims were more audacious than just saying He's the source of warmth in every Thomas Kinkade painting? What if this claim was His biggest ever?

In Hebrews it hints that Jesus "holds the universe together," which means He's calling himself gravity, but this is even more earth shattering.

For God to create this universe, He had to exist outside of time. He must be eternal. He must be the most powerful force anyone on this planet's ever heard of. But what if God didn't just invent light? What if He *is* light?

Jesus says He's the light of the world.

Light is outside of time.

It all fits!

It's been sitting in front of us all along but because the PiLCs and the theologians are in the middle of a Hillbilly feud, they've never bothered to compare notes.

Jesus literally is the light of the world. He travels at 670,616,629 mph. Awesome! I would dedicate my life to following Him, but I'm too out of shape to catch up!

If this idea is true, imagine for a moment the power that comes with the word Jesus. This should blow the 'nice, meek, unassuming' Jesus out of the water.

He was, indeed, meek. But the definition of meek is a powerful animal who is under control. A trained horse is meek, but you treat them as weak at your peril. A horse is unbelievably powerful, but a trained one will only use that power when called upon.

Imagine Jesus like that to the one billionth power! He is the most powerful force in the universe who humbled Himself to the point of death.

When He was on trial, He could have wiped out any person who came against Him. Imagine Superman's heat vision. That's a taste of what Jesus could do. He also had legions of angels at the ready, willing to do His bidding. Despite that, He managed to keep it all under control.

Note that Jesus never got angry during His whole trial, scourging and crucifixion. He only showed anger when someone insulted His Father or oppressed the innocent. When He, Himself, was wronged, He did nothing. He knew why He was sent here and He was big enough to take it.

For that, I will be forever grateful.

Is this grandiose theory imperative to your salvation? Do we need to agree on this rather grand idea? Most certainly not.

My intent is shake you up a little in order to help you see Jesus in a different way.

Unfortunately, I believe His character has been redefined by our attention deficit disorder modern culture. Jesus never used a cell phone or a computer, He never ordered from Door Dash, so He must be weak and insipid. That's the trap I want you to avoid.

Take a breath, step back and see Jesus for Who and What He truly is. My conclusion is that He's worthy enough to be worshipped.

††

Fun Fact: Jesus raised three, count 'em, three people from the dead! The first was a widow's only son at his own funeral in the town of Nain! The second was a synagogue leader's daughter. Jesus was told Jairus' child had died, so He went to the leader's house and raised the young girl. The last resurrection was His friend Lazarus. He'd been dead for four days, but Jesus called him out and Lazarus walked out from his grave! The most miraculous thing about all three events was that not a single person who cheated death signed a book deal!

Why Didn't Jesus Just Come Today?

A very valid question I need to address is one of utter simplicity: with all the social media and telecommunications available in our modern age, why didn't Jesus just come today?

He could have hit the talk show circuit, done a couple of miracles, got His message out and then zipped right back up to heaven!

Here are a few reasons why I believe God, in His infinite wisdom, chose to incarnate His Son when He did, rather than wait a couple thousand years for the internet to be invented.

Top 10 Reasons Jesus Wasn't Born in The Modern Age:

10) Disciples always tweeting during miracles.

9) Sermon on the Mount too long to go viral on YouTube. Lost out to a cat video.

8) Calling people 'sinners' considered intolerant hate speech.

7) This time around, the whole virgin story would be even more of a miracle!

6) Casting demons into innocent pigs would anger PETA.

5) To feed 5,000 people, He'd have to individually wrap and label nutrition content of loaves and fishes.

4) People would complain if Judas didn't at least receive a 'participant' trophy.

3) The Christmas season already way too overcrowded to try to squeeze in a savior.

2) Nearly impossible today to find three wise men.

And the number one reason Jesus didn't come today...

1) We didn't pay attention then, what makes you think we'd pay attention now?

Come on Down!

One of the explanations of why Jesus entered into human history when He did can be explained with one simple word: peace.

For the first time in hundreds of years leading up to, and then for only a few years after the birth of Jesus, there was a tenuous world-wide peace courtesy of the Romans.

Both before and after His life can be summarized in another word: chaos.

In Monty Python's 'Life of Brian' there's a brilliant scene where a rebel force complains about what a horrible occupying force the Romans are. After listing the multitude of improvements Rome has brought to their land, the ire against their oppressors dies down. But still, they hate them! And comedy ensues.

Before the Romans came along, it was pretty much every nation for itself. Due to the ever-present threat of thieves and robbers attacking travelers, long journeys were next to impossible. But with the Romans came fantastic roads (some of which are still in existence today) and a policing force that minimized highway robberies.

The Roman Empire didn't set out to make spreading the gospel easier, nor did they have any intention of helping God evangelize the world, but that's exactly what happened.

That's something that needs to be stated; God can use His enemies to accomplish His will.

The best example of this was when Joseph was sold into slavery to the Egyptians by his brothers. After a series of unfortunate events, he rose to power and ultimately saved his family from a world-wide famine. Later, when Joseph faced his brothers, who were quaking in their sandals waiting for their brother's severe retribution, he uttered the ultimate line, "What you intended for evil, God meant for good."

Keep that nugget tucked away; somehow God can make absolutely everything work out for good—for those who love Him.

Back to my point. If Jesus had come just 100 years before His birth or 100 years later, there was and would be no world peace and, because of that, the good news would have been, despite the best laid plans, stuck in Jerusalem.

While we have a hard time imagining it, the perfect time for Jesus to come was over 2,000 years ago. If nothing else, God has always had incredible timing.

Another benefit of the Roman Empire was their incredible creativity when it came to public executions. They had a rather expansive kingdom, and one of the ways they kept the local riff raff in line was by making all punishment for crimes against the state a very public spectacle. The Salem witch trials had nothing on them.

In case you didn't know, the Romans invented crucifixion. It wasn't quite as dramatic as dipping people in pitch and then lighting them on fire to illuminate your gardens at night like Nero did, but it got the job done.

One of the gruesome facts about crucifixion is that death comes about through suffocation. In order to breathe, you need to push yourself up on the cross. When your legs give out, you collapse, your lungs aren't able to take in enough air and you asphyxiate. Now, if your back happens to be whipped to shreds as Jesus' back was, it dramatically cuts down the time on the cross.

It's an unbelievably horrible way to die, which is why it served the Romans perfectly!

See, Jesus had to die publicly. His death couldn't be hidden. The whole world had to see Him die. Otherwise His subsequent resurrection would have come into question.

It's another reason Jesus couldn't have come today. If a bleeding-heart do-gooder took up His case, His execution would have stalled in the courts indefinitely and we'd never have Easter!

Somehow, I don't see a world-wide movement of people following a guy languishing on death row.

No, justice had to be swift, and the Romans were just the guys to do the dirty deed.

So, after the scourging and hanging Jesus on a tree, the Roman professional killers pierced His side with a spear, blood and water came out, and they pronounced Him dead as a door nail. If He weren't, they would have broken His legs in order to get Him to suffocate by sundown.

Which, FYI, was another amazing prediction made thousands of years before Jesus' death. This one is found in Psalm 22.

A chapter before David talks about having no fear as he walks through the valley of the shadow of death, the man after God's own heart lays out how the Messiah of the Hebrews would die on a tree, that soldiers would cast lots for His clothing and that while His bones are pulled 'out of joint,' none of them would be broken.

To us, predictions like that are nothing short of amazing. To someone who is outside of time, I suppose it's nothing more than accurate reporting.

So, yes, Jesus actually died on the cross. He didn't swoon. He didn't faint, only to be revived in the coolness of the tomb. The Roman soldiers were well trained. They were experts in death. It may not have been the dream job they signed up for at the Roman Job Fair, but it paid the bills.

And after all of that, three days later He came back from the dead. Drop the mic. Coolest encore ever!

A Summary of Sorts

In the name of clarity, I'd like to make a few final observations.

Jesus is not intolerant. Regrettably, a few people who follow Him may well be, but Jesus Himself is the very essence of inclusiveness. His entire purpose is to give unlimited grace to everyone on the planet, regardless of race, creed or gender.

Jesus created the entire universe, from the largest galaxies to the smallest atom. He invented time. And dimensions. Speaking for myself, I can't put together an Ikea dresser.

To help His creation know who He is, He broke through time and space and was born as a human.

His mission was simple: tell the world God wants a relationship with us—even though everyone quite naturally runs after their own desires instead of His.

After spreading His message for three years He allowed Himself to be sacrificed for us and promptly brought Himself back from the dead.

FYI, He knows the world and the people in it are royally screwed up. It's not the way He wants it. But out of respect for us He gave mankind the freedom to reject Him.

Unfortunately, that freedom means the world can be quite messy, but it also makes it so much richer when we finally choose to be with Him.

The good news is that He has promised that when the time is right, He will put His kingdom back together again.

Through the ages, His followers have made a million mistakes; but they also started the first orphanages and hospitals and every day untold numbers do their best to selflessly serve the hungry, the oppressed and downtrodden.

He was a Man who never posted on social media but somehow gained millions of followers who encircle the globe.

I'd encourage anyone reading this to not reject Jesus out of hand, but rather, to investigate His claims.

And maybe when Christmas rolls around again, you just may discover the reason for the season.

As a side note, on Christmas, my wife and I do our best to make it as authentic as possible. We decorate the house in straw and cow patties, keep sheep in the garage and when people come over to visit we shout out, "There's no room at the Inn!" and then slam the door in their faces. Ah, the warmth of the holidays.

It's entirely too easy to mock Jesus and put Him down, but to do so only shows your ignorance. Instead, put Him to the test. Examine His statements. I believe you'll be pleasantly surprised.

Look at the astounding thing Albert Einstein said…

"I am a Jew, but I am enthralled by the luminous figure of the Nazarene. No one can read the Gospels without feeing the actual presence of Jesus, His personality pulsates every word. No myth is filled with such life."

I will go to my grave believing that Jesus was an actual historical figure who performed many miracles while He was here, was crucified, died and rose again from the grave. This is not conjecture. This is not myth. This is what the entire Bible and Christianity's whole faith is based on.

People seem to be amazed by the resurrection. Speaking for myself, I don't think it's God's biggest miracle. If God is outside of time and made the entire universe, bringing a body back from the dead is child's play to Him.

Now, for Jesus to willingly go through the torture He did and to take on the sins of every single person who ever was, or would be born, to my mind, that's just flipping amazing. He did it voluntarily. He was totally innocent and took on the wrath of God for all the sin and evil in the world.

That, ladies and gentlemen, is worthy of praise.

With all that said, let me be clear. Belief in Jesus is the big stumbling block to the Christian religion.

It's not about having enough faith, it's not about avoiding sin, it's certainly not about how many rules you follow!

To be a Christian, the very simple, incredibly difficult task everyone has to accept right up front is that, listen closely now—You-Are-Not-God.

There, I said it. And that's what keeps most people away from this particular religion. They may rant on and on about different rules or argue about tangential items, but the reality is, people have a very hard time accepting the fact that they are not the personal God of their own universe.

To accept that someone or something is greater than you is the very first very uncomfortable step in a long road toward finding who you were meant to be.

Yet another misconception about Jesus is what His actual job is. Yes, he came to introduce us to God and die for our sins. Check. But what about now? In other words, what has He done for me lately?

As to His day-to-day job, Jesus is an advocate for you. Literally, that takes up most of His time. When you pray and have a desire so deep you can taste it, Jesus is the one who takes it to God.

Multiply that times several billion people bumping around on this planet and you can just imagine how busy He is. Good thing He's as fast as light.

Take that one scene from *Bruce Almighty* where Bruce looks over a million prayers and multiply that times a billion jillion.

Now, your prayer may not get answered the way you want it to. There's an old saying about prayers: they get answered in three ways: 1) Yes, 2) No, and 3) Maybe later. Then there's my favorite, #4) Are you crazy?

But even if your prayer seems to fall on deaf ears, I guarantee you it hasn't. It was heard, considered and acted upon. It had to be. You have an advocate who cannot break His word, who has promised to represent you before the almighty God.

Pretty cool in my book.

Recipe—Jesus

1. Be one with the Father.
2. Step down from heaven to take on human form.
3. Be born of a virgin.
4. Be sinless.
5. Be singularly focused on mission to save humanity.
6. Mingle among humans. Explain who and what God is.
7. Chastise any and all who think they're "all that."
8. Show love to the unloved.

9. Sacrifice self.
10. Resurrect self.
11. Sit on the right hand of God the Father almighty.

Fun Fact: In the category of 'Those Most Unlike Jesus,' the leading contender for this prize would be the suspected Anti-Christ, the Roman Emperor Caesar Nero. In the Hebrew language, his name adds up to 666, which, according to the Bible, is the mark of the beast. This is not too surprising, since Nero had his own son and mother killed, set Rome on fire so that he could rebuild it and liked to dip Christians in pitch and then burn them to light his garden.

Section III
The Conundrum

Fix it!

Now we run headlong, smack dab into the biggest problem of all: if God did, indeed, make every miraculous thing in this endless universe, and if He is so all-fired good, then why is this world so broken?

Granted, our domicile is not entirely busted. It still works, but it no longer runs like a Swiss watch. It hacks and coughs like an old man clearing out phlegm left over from the cold war.

I'm not just talking about our physical planet. I'm also including the majority of the several billion people walking around on our celestial home. Our lives are too often pockmarked with pain and unfulfilled wishes. What's up with that?

We have been given a gift that appears to have fallen out of warranty. We all learn quite early on that perfection is a pipe dream reserved for romance novels and airbrushed Instagram selfies.

We long for the Hollywood fantasy but are stuck living in a low-rent community theater production. We want Marilyn Monroe but end up with a past-her-prime bleached out B-movie star in Spanks with fake lips and a run-down pink Corvette.

In short, life is not all it's cracked up to be, and we at least deserve to know why!

Seven Deadly Sins Adjacent

As you are most likely aware, the word 'sin' has fallen out of favor of late. More often than not, it's mocked. And for good reason. How many over-the-top Bible thumping preachers have we seen on TV crying crocodile tears begging us to stop our sinful ways? Maybe a few were sincere, but the majority sure looked like parodies waiting to happen.

As I've stated previously, to have a relationship with your Creator, you must begrudgingly admit that you are, in fact, a big, fat, stinking sinner (actual words from the Bible. No exaggeration intended whatsoever!)

So, if you are one, let's break it down.

First off, you're not alone. Everyone on the planet falls into this category. To 'sin' means to miss the mark. There is a bullseye in life, and even if you hit the target 99 out of 100 tries, that one off day still puts you in the same boat with the rest of us losers.

What I find interesting is our culture's insistence that everyone is perfect and no one needs to change anything! If that were true, five million therapists would go out of business tomorrow.

When I was growing up, we had two examples to show us what we should and, conversely, what we should not even think about doing. They were called the 10 Commandments and the Seven Deadly Sins.

One of the interesting reversals in our modern culture is that we can't seem to erase the Top 10 Cs fast enough and the Seven Deadlies are now inexplicably celebrated.

Lust is now applauded, gluttony is a brave life style choice ("Fat shamer!"), vanity has been embraced by an entire generation of endless selfies and pride has more parades than the 4th of July.

For good or ill, what we are witnessing is the death of shame. In many ways, that's a good thing. Shame can cause serious psychological problems and was used for far too long by sadistic teachers to keep impressionable kids in line. I doubt if Pink Floyd's *We Don't Need No Education* would have been written without a steady diet of boarding school shaming.

Before we bury shame forever, I believe there are several behaviors we *should* all be ashamed of!

Racism, sexism, ageism, in fact, pretty much all the isms are examples of nefarious people using their short-lived power to get other people to bend to their will.

When any of these cases are brought to light, to a person, we all feel like we've been punched in the gut (narcissists being the notable exception).

As such, it shouldn't be too hard to understand why the Bible says that everyone has fallen short. Tim Keller says our brokenness is the one area of religion of which we have empirical proof.

Our issue seems to be how much we can get away with. The official term is rationalization. I call it the Hitler defense. "Well, sure, I may have kicked that dog, and cheated on my wife, as well as my taxes, and hate anyone who doesn't look and think like me, but I didn't kill six million Jews! So, basically, I'm a good person."

I agree that there are degrees of sin. Swiping a fiver from the offering plate is nothing when compared to genocide, but the fact remains that neither behavior quite reaches the standard of perfection.

That, of course, is the point. God wants you to come face to face with your own failings so that you will finally admit you can't do it on your own.

Self-sufficiency is a wonderful trait, but it can also be a trap. How many parents have stood patiently by while their child struggled with tying their own shoes while emphatically insisting, "I can do it!"? Of course, with the age of Velcro, that example's officially passé, but the point remains.

Don't get the idea in your head that God wants us to be passive couch potatoes either. While it may be mildly depressing to face the fact of ultimate failure in the perfection department, giving up apparently isn't an option.

So, which is it? Are we supposed to be totally dependent or willfully independent? The answer is 'yes.' God's very clear that He wants us to work toward perfection, no matter how impossible the end goal.

God wants a partnership. He wants to come alongside. He'll

give advice on, say, how to carve and whittle down the race car for the Cub Scout pinewood derby, but He won't cheat and hollow out the back and add weights on the front end to help you win. (Not that I have any deep scars from my own humiliating childhood experience racing against other fathers in my troupe who valued their son's winning over my own dad's unbelievable never-bending sense of fairness.)

In summary, the world is, indeed, broken, and the inescapable fact is that we are broken right along with it. So now what?

While this thought is in no way popular, I believe we need a clear-eyed view of exactly who and what we are. That's a tall order because it's in our very nature to believe that somehow, against all rational odds, just as Al Franken's self-help character said on SNL, we are, indeed, good enough, smart enough and, dog gone it, people like us!

Semantics

I have a love/hate relationship with the never-ending soothing semantics society throws at us. Today you can make the most horrific event or action sound wonderful simply by rephrasing the words. It's no longer what you do, it's what you *call* what you do.

In a way, it's fairly brilliant. In order to excuse any behavior, all you have to do is redefine it.

"Your honor, my client is not guilty of murder, he merely accelerated the victim's reincarnation process."

That's right, we're not going to hell in a hand basket, we're simply advocating an alternative post life location. In a hand basket.

Last year they opened up a gentleman's club right next to our post office. Let's be honest: how many 'gentlemen' actually frequent those establishments? I like to imagine the entire place filled with fussy English butlers wearing tuxedos saying, "Oh, I say, miss, you're practically naked! You'll catch your death! Here, take my coat until suitable clothing can be found!"

It may be hard to believe, but I wear it as a badge of honor that I've never been to a 'gentleman's club.' I tell people that while God would certainly forgive me, He and my wife don't see eye to eye on that particular issue.

Fun Fact: In 1631, a publishing company printed a run of Bibles with the typo, 'thou shalt commit adultery.' They sold out immediately. Today only nine of these 'Sinner's Bibles' are known to exist but the pent-up demand for them is huge!

The Downgrading of Evil

One of the other alarming emerging trends of our modern culture is that evil just isn't what it used to be. Evil used to mean sadistic war criminals, or demons from *The Exorcist* who made young girls walk down the stairs backwards like a spider.

Evil was formerly a great descriptive word saved for the most heinous of crimes. A midnight abduction for nefarious purposes? Definitely evil. A polarizing political figure advocating fiscal responsibility? Eh, not so much.

Evil was also something you did not want to wake up! Every other horror movie of the last decade seemed to have a tagline about waking up evil. As if evil really needs its beauty sleep!

"Look out, evil hasn't gotten its full eight hours! It's going to be cranky! Run!"

But modern evil has been downgraded to the point where anyone who disagrees with you on Facebook is now labeled with the 'E' word.

"I sure do love me some Chick Fil A."

"Fascist scum! In your free time do you drown kittens? Why is no one policing these sites?"

Regardless of how you define it, in one form or another, evil seems to exist. It is much like the popular description of pornography: "I may not be able to describe it to you, but I know it when I see it."

What I find interesting is that the majority of the evil in the world (with the possible exception of snakes and mean little yappy dogs) flows from man and woman kind—but we just love to blame God.

Personally, I'm not convinced it's His fault. It's not like we haven't received fair warning about where our bad choices will eventually lead us.

If you think cheating or lying or being a proud idiot is the definition of a good time, the Bible plays the role of Jiminy Cricket.

Take a cursory glance through the Psalms and Proverbs. They're packed with sage advice.

When Solomon said there was nothing new under the sun, he was probably thinking about the predictable evil men choose on a daily basis.

Bottom line, evil is real, and 99.9% of the time, it is us.

The Spectrum of Humanity

A recent example of the whiplash we all experience on a daily basis would be two vastly different pieces of entertainment I recently experienced.

The first night was a one-man show about C.S Lewis called *The Most Reluctant Convert*, while the next night I found myself in a comedy club/bar/den of iniquity. The two could not have been further apart on the enlightenment scale.

The C.S. Lewis play was a thoughtful, well researched production that dramatized how Mr. Lewis was dragged kicking and screaming from an atheistic materialist worldview over to the tenets of Christianity.

It was intellectually stimulating and provoked a lot of discussion with my wife on the way home and with various friends after the fact.

The next night I went to check out a comedy club to see if it was the right kind of place to try out my material. I had a Facebook friend who was headlining, and I thought it would be a good time to go check out her act.

I couldn't stay long enough to even see her.

In the early part of my career, when Neanderthals roamed the earth, I performed in a lot of clubs. Comedy was hot then, but it was hard to relate to people with such limited interests (sex, drinking and more sex), so I stepped outside for about two decades.

But if this club in the San Fernando Valley was any indication, we're evolving backwards.

Generally, I can accept a fair amount of cursing. I've heard it all before and, if it helps a joke, I'll live with it. In fact, sometimes a well-placed curse word can take a mediocre gag over the top. This was not that.

Lenny Bruce and George Carlin pushed the comedy envelope for a reason. They were trying to shake up the status quo, and it didn't hurt that they were brilliant. I may not have agreed with everything they ever said, but you have to respect their courage, conviction and imagination.

However, the comics on this particular night didn't use their words to elucidate or educate. They used them as blunt tools with which to bludgeon their audience over the head.

Evidently the only relatable material these wanna-be comics could come up with revolved around porn, penises and lesbians. Half way through my two-drink minimum, I felt as if I had been tricked into watching the Crack Whore Comedy Tour.

I saw the lowest forms of humanity doing their best to drag the rest of us down to their level.

I left there depressed and in great need of a shower. I had to come home and watch some old episodes of the Lawrence Welk Show to cleanse my pallet.

This dichotomy of entertainment wasn't lost on me. Over the course of 24 hours, I saw the best and the worst humanity has to offer. This is one of the reasons there is a groundswell of clean comedy. Our slogan should be, 'We may not be the funniest people you've ever heard, but you won't need to be inoculated after the show!'

What Divides Us

The list of how our world seems to be falling apart could go on forever! In our current climate, we are divided by our opinions on global warming (and what should be done about it), abortion, politics, naked selfies, diversity, sexuality and should communion come with both gluten and gluten-free options?

All of these issues are worthy of further discussion, so please understand I'm not putting down your possible personal pet passion. What I am saying is that as a culture, we seem to focus an inordinate amount of energy on things that by their very definition are tangential.

I'm not discouraging you from doing everything you can to make this planet a better place to live, but to my way of thinking, it's all about *focus*.

According to God's instruction book, we were put here for one reason: to love our Creator and to love our neighbor as ourselves. Anything we do that falls outside of those guidelines is strictly extra-curricular.

We need to focus on what's really important. To paraphrase the Bible, what good would it do you to run a fortune 500 company, win the Kentucky Derby, or take home an Academy Award if, in the process, you ignored your true purpose and ultimately lost your soul?

I'm not saying you should become a nun (nothing against nuns, if wimples are your thing). I am saying that your life could well be out of balance.

Anyone who's ever gone down the rabbit trail of Facebook, Instagram, Twitter or late-night channel surfing knows of what I speak. We live in a world of distractions. Some are worthy, others are blatant time-sucks. We have to hold them all at bay as we work out our destinies.

Will you ever get it right? Absolutely not. It is a life-long task at which you will, in all likelihood, only get incrementally better the longer you live. But keeping your life in balance is a worthy pursuit.

Consider All of This, What, Exactly?

Most people find it rather strange, if not impossible, to fathom why a supposedly perfect, all loving God would allow so much angst and misery on the planet He says He created.

After that, the questions get even harder; if God is loving, then why doesn't He fix this place? Is He even watching? Is He powerless? Or worse, does He not care?

This is a very tough sticking point and one that is not easily explained away except by trotting out some time-honored clichés, such as, "That which doesn't kill you makes you stronger" and "When the going gets tough, the tough get going," and last but not least, Christopher's Robin's immortal words to Pooh Bear, "You're braver than you believe, and stronger than you seem, and smarter than you think."

A possible hint as to why God seems to revel in our endless struggle comes from Dr. Martin Luther King, when he said, "The ultimate measure of a man is not where he stands in moments of comfort and convenience, but where he stands at times of challenge and controversy."

The Bible weighs in on this issue in James where we are told to "consider it all *joy*, when we encounter various trials and tribulations, for the testing of our faith will produce blah, blah, blah." (I believe this comes from the, pardon the pun, King *Lames* translation).

If you're like me, every time someone says pain and suffering are good for me, I want to slug them. Repeatedly. And while I'm kicking them, scream out, "After just a few more body slams, you should be feeling fantastic!"

The fact of the matter is: pain sucks. This is why the majority of our lives is devoted to pain avoidance. I give you aspirin, TV, movies, board games, vacations, romance novels, the list goes on and on.

Why is there so much pain in the world? Why is there starvation and poverty and death? Why does that person have a Porsche and I'm clipping coupons?

Seriously, if God can't fix this, or worse, doesn't want to fix it, then why even believe in Him? Sometimes I want to invoke the landlord clause, "We agree to keep the place reasonably livable, but the upkeep is your responsibility!"

In this state of confusion, I turn again to C.S. Lewis. On this subject, he says, "Is this state of affairs in accordance with God's will or not? If it is, He is a strange God... and if it is not, how can anything happen contrary to the will of a being with absolute power?"

That's a big one.

The Problem of Pain

No matter how many PR campaigns it launches, pain will never win a single popularity contest. The harsh truth is that no one likes it. I suppose a few twisted individuals actually look forward to it, and Bill Murray was hilarious in his masochistic bit in the movie *Little Shop of Horrors*, but the majority of humanity tries their level best to avoid it at all costs.

So, why do we have it? If God is truly a good God, couldn't He just zap it away?

As with everything else in life, there would be consequences for that particular action.

Even though it pains me to do so, let's look at the upside of suffering, shall we?

C.S. Lewis says, "God whispers to us in our pleasures, speaks in our conscience, but he shouts in our pains; it is his megaphone to rouse a deaf world."

If you have teenagers, you understand this. Sometimes you have to build a fire under their butts to get them to actually move!

If there were no pain, no discomfort, no challenges, no suffering, we would, in all likelihood, be shallow, self-centered creatures.

Not you, of course, but the rest of humanity would find it difficult to be altruistic were they not given a very hefty push now and again.

If all we saw around us were endless perfection, then there would be no call to action. Not to say people in Hawaii and Bali never get up off their sarongs to help their neighbor, but if it were me, I'd have a hard time putting down the pulled pork.

A friend of mine has a theory that in the modern age, there

has never been a world superpower located on the equator. His hypothesis is that countries need to suffer through some kind of hardship, like freezing temperatures in Siberia or Nebraska, for example, in order to make them stronger.

Somehow delaying gratification and storing up food for the winter helps a country look at the big picture, and since everyone in that nation understands sacrifice and hardship, then the next logical step is stockpiling nuclear arms. Or something like that.

Pain, in small doses, can be a welcome friend. It can help you avoid much larger pains down the road.

Humans get bone tired when our bodies need to sleep. We feel pain when we put our hand over a flame to remind us that fire is something to be avoided. We have our hearts broken so that the next time we won't be so massively stupid and ask the head cheerleader to the prom.

In his book *Walking with God through Pain and Suffering*, Tim Keller says that while everyone suffers in this life, the Christian world view brings not only a greater hope, but a freedom in the midst of our pain. He postulates that Christianity ultimately promises a restoration of life. The pain down here is worth it because eventually we get our lives back.

The very real difficulty is that most of us don't want to wait. We want our lives back now!

Fun Fact: 20% of the world's population are afflicted with chronic pain—with back pain being the number one complaint over 25% of the time. 80% of Americans say they have lower back pain, while Europeans list this as the main reason they take early retirement.

Fun Fact: The best reason to get an education is to avoid pain! Quite possibly manual labor is the smoking gun here, because people who don't complete high school are *370%* more likely to suffer from chronic pain than people who possess a graduate degree!

The World Is Broken III

Still, Does it Have to Be This Hard?

Hopefully you have a begrudging acceptance of the fact that while suffering can often be a pain-in-the-butt, it seems to be a necessary evil.

But does there have to be so much of it? The question still remains as to why the majority of our existence seems to be filled with off-the-charts toil and trouble.

Sometimes the answer's as plain as the nose on your face; first, as previously stated, the world is broken. It could well be that God doesn't want you to get too comfortable here. He wants you to long for a better place.

The other reason for evil is that it's a great life lesson. When you see someone throwing a red-faced kicking and screaming tantrum or doing something else suitably despicable, most of us think to ourselves, "Note to self; don't ever do that."

I think learning to hate evil is a hallmark of humanity. When we see it, most of us know instinctively, 'that's not right!' And if we are then moved to action to stop said evil, then we're on the path of God! True love is not selfish; it is altruistic.

That is one thing we've got over the animal kingdom. I can't remember the last time I heard of a racoon throwing itself over a grenade or of a shark sacrificing itself so that a swarm of tuna could avoid a fisherman's net.

But humans? In the most unexpected ways, we're lousy with

compassion. And sometimes you need a broken world in order to see, by comparison, what true goodness should look like.

Despite hundreds of history's examples, all anyone really needs to know about evil is that it's a temporary bump in the road. It may seem terrifying, but just like every opponent in every *Rocky* sequel, it will be defeated someday, once and for all.

I hope this doesn't sound like a cop out, but I think one of the main reasons God allows so much pain and suffering down here is that it must be good for us.

I'm not trying to be a pious pie-in-the-sky optimist here. Really, I didn't drink any Kool-Aid this morning.

What I'm doing is trying to see things from God's perspective.

With free will comes free choice. Yes, God could eradicate all evil and suffering, but to do that He'd have to take away free will, and more importantly, us! Without the possibility of rejecting God, then there's no way God can ever know if our love for Him is real.

I think sometimes He allows very difficult tests to befall His followers to see if they really do love Him. I'm not saying I like it, I'm saying I think I understand it. He needs a testing ground to separate the sheep from the goats, the wheat from the chaff, His true followers versus (insert name of disgraced TV evangelist here).

Another reason could be that the work we do down here is to prepare us for the life ahead. I swear I have no idea what my job in heaven's going to be, but I'm volunteering to be C. S Lewis' chauffeur. Assuming he needs one.

According to God's current playbook, for any of us to have true freedom, we have to be able to choose between good and evil. God has to allow a few people to go off the deep end for the rest of us to see it and decide that we refuse to ever live like that.

Out of the endless cases of evil that we've all seen, haven't we also seen goodness, mercy, compassion, justice and love rise up out of the ashes?

When babies were being abandoned by the river in Roman

times, compassionate people gathered the babies and started the first orphanages.

When Europe's population was dying in droves because of the black plague, others stayed behind to help, which led to the first public hospitals.

So, I guess (sigh) that evil is (double sigh) in its own way (quadruple sigh) actually good for us.

But don't quote me on that.

Free Will

I was talking to a friend the other day and he posed a very good question: if God is truly good, why would He include the tree of knowledge in the garden?

One doesn't have to be all-knowing to figure out that eventually the temptation's going to overwhelm some poor schmuck and then within minutes they'll open up a 24-hour liquor store.

At the very least God could have made the tree hard to get to! Put it at the top of Mount Everest! Maybe surround it with a hedge of thorns! Adam and Eve were naked, after all. Or make the forbidden fruit taste like Brussel sprouts. That would have kept humanity safe for centuries until wrapping them in bacon was discovered!

Taking the story for what it is, maybe we need to get off the details and look at the meaning. It seems God is telling us a story about what a mess free will is and the inevitability of choice.

C.S. Lewis says, "Why, then, did God give them free will? Because free will, though it makes evil possible, is also the only thing that makes possible any love or goodness worth having."

This is where we get to the 'robot speech.' If God had wanted everyone to automatically love Him, then He may as well have created a race of robots, creatures with no will of their own.

When Sting sang, "Free, free, set them free..." he learned what God has known all along.

The Matrix showed us a world that looked perfect on the surface, but the reality for each person living in that utopia was, in fact, something much closer to slavery.

Take a wild guess: what does God want from everything and everyone He creates? Anyone?

If you blurted out, "He wants a relationship!" then you get bonus points. Why do you think so much of our time down here is spent building and repairing relationships? It's all a big practice run for when we get to the other side.

Apparently, there is no scenario in which a subject of God can have both free will and be 100% obedient to their Creator. Without the ability to choose to allow or deny, all love is suspect.

So, weighing the options, God chose the harder path. He chose to allow everything that has breath to either accept or to bitterly reject Him.

Not that He's some wallflower wringing His celestial hands, hoping we'll notice Him over by the punchbowl. He's definitely sweetened the pot for those who choose Him.

"Hey, if you accept me, you'll get peace that passes understanding! Plus, when you die, you'll get a mansion! Seriously, an entire mansion! The streets up here are paved with gold! There are no more tears! Ever! Come on, what do you say?"

Of course, while that may sound appealing, life down here seems to always get in the way. I'm sure you've heard the biblical saying, "the spirit is willing, but the flesh is weak." I don't even have to apply that to my application for holiness. I fail on things like diet and exercise and kindness and a dozen other good-for-me goals pretty much daily.

I bring up this frustrating reality for one overarching reason: I believe the first step to a correct world-view and a sober judgment of our place in it, begins with an assessment of who and what we are.

Once you do that, and you invariably come up short, the dilemma that befalls us all is universal in its frustration.

"What do I do now?"

Fun Fact: 700 people die every year by falling out of bed! Statistics are not available as to whether those people jumped or were pushed, but if snoring was involved, I suspect foul play!

The World Is Broken IV

Making the Best of It

This world is our classroom. We are all in the school of hard knocks. While our lives are undoubtedly a wonderful gift, they can also be seen as one long, sometimes tiresome test. That's why, at the end, God loves to say, "Well done, good and faithful servant. Enter into the joy of your master."

That phrase implies that we did something. We accomplished something and He's giving us an atta-boy!

What a complete joke! We did nothing! He's done all the heavy lifting. The best we can do is basically survive the journey for as long as possible without mucking it up too badly.

I may not understand it, but that's where trust comes in. If God did all that He says He did for me, I can put aside (a few of) my questions until I see Him face to face. I have complete confidence that when I'm inside the pearly gates, He'll shoehorn me in a huge lecture hall with the rest of humanity and show us all where we missed the boat. That should take up about the first millennium of eternity.

On an award show recently, I heard someone say, "We live in troubled times." And my first thought was, "Really? Define 'troubled'."

Now, if we lived in an era when Vikings could attack your village at any moment and drag off the women and children, then I'd say you lived in troubled times.

Or if you lived in London during WWII when the Nazis

blitzkrieged the crud out of that city, then I'd agree that you lived in troubled times.

Or maybe if you lived during the civil rights protests in the sixties, or the Vietnam war, or when the Kennedys and Martin Luther King Jr. were killed, or at any time during the entire cold war with Russia and you had to hide under your desk during school drills (since we all know desks are the first line of defense against nuclear bombs), I'd be the first one to say you lived in troubled times.

But today we have historically low unemployment, peace in our country, LGBTQ+ rights, astounding medical advances, women and minorities making strides in all areas and Chick Fil A finally opened in California.

Granted, we have a lot to work on: global warming, the homelessness crisis, sexual trafficking and a host of other problems means we have to be diligent in our efforts to make this a better place to live.

But honestly, compared to the tension in the past, this particular time period seems pretty flipping sweet!

Put Up or Shut Up

I believe the conclusion is inescapable: the world is broken.

That being said, what are you going to do about it? And who are you going to blame?

What if the point is that we're supposed to get up off of our collective butts and go out there and try to fix whatever we see that isn't working?

Maybe the point is that we're not made to sit on the sidelines and complain.

Maybe, just maybe, the world, such as it is, is a gift. It gives us something to do. Something we can feel good about as we dive into our long list of needed repairs.

I have a friend who gets up early every Thursday morning to drive to a church parking lot in order to help homeless people take showers. He's not scrubbing their backs or anything, but every week he shows up and orchestrates a mobile shower facility for the down and out.

Now, will those people get dirty again? Will they no longer need to exchange their sullied underwear and socks? Has my friend stopped body odor for all time?

Regardless of the lack of a permanent solution, he's making a difference in the lives of those people every single week.

He's living out the great commandment: to love his neighbor as himself. We all should be doing as much.

Yes, the world is broken. And I put it to you that it's a test to see what you're going to do about it.

I've got another friend who spends half of his year working at an orphanage in the Dominican Republic. The people he helps live next to a garbage dump. They go to the dump every day searching through mounds of trash, hoping to find something they can use, sell or eat.

My friend works there because he wants to help. I send him money every month (okay, not every month, because, you know, sometimes things get tight), and my conscience is clear.

I'm a hypocrite who lives quite comfortably on the slippery slope of a semantic society.

If you look up 'spiritual armor' in today's modern translations, you'll find the Helmet of Rationalization, the Breast Plate of Relativity, the Sword of Excuses and the Shield of 'Hey, be nice!'

Sadly, I fit right in.

I Try to be Good

Regardless of what I learn, or espouse, I still do my best to try to be 'good.' Or, to be more specific, I want you to think I'm good.

The reality is, no one's good. We're all pretending. If you knew the secret thoughts of everyone in the world… you could make a lot of money blackmailing them.

"Do you really want your best friend to know what you really think of her? Pay up!"

To convince ourselves we're good, we put ourselves on a sliding scale next to heinous humans like Himmler and Jeffrey Dahmer.

Compared to them I'm one of the disciples. Turns out it's Judas, but still: top 12!

If you want to see if you're really good, stand next to Billy Graham, Mother Teresa and Jesus! Compared to that crowd, I'm the whore of Babylon.

BTW, how big of a whore would you have to be to be named your city's best? "I'm sorry, you may be one of the best whores in the county, but you'll never be the whore of Babylon! Keep trying!"

That is one reality show I'd watch.

These are the kinds of things I think of. Because I'm not good!

Jesus knows my every thought and I feel so sorry for Him.

Think of all the ways we fall short! We lie, cheat, steal and envy others. And those are our pastors! They get paid to be good! What chance do the rest of us have?

If gossip was a capital offense, we'd all be on death row. And that still wouldn't stop us! "Can you believe she's wearing *that* to her execution?"

I'm not good! I know that! But I've been thinking. If I embrace my not-goodness, then you can't sin-shame me!

I am proud of who I am. Which is also a sin, so it just compounds it, but let's ignore that.

The other day in church our Pastor told us we should all be more authentic. That we should honestly confess all of our shortcomings to God.

Why? He already knows! Let's leave well enough alone! My reminding Him is not going to do anybody a bit of good.

If you want to know why people reject Christianity, it's because it keeps telling us that everything we do is wrong!

And the minute we do something right, we get warned about pride!

Welcome to Christianity—where the sins are endless! Lust? Anger? Envy? Come on in!

Despicable you? Despicable all of us!

Welcome to the religion where you'll never get it right! Sign me up!

Bad P.R.

I think Christianity needs a new PR agent. We have unbelievably bad press. Maybe we were loved and respected at one time, but of late all the long-suppressed resentments have come out in full force.

Our problem is three-fold:

1. People think Christians are idiots
2. People think Christians are hypocrites,
3. People think Christians are haters.

See what I mean? Bad PR!

The Bible makes my job very clear: I am to be an Ambassador. I am a representative of the Christian faith.

Tim Keller states it best. He says if people aren't attracted to your version of Christianity, maybe you're doing it wrong.

Ouch!

As far as I can tell, I have one job in life. As I've stated repeatedly, my primary job is to love the Lord my God with all my heart, soul and mind, and to love my neighbor as myself.

Everything in life either falls under that category, or it doesn't. If I put something like money, fame or power in front of God, I've got to see my mistake and correct it as soon as possible.

Of equal importance is loving your neighbor as yourself. The Bible says that God hates two things: idolatry (putting something above Him) and wickedness to our fellow man (not treating our neighbor as ourselves).

Granted, these two goals are impossible to hit on a consistent basis. The bar is set impossibly high. I fail at this more times than I'm willing to admit here.

But any time I come across as hateful, or ignore a stranger's need (which is my regular go-to), or solidify someone's prejudice against Christians, I've just failed as an Ambassador.

Moving On

I know the issues I've listed above don't even begin to scratch the surface of the real problems we face in our world today. From pay inequality to gender politics to racial reconciliation, we have our work cut out for us.

But rather than lose focus and get stuck in what could quickly turn into an endless, blathering eye-rolling rant, let's move on from what's wrong with the world to the one point that really matters: what's wrong with you? (And what are you going to do about it?)

Recipe—One Broken World

1. People should follow their base desires instead of being concerned for others.
2. People should harm those physically weaker than themselves.
3. People should mock everyone they can.
4. People should cheat, lie and steal until they get what they want.
5. People should reject God and His free gift of grace.
6. People should call everyone who disagrees with them a Nazi.
7. Cut people off in traffic, extending middle finger if anyone questions your right to do so.

Fun Fact: Those who think nothing good can come from war need only look at WWI. At that time, the government encouraged women to stop wearing corsets and switch to bras. The metal that had been previously used to construct corsets (28,000 tons of it!) was instead used to build two battleships! Since that time, women all over the world have been breathing considerably easier!

Dive! Dive!

I think we're probably in agreement that the world is broken. There is always hope, but the obstacles to reaching Nirvana seem to be insurmountable.

Not that I want to discourage anyone who feels a burning in their gut to tidy up our home. By all means, go change the world. It needs it. Desperately.

But trying to save the world can sometimes be an unhealthy distraction from what I believe is the true, underlying problem: you are also broken and in need of repair and/or rescuing.

There, I said it. You're not perfect. You need help. If I've insulted you, you are either living in a bubble or haven't looked in the mirror lately.

To circle back to one of my main points: the overwhelming obstacle in having a relationship with the Creator of the universe is that He insists on one fairly large sticking point—we have to admit that He's God and we're not.

To do that means we need to admit to ourselves that we're seriously flawed. That means we have to stop rationalizing our behavior and take a good, hard look at ourselves.

Gulp.

As we begin to come in for a landing, I'll dive deeper into this oh-so-fun subject.

Our Nature

Recently a friend posed the question, "Why are we born so selfish?" It seems that as humans, our go-to is self-preservation. Altruism will always take a distant back seat to covering our own heinies.

My answer, while flippant on the surface, is one that I think bears up under scrutiny. God wants to see our improvement. If we all started off perfect, there'd be nowhere left to go.

For reasons only He knows, our Creator has designed life as a series of never-ending tests that fall under the category of, "Do you love me more than that?"

We start off as selfish, self-absorbed little snots. Some of us never mature out of that phase. But if we let it, life has a way of beating the selfishness out of us. That's sort of the point.

The two-dollar theological term here is *sanctification*. That's the life-long process we all go through as we slowly but surely morph into the image of God's son.

Picture a long horizontal line. On the far left is you. On the far right is Jesus. God's goal is to take you from where you are and push you kicking and screaming over to the other side where you become more like Him.

In between you and your goal of perfection is a pesky thing called reality. The world and all of its temptations and distractions are a huge impediment towards perfection. So is your unfortunate tendency to be human. The bottom line here is that you will never, ever, ever, be able to make it to the other side by yourself.

Most of us spend an inordinate amount of time on self-improvement. We think if we just try a little harder or get the right break, life will somehow work out. Sad to say, despite what society's selling, that's not how it's designed.

C.S. Lewis compares life to a car. He states the obvious when he informs us that it runs better with petrol. (In America, we say 'gasoline' unless you can afford a battery powered Tesla.) You can waste an awful lot of time trying to get the car to run on other materials, but, in the end, it's always smarter to read the instruction manual and, whether you like or not, operate the car as its Designer intended.

Universal Standards

A good clue that there's something greater than our basic instincts for survival is the world-wide agreement on certain points.

Pretty much everyone agrees that murder and rape are wrong, that you shouldn't steal and that common core math comes from the seventh circle of hell.

But why do we agree on anything at all? If evolution is correct, and you play out survival of the fittest to its logical conclusion, there shouldn't be anything close to a universal standard of right and wrong.

If we are nothing but evolutionary beings, then whatever helps me survive is the ultimate good, and everything else on the list is just social niceties that we live with until they come into conflict with my need to please my number one: namely, me.

The philosopher Immanuel Kant addressed this when he said, "Two things fill me with wonder and awe—the starry heavens above me and the moral law within me."

For C.S. Lewis, this is one of the proofs of God that finally pushed him over the edge. He explained that all people seem to believe in a 'Law of Nature,' where we believe some things are good while others are less so.

He says, "Human beings, all over the earth, have this curious idea that they ought to behave in certain way, and cannot really get rid of it. Secondly...they do not in fact behave in that way. They know the 'Law of Nature;' they break it. These two facts are the foundation of all clear thinking about ourselves and the universe we live in."

C.S. also points out that whenever we break the 'Universal Law,' we inevitably make excuses, like we're hungry, or tired, or any of a number of extenuating circumstances.

But whenever we have a good day, or behave the way that puts us in the best light, well, that's because that's who we *really* are!

The obvious conclusion is that exactly the opposite is really true.

The Apostle Paul lays out this point in Romans 7 when he talks about the dual nature of his own personality. His pretzel logic takes us on a very insightful tour of his psyche as he describes that what he wants to do, he doesn't do, but he does do what he doesn't want to do, so by doing the very thing he hates, it's proof that it's not him doing it, but the sin inside of him!

I wouldn't suggest picking up Paul for any light reading. You'll likely get a hernia.

Regardless, Paul and C.S. are in total agreement. There is a 'Universal Law' that rests in each of us, and we spend all of our days either obeying or disobeying it. Over time, your personality will become entrenched in either the light or the dark, depending on which dog you feed.

Welcome to the human predicament.

The Downside of Pride

Which brings us right back to pride. We don't want to accept God because, in truth, we would much rather fill that vacant role ourselves.

Pride is the ultimate self-caught communicable disease.

I've seen horribly insecure people crippled by pride. They're not getting the recognition, praise, or whatever dangling carrot they think they deserve, so they turn inward and start seething and burning with envy.

Narcissists are almost too easy to spot. They wear their pride on their sleeve; "It's all about ME! Not you, ME! I would love to have a conversation as long as the focus is on ME! I would believe in God if He spent more time worshipping ME!"

My main point is this: the very first step toward God is a little thing called humility.

You recognize that God is God and you are not.

You don't have to agree with all of His policies.

You don't have to like His plan for humanity's redemption.

Ultimately, your opinion is totally irrelevant. Which is why it's so darn hard to accept! And why He insists on your need to become humble.

All you need to be a Christian is to acknowledge that you're tired of running life your way and want God to step in and point you in the right direction.

You're Not Alone

Despite an intellectual understanding of everything I've presented, the odds are you still don't want to give your heart over God. I totally get it. You're in good company. The Bible freely admits no one seeks after God.

Josh McDowell says there are three major reasons people reject the good news: ignorance, pride or a moral problem.

At this point in the book, you can now cross 'ignorance' off of the list. By having a working knowledge of the rudimentary concepts I've laid out, you now at least know the gist.

But please understand, I've barely skimmed the surface. I think it takes a lifetime of in-depth study… and humility… and awareness… and a willingness to change… and discipline… and drive… and patience to begin to understand God and His creation.

Or, it could be that I'm just shallow and slow.

I've already touched on 'pride,' but essentially it can be seen as a myopic love of self to the exclusion of all others.

Finally, the 'moral problem' issue is fairly self-explanatory; instead of reining in your lifestyle, you'd much rather continue doing whatever semi-heinous thing you're currently doing. Good luck to you. History has shown there are *never* any negative consequences following after one's own lusts and desires (insert dozens of obvious sarcastic examples here).

I get it. Accepting what I've laid out is a fairly large pill to swallow! You might even half-heartedly begrudgingly accept what I'm saying, but you know as well as I that if you totally bought in, you'd have to deal with your family and your friends, not to mention your total social circle.

Peer pressure is a very real thing. We like to pretend we outgrew it in Jr. High, but the reality is it only gets stronger over time. If any one of us steps out of line at any time in any area, we will be ostracized in a heartbeat. Thank you, social media!

Unfortunately, God doesn't really care. In fact, the more difficult the obstacles you must overcome to get to Him, the happier it makes Him. He's got some kind of hang up on sacrificial love.

Fun Fact: It's estimated that the average American breaks the law three times a day—the most popular of ways are pirating music, jaywalking, smoking marijuana, littering and underage drinking. To most, these might seem like minor statutes, but when the entire population is factored in, a billion laws are broken each and every day. No wonder the police are exhausted!

I Don't Wanna Believe! II

Three Types of People

Not too long ago as I read Tim Keller's book *The Prodigal Prophet*, I was hit upside the head by his description of the story of Jonah as a precursor to the parable of the Prodigal son.

This may not seem like a big deal to you, but I was previously unaware that God told us the same story not just once, but three separate times (that I'm aware of)!

When He does something like that, it behooves us to pay attention.

(Note: I am on a personal quest to save the word 'behooves' from extinction, before it goes the way of its disappearing literary cousins, 'tarnation,' 'gussied up' and 'heavens to Betsy!' Joe Biden's already done his part to save 'malarkey.' I'm just here to keep these poor, innocent words from going extinct.)

Anyway, according to Keller, in the first half of this very short four-chapter book, Jonah is just like the prodigal son. He rebels against his father and goes his own way.

You know the story: he hops on a boat, gets thrown overboard and is immediately swallowed by an ancient relation of Monstro, the whale who starred in Pinocchio.

A lot of people get hung up on this part. The fish is not the point. There were no cruise ships going by when Jonah booked a boat going in the opposite direction of his final destination. So, God sent a fish. The great beast wasn't punishment; it was transportation.

In the second half of the story, after Jonah is unceremoniously vomited on shore, the semi-digested prophet of God becomes like the Elder brother, the selfish, whiny moralist.

Jesus revisits this tale in the New Testament with one of His more famous parables. Then Paul further unpacks the universal characteristics of these types of people in Romans 1–3.

Something tells me that maybe this story is somehow important. When God wants us to pay attention to what He's telling us, He tends to repeat Himself.

Although I'm still looking for the translation where He says, "And lo, it doth verily *behoove* thee to listen to the Lord...!"

There are exceptions, of course, but this thrice-told story states that generally the majority of humans are either...

1.   Rebels
2.   Moralists, or
3.   Broken People Who Have Humbly Accepted God's Gift of Grace (We'll call them BPWHHAGGOGers for short. It just rolls off the tongue, doesn't it?)

Your basic, run-of-the-mill *rebel* is the person who's literally and figuratively given the Italian salute to God. These people are determined to go their own way, regardless of the sound advice they've been given to the contrary.

In the story of the prodigal son, the rebel's the guy who asks his father for his half of the inheritance early. In doing so, he's basically telling his dad, "Hey, I kind of wish you were dead so I could cash out and go live my life."

Though it pains him, the father grants his son his selfish wish, splits the family fortune and gives his offspring half.

The son goes out, sews his wild oats, and, big surprise, squanders the whole kit & caboodle (another dying phrase). He ends up living with a bunch of pigs. Not some roommates with hygiene problems, but with actual pigs. This becomes even more ironic when you understand the Jews didn't eat pork.

The rebel has now officially sunk as low as one can possibly sink.

After a while he 'comes to himself.' This is that moment of clarity most of us get the night before a big exam or an IRS audit.

Meanwhile, his elder brother's back at home playing the *moralist*. He's the guy who has obeyed the rules his entire life but resents pretty much everything.

Why he does it is anybody's guess. He apparently hated his dad just as much as his younger brother did, but he never had the guts to admit it. Or he lied to himself and pretended he was fine. Or he liked to feel superior to his wayward sibling. I suspect he was just waiting around to cash in on his inheritance.

Either way, he looked down on his brother and his repugnant actions. You see, moralists believe they're going to be rewarded for their work. They don't smoke, they don't chew, they don't go with girls who do.

But the father wasn't fooled. He saw into the moralist's heart. The dad knew his elder son didn't love him.

The point here is that while we generally condemn the rebel, it's the moralist who is actually worse off than the one who's determined to sew wild oats.

God can respect someone who's honest. He'd much rather have you be hot or cold than lukewarm.

Famous rebels from the Bible would be Cain (who never turned around as far as we know) and Samson (who eventually became a blind BPWHHAGGOGer).

Jonah was a rebel who became a moralist. The apostle Paul and all his Pharisee pals fell into the big M category as well. Paul and Nicodemus found their way out. Nic on his own terms; Paul had to be blinded and knocked upside his head.

It's not too difficult to find moralists in this world. They're usually self-appointed, and they spend an inordinate amount of time telling everyone else how their lives should be run. (Present company excluded, of course.)

Which brings us to category number three: the *BPWHHAGGO-Gers*. The broken person is someone who most likely started out as either a rebel or a moralist. They've tried to go their own way and have come up short.

The broken person has come to the end of themselves. This is where the prodigal son was when he found himself living with pigs in a foreign country. He said to himself, "Even my father's servants eat better than this. I will go to my father and beg to be his servant."

He wasn't going home to demand to be taken in as a son. He knew he'd blown it. He knew the extent of his sins and he was willing to accept the consequences.

He was now exactly where God wanted him to be. You may not like the journey the prodigal son had to go on before he came to the end of himself, but you must admit, most of us are awfully stubborn. It can sometimes take extreme situations to get us to actually ask for help.

In the story of Jonah, our lead character refused to do what God told him to do. And he was a prophet of God! It was his job to obey! God wanted to use Jonah to spread His message of love to the enemies of Israel but Jonah would have none of it.

Here's where God delivers one of my favorite lines from the entire Bible. After the people of Nineveh repent, Jonah's watching from afar, stewing in his own juices. He's super miffed that God forgave such a repugnant nation. (Think of a group of Nazis sitting in the front pew of a synagogue. They were that bad.) And now Jonah's grumbling under a withered plant.

As he curses God, the people and his horrible life, God gently says, "Is it good for you to be so angry?" That's it. That's all the chastisement the petulant tantrum thrower got. But it says it all.

We shake our fists at God and everyone around us because we're not getting what we want at the moment.

And God, who made the universe, the world, our bodies and our souls, simply asks, "Why art thy panties in such a bunch?"

Broken people get this. They understand how far they've fallen and how good God is. Every day we wake up, look around, see we're still alive and thank God He didn't strike us with lightning while we were sleeping.

I'm not saying those of us in the broken people group are any better than the other two categories (which is a lie, I think I'm way better than your average run-of-the-mill moralist), but we do know one thing: we can't do it on our own.

You may think us weak, but that's okay. We may not like the lengths God had to push us to come to the end of ourselves, but, again, that's okay.

By accepting the fact that God has been drawing us to Him all along, we understand that who we were *before* pales in comparison to who we are *now* and who we are *becoming*.

We were empty, now we're filled. We were aimless, now we have a direction.

Please don't think for a minute I've arrived. I haven't. I know I have tons of issues to work out. But we BPWHHAGGOGers know who our Father is and we trust He'll help us steer clear of the major pitfalls of life—and help us deal with it when we don't.

As I stated at the beginning, any religion worth its salt should try to answer a few basic questions: Who am I? Why am I here? And, as a bonus, where do I go after I die?

Christianity is the only religion that features someone who actually died and then three days later brought Himself back to the land of the living.

While other religions may well have a myriad of wonderful attributes, to use an automobile metaphor, I'm voting for the one that claims to have actually created the car and its engine (and, as a bonus, provides an instruction manual), rather than any group of well-meaning individuals who have carefully studied the automobile and have determined what they sincerely believe will make it run.

†††

Fun Fact: The average American dies nearly $62,000 in debt. My accountant has estimated that I can officially retire 15 years after I'm dead.

Lessons from Jury Duty

I'm going to make a statement here that will be considered blasphemous by many in today's society: the most important thing isn't diversity.

Yes, everyone's voice should be heard, but ultimately, we need to listen to the *right* voice, not the one who shouts the loudest, or whose feelings will be hurt if we ignore or discount their views.

When the Oprah Winfrey and Jerry Springer shows were in their heyday, we began something I like to call 'morality by majority.'

Before Oprah started giving out cars, she'd bring guests out on her stage, they'd state their case, cry copious amounts and wait for the jury of their peers seated in the audience to pass judgement.

Jerry's show was the same thing, only aimed at more of the WWF demographic. It was often hard to tell who was being interviewed and who was in the audience. When the crowd got fired up enough (usually well before the first commercial break), they stood up and yelled at the white trash couple on stage who were accusing each other of sleeping with their cousins.

In both cases, many voices were heard. We watched the daily train wrecks and thanked whatever God we worshipped that our lives weren't as bad as the ones on display on our boob tube.

But something happened along the way. We began to assume that the people in the audience were right. We accepted mob rule, which is never a good idea. Emotions ran high, which is another red flag.

303

Now our entire social media platform is mob rule. Whoever shouts the loudest or pulls out the Nazi/racist accusation card first wins!

I put it to you, regardless of popular sentiment, right will always be right and wrong will never cease to be wrong, no matter how diverse our voting blocks are.

When I served on a real jury (not the Oprah/Jerry kind), I got a great view of humanity. Not of the person on trial—we all agreed unanimously that he was an unmitigated jerk.

No, I got a great view of humanity by looking at the jury itself.

First, there were the people who lied through their teeth to get out of doing their civic duty. One guy told the judge he was a racist. That was his opening remark. Not, "hello." Not, "how are you, your honor." Nope. He opened with, "Hi, I'm a racist."

He also hated cops. And anyone who was ever arrested. He wasn't too fond of being in a confined space with 11 other people either.

The judge asked him if he could put all that aside for the trial, and he said he couldn't. It was so obvious he was doing whatever he could to get excused, I was waiting for him to start answering the judge in Klingon.

My son's a cop, and they still took me! But the lying self-proclaimed racist got excused!

After much agitation, the court settled on a group of people who were found to be acceptable to both the defense and the prosecution.

Over the next few days, 14 people unable to get out of jury duty heard the exact same evidence. We all saw the very same testimonies. I will point out that I was the only one taking notes, but I assumed everyone else at the trial, against all odds, had photographic memories.

It should come as no surprise that our conclusions in the deliberation room were wildly different.

So much so that we were totally split on our verdict. That didn't concern me so much as the group's inability to focus on the matter at hand.

Certain people kept inventing new scenarios the defendant *might* have done. And if he did that, how the people he was threatening *might* have responded. Once that train of thought was introduced, it took the power of Superman to bring that locomotive to a grinding halt.

Periodically I had to be the adult in the room who would stop these flights of fancy and bring the jurors back to the task at hand. Which, to my mind, was very obvious: based on the evidence, was the defendant innocent or guilty?

There was no mob mentality at play here. In truth, there was very little mentality. The majority of people in the room, in my opinion, misread the evidence given to us and conveniently added their own spin.

But that's our judicial system. It was luck of the draw. Any time you get a group of people too honest or uncreative to get out of jury duty, you take what you can get.

But the whole affair made me think about our world today. The biggest question confronting every man, woman and child is, at its core, very simple but has life-changing ramifications: is God real or not?

Unfortunately, we are bombarded with a constant stream of distractions that renders almost any verdict on the evidence at hand impossible.

The attorneys for both the defense and prosecution were a perfect metaphor for the spiritual battle going on around us on a daily basis. When one side presented their case, the other side immediately jumped up and did their best to convince us what we just heard was a complete lie.

Each lawyer was so heavily steeped in hyperbole, they wouldn't let a single sleeping dog lie without kicking him several times.

When their own witnesses contradicted themselves, or tripped over a previously stated fact, they presented the shoddy testimony as a minor misstep, or an oh-so-innocent faulty memory.

But when the other side made a mistake, oh, they were accused of being hell-bent liars on par with Hitler and his cronies! Who knows who they schemed with before the trial to concoct such heresies? Their testimony should be taken out behind the courthouse and shot!

No wonder my fellow jurors had a hard time separating fact from fiction in the deliberation room.

Not to over spiritualize it, but C.S. Lewis put it best in *The Screwtape Letters* when the head demon was recounting how he almost lost one of his charges to 'the Enemy' (for the uninitiated, the Enemy in his book is God). He knew he couldn't counter with logic, so he suggested that his charge should take his new, unexpected thought on the Enemy very seriously, but not until he'd had a good lunch.

Screwtape then brags that by the time his charge was out on the street, with the bustle of the city and the newsboys shouting the current headlines, the distracted man never gave God a second thought.

What are your distractions? Bills? Relationships? TV? Facebook? There are a million ways to avoid the big decisions of life. Focus and look at the evidence placed before you in order to make an informed decision.

But not, of course, until you've had a good lunch.

The Horror!

If you are the type of person who has, up to this point, summarily dismissed any idea of God, but can now see the slightest possibility that some type of Creator, may, in fact, be more real than less so, then that fact most likely fills you with abject terror!

Robert Jastrow from his book, *God and the Astronomers*, sums up this waking nightmare when he says, "For the scientist who has lived by his faith in the power of reason, the story ends like a bad dream. He has scaled the mountains of ignorance; he is about to conquer the highest peak; as he pulls himself over the final rock, he is greeted by a band of theologians who have been sitting there for centuries."

The reaction has to be a mixture of elation at finally finding the answer you've been searching for your whole life mixed with a healthy dose of, "Crap! Now I have to deal with those people?"

There can be no doubt that science has done an absolutely astounding job of figuring out the 'how.' I stand in amazement at their accomplishments. In no way does having a Designer behind the creation diminish that. But once religion begins to answer the 'why,' it does tend to put science into its proper perspective.

Detractors

I became a huge fan of George Carlin when I was a younger man. When he dropped his *7 Dirty Words You Can't Say on Television* routine, as a rebellious teenager, I sucked it up like a sponge.

He was hip, cool and definitely anti-establishment. He was also highly intelligent. His command of the language was always impressive, and watching him go after any particular topic was always a joy to behold.

Until he started coming after God.

I get it, he was angry. Things happened over the course of his life that justified a lot of that anger.

He had a rough upbringing with some very strict knuckle-wrapping nuns, and much later his wife was taken from him by a horrible disease. To his mind, there was no God, because not a single one of his prayers was ever answered.

Sad to say, George is a perfect example of someone who claims God doesn't exist, then gets angry when that same God, for some inexplicable reason, seems to ignore his most heartfelt prayers.

On life's two-way street, what did you expect? That's simply the God of the universe giving George the dignity of his decision to deny his Creator's existence. Subsequently Carlin suffered the consequences of that decision. It's cause-and-effect at its most basic level.

As he came near the end, Mr. Carlin went out of his way to let everyone know there was no love lost between him and his Creator.

He ended a pair of his last specials on HBO with the very same rant against God. For a guy who built his reputation on coming up with a constant stream of fresh material, repeating the exact same routine on two different specials was noteworthy.

For hundreds of years, using humor to shame people into believing God doesn't exist has been a time-honored tool. We all want to be part of the cool crowd, so we mock. Facts don't matter. Acting tough and giving the middle finger do.

That being said, while George was certainly funny and without a doubt preaching to the choir, he was confused and/or misinformed on several issues.

He said, "We're supposed to believe in an invisible man in the sky…" We laugh because the idea sounds so absurd that we're immediately on George's side.

But wait a minute. Why shouldn't I believe in an invisible man in the sky? This is not a fantasy creature we're talking about, like Santa or the Great Pumpkin.

Personally, I want my God to have the power to be invisible. Sure, I think I can handle having Him appear and disappear at will, but that would seriously freak out most of humanity.

The obvious point George didn't see was his own audacious hubris. If he couldn't see it, touch it or feel it, then it must not exist!

Using that logic, we are the ultimate judge of our own reality. We humans, who can only see a small sliver of the electromagnetic spectrum, who can only hear within a limited range, who exist in four dimensions, who can't even see in the dark or breathe underwater, we are the ones, out of all of creation, who should be trusted to know what is and what isn't true based on our very limited observations.

Really? Maybe we should spend a little time getting over our fine selves. If there are other dimensions, who's to say God can't hide Himself in one of those until He's good and ready?

Maybe God's resting in our dimension, but can only be seen through Ultra-violet glasses. Which would mean heaven is one big day-glow party. Which might sound cool at first, but after a few thousand years, I think it would get old.

What about all the other animals on the planet? Many creatures have far greater skills at discerning danger than humans do. The instincts of animals far outweigh our own. To quote the four-year-old boy in *Jerry Maguire*, "Did you know bees and dogs can smell fear?"

To really bring home the point, Jesus wasn't invisible. Nor did He spend the majority of His life floating in the sky. He was clearly seen by thousands of people. He stated in no uncertain terms that He was the visible representation of an invisible God.

None of that mattered to George. He simply didn't want to get his facts straight. He went to his toolbox and used diversionary tactics, but after one ponders over it for more than a few seconds, it just doesn't hold up.

Sigmund Freud argued that belief in God is just wishful thinking. C.S. Lewis would argue right back that having a God-shaped hole in our heart is actually proof of His existence.

Albert Einstein, someone who, if history is correct, was never a particularly religious person, still understood the value of a broader worldview. He said, "Science without religion is lame, religion without science is blind."

When it comes to famous atheists who love to vent their spleen on the very idea that there might be a God, George Carlin would be considered a rank amateur. Richard Dawkins and Sam Harris come to mind as the leaders of that particular parade.

Both make very good points that are, from my perspective, often unencumbered by the facts. Still, you have to admire their tenacity as they tilt at windmills. They want to be right so badly that they grab at any straw that will support their presupposition.

The way I see it, atheists are people who use their God-given intellect to attempt to prove their Creator doesn't exist.

Many years ago, Newsweek magazine printed a debate between

outspoken atheist Sam Harris and Saddleback's 40-Days-of-Purpose Pastor Rick Warren. The ending quote from Warren is one that has stuck with me for years and one that I think encapsulates the atheist/believer debate.

Warren said,

"I believe in both faith and reason. The more we learn about God, the more we understand how magnificent this universe is. There is no contradiction to it. When I look at history, I would disagree with Sam: Christianity has done far more good than bad. Altruism comes out of knowing there is more than this life, that there is a sovereign God, that I am not God."

And then Rick brought it home with a grand slam. Indicating Mr. Harris, he said,

"We're both betting. He's betting his life that he's right. I'm betting my life that Jesus was not a liar. When we die, if he's right, I've lost nothing. If I'm right, he's lost everything. I'm not willing to make that gamble."

Fun Fact: Apparently, atheism has peaked. There are fewer atheists in the world today (138 million) than there were in 1970 (165
million). If the experts are to be believed, atheism should fall below
130 million adherents by 2050. According to Steve Martin, this
trend could be reversed if they had just one good unifying song.

I Don't Wanna Believe! IV

Christians—Society's Punching Bag

Since I've given you some fairly good reasons as to why you should accept the teachings of Christianity, I think it's only fair that I lay out a few of the negatives associated with this particular faith.

This is not a whiny complaint, but it is an unfortunate piece of modern reality that may well influence your decision: Christians are fast becoming the world's favorite punching bag (List this as Determent #1).

Despite the long list of good deeds Christians have brought to our planet, we are now seen as the bad guys. Possibly it's because it's common knowledge that we've been directed to turn the other cheek (and since we've got four, we have a lot to turn) which makes us an easy target.

Not too long ago I saw a YouTube video where a young man was brought in to talk to journalists about bullying.

Instead of talking about his chosen subject, he decided to bully the Christians in the audience by insulting and degrading their beliefs.

This young man seemed to be totally oblivious to his own hypocrisy. I can only assume, because he was on the receiving end of bullying at some point in his life, he felt perfectly justified in spewing bile on anyone on the planet who happens to believe in Jesus.

Let me get this straight: whenever anyone disagrees with you and

312

mocks you for it, that's called bullying. But when you do the very same thing to people you disagree with, that's somehow justified? Please, tell me more about this 'tolerance' of which you preach!

Aren't people fascinating? We are so quick to point out the faults of others while, at the same time, we are basically blind to our own failures. Don't think I'm excluding myself here. I have a long list of problems that I sincerely try to own.

One of the main charges the world loves to throw at Christianity is that we are hypocrites—and that's what I take exception to.

Simply put, to become a Christian, one must accept Rule #1— You have fallen short. Waaaaay short. And there's nothing you can ever do to measure up.

As depressing as that sounds, it's sort of freeing. By fully accepting the fact that we're not perfect, the Christian can spend the rest of his or her days trying to improve their lot, while, at the same time, understanding that no matter how hard they try, they'll never even get close to being perfect.

Which, to my mind, takes most us out of the hypocrite category. But, yes, before you go off on your own rant, I fully acknowledge that as a group of followers, alongside our list of positive attributes, we have an equally lost list of failures.

My personal favorite example of hypocrisy was dramatized by a popular televangelist we'll call Swimmy Jaggert. (The name has been changed to completely disguise his identity.)

I was flipping around the dial one day when I happened upon good ol' boy Swimmy.

On this particular Saturday afternoon, Swimmy was listing the many evils of going to the movies. Not just R-rated movies, mind you, but all kind of movies, like *Bambi* and *Snow White*. I think we can all agree the *The Teletubbies* comes from the dark side, but Disney movies? Come on!

To Swimmy's way of thinking, if you took your family to see a perfectly innocuous G-rated film, well, that set up the habit of watching commercial filth. Then it will only be a matter of days before you and your offspring will be sneaking into dens of iniquity to watch the likes of *Forrest Gump* and *Titanic*.

If that were where he left it, we could have agreed to disagree. Granted, I thought Swimmy was unencumbered by intelligence, but I still could have accepted his reactionary thinking under the categories of, 'live and let live' and 'you must have been dropped on your head as a child.'

But then Mr. Jaggert continued. Without dropping a beat, he then held up his latest record album (yeah, this happened a long time ago, in the days of actual records) and began urging people to buy his holy platter to help support his ministry.

At that point, I started yelling at the TV screen. I said, "Wait a minute, Swimmy! If they buy your record, won't they be conditioned to listen to music, which will eventually lead them to Led Zeppelin and AC/DC? And after that, maybe even the hard-core stuff like Kiss and Abba! It's a slippery slope, my friend!"

All of my yelling was for naught, as Swimmy was later caught with a prostitute in a hotel room watching a bootleg copy of *Dirty Dancing*.

So, if I had a bottom line here, I guess it's this: in one way or another, we're all hypocrites. What I hope the majority of Christians convey is a very real version of that schmaltzy bumper sticker we've all seen while driving: "Christians aren't perfect—just forgiven."

Full disclosure: I yell at people in traffic every day for doing the very things that, when I commit them, I think are perfectly innocent and justifiable. I am the king of pots who loves to call all kettles black.

I have a true talent for seeing specks in other people's eyes while looking around the log in my own.

#Hypocrite!

Not My Kind of God

Determent #2. I absolutely love it when people say they reject

God because He doesn't fit their image of what they believe a good God should be.

I always imagine God up in heaven smirking, saying, "Really? Well, what would you like?"

The answer is usually one that sounds good but doesn't hold up in the long run.

Every time I hear someone say this, I always imagine a young child walking downstairs and announcing something like this to their parents…

"Mom, dad, I need to tell you that I can no longer accept you as my parents. I find your decision to take away my iPhone both cruel and unusual punishment and, as such, I must rescind my previous acceptance of you as my parents. I need you to find another place to live until acceptable parental substitutes can be found. I hope you can both respect my decision. Now, what's for breakfast?"

Speaking for me, I don't want some namby-pamby god who bends to the will of his people. People are selfish. They're short sighted. They change their minds depending on which way the wind is blowing and what they had for lunch.

Personally, I don't want a God that I designed. I have a finite mind. I can't see past tomorrow. I would much rather have a God who claims to have my best interests at heart and can see the future. Even if He doesn't always give me what I'm asking for, I can have confidence in a God who has the wisdom and fortitude to ignore me—for my own good.

Not to beat this particular dead horse, but God is a great deal more concerned about your character than your comfort. If being shut down, turned down or flipped around makes you a better person, you can almost guarantee that's going to be Plan A in God's playbook.

The Standards!

If you have an honest heart-to-heart with anyone who's been

in the faith game for any number of years, sooner or later they'll bring up Determent #3: The standards are crazy!

For example, just having normal, everyday lustful or murderous thoughts is, let me perfectly clear, just as bad as actually doing them! Well, slap on the cuffs and throw me in the slammer, because I'm a wanted fugitive.

My question is: then why don't the same all-or-nothing standards apply to my almost-good-deeds?

Taking that standard to its logical conclusion, if I even think about giving money to the homeless guy, then surely that good-deed thought should count for something, right?

If I say I'm going to help you move, but then I don't, I think I should get at least half a good-deed credit.

Nope, not in this game. For some reason, merely thinking of good deeds and then not following through is even worse than not thinking of them at all.

Everyone always seems to be sending out good thoughts to people in disaster areas. Are they good for nothing?

My problem is, throughout the Bible, it tells us to be good. Then it says that no one is good, no, not one. That's like having a class in high school where they tell you that you need to pass, but sadly, no one has ever managed to get anything above an F+. Way to motivate us!

Despite my frustration, I understand why it lays it out this way. We all need the grace of God. Got it. We also need to understand that our own efforts will always fall short.

Then why doesn't it say, "You'll never make it on your own! Just accept it! Do whatever you want!"

Personally, I think that tactic would get a lot more converts!

   Fun Fact: It's actually illegal to die in the town of Longyearbyen, Norway. In fact, if you're terminally ill, they will ship you off the island. The reasoning is that back in the 50's they discovered that because there was so much permafrost in the area, buried bodies weren't decomposing. This meant that various and sundry viruses could survive in the corpses and, when the ground thawed, infect the living.

Public Prayer

The most recent statistics are quite sobering. Not too long ago, at least 75% of this country identified themselves as 'Christian.' That number has now dropped to 65%. Only God truly knows how many of those self-proclaimed 'Christians' really believe in Him, but regardless, people are apparently leaving the faith in droves.

Culturally, religion is taking a beating. Way back when, it used to be part of the fabric of our country. Now we bend over backwards to pretend it doesn't exist—mainly, I assume, because we don't want to offend anyone (and also because we don't want to get sued).

I performed at a dinner one time for a program called *D.A.R.E.* Which I believe stands for 'Drugs Are Really Exciting.' It's a horrible name. I have no idea how they get funding.

They asked me to pray before dinner. But because they're a government sponsored organization, they said I couldn't mention any specific deity's name.

I told them it wasn't a problem, I start praying and, in the middle of it, I realized I had no idea how to close this prayer.

It started getting longer and longer and longer, and finally I just said, "We pray these things in your name. Hopefully you know who you are."

In Praise of Mediocrity

There's a great story in the Bible where a master divvies up some money amongst his servants, instructing them to invest his money. He gives one guy 10 coins, another five and the last guy gets one. The parable is about how we are to wisely use the talents God has given us, not about how unfair the original distribution was.

The point is that God knows exactly what He's given you. You may well be a person who is overflowing with talent. You might be the person with an average amount of talent. Or you might be better suited to the position of team mascot.

The perfect example here is Hollywood's multi-hyphenate Judd Apatow. He started out as a stand up, rightly assessed his talents and decided he was not the up-front guy but instead chose to pursue a career behind the scenes. He wrote for other stand ups, produced some shows and eventually became a very influential writer and director. Yes, he followed his dreams, but he correctly assessed his talents as well.

After my own realization that I was given far fewer talents than I wanted or needed, I eventually accepted a philosophy that has kept me grounded through several of my own personal storms...

John 15:5, *"I am the vine; you are the branches. If you remain in me and I in you, you will bear much fruit; apart from me you can do nothing."*

Philippians 4:13, *"I can do all things through [a]Christ who strengthens me."*

This one-two punch is a great reminder for me. On my own, I can accomplish literally nothing. But when I invite God along for the ride, who knows what we can achieve!

In short order, I'll be bearing fruit! Which, in time, could ferment into wine! Now you're talking!

I may well be the servant who was only given one coin. Instead of grousing about how unfair the whole system is, I'd much rather invest the paltry sum I've been given and see where the adventure takes me!

God is looking for willing soldiers to get out there and go where He sends us. Taking this to its logical conclusion, a lot of our assignments are not going to fall under the category of "plum." Many will be mundane, others darn near underwhelming.

I know I will never be the big star. But, hey, I'm on the team!

The Big Lie

Tim Keller boils all this down to one succinct point: we are wired to worship God. Because of that fact, anything we put above God will lead to our eventual downfall. The biblical term for this is idolatry.

He says that idolatry is when we take a *good thing* (follow your dreams, make a lot of money, find the perfect spouse, pleasure is the only reason to live!) and make it the *ultimate thing*.

This big lie in our culture has been slipped into our drinks like a roofie. It claims that not only are we good enough as we are, but that we can do anything we set our minds to.

An add-on to that lie is that true happiness will come if we only sacrifice everything to achieve our dreams.

God begs to differ. He says we can accomplish nothing without His help. And that our true joy will only come if we pour out ourselves as a sacrifice.

You may well be tired of C.S. Lewis by now, but after everything I've thrown at you, he sums it up best. He says, "Life with God is not *immunity* from difficulties, but *peace within* difficulties."

That's the bottom line. Christianity is not a magical religion that will erase all of this world's problems. It is a tool that helps you cope with this sometimes wonderful yet often cruel, cruel world. It helps you accurately assess what is and what is not important. It helps you become a better person inside and out.

And when your life is over, yes, it will usher you over to a magical place where every desire of your heart will finally be answered.

That's the promise: a better life here and the best life ever after.

Considering the alternatives, it's a pretty good deal.

Recipe—Rebel

1. Reject God.
2. Go have a good time.
3. Wake up in pig sty.

Recipe—Moralist

1. Think you're making it to heaven on own efforts.
2. Look down on anyone who isn't you.
3. Be impossible to live with.

Recipe—Broken Person

1. Accept that God's God and you're not.
2. Accept free gift of grace.
3. Spend entire life attempting to receive free gift without trying to earn it.
4. Love justice, show mercy, walk humbly before God

Fun Fact: The coins the Biblical master gave his servants to trade were thought to be minas. Each mina weighed between eighteen and twenty ounces. It was worth one hundred denari, or fifty shekels, amounting to about four month's wages. No wonder the last servant was scared of losing it! That was a whole lot of coin!

The Wrong Question

There's a point in the first *Indiana Jones* film where the lead character is sneaking around a Nazi infested Egyptian burial site. After looking at the front and the back of an ancient artifact, he concludes that the Nazis are, "Looking in the wrong place. They're looking in the wrong place!"

This exciting discovery leads to the unearthing of the original 10 Commandments and a lot of snakes. Adventure ensues.

Not that I've ever been in any situation close to what happened to good ol' Indy, but that particular quote seems to come up time and time again in my life.

As someone who's been in show business my entire adult life (admittedly on the farm team, but in show business nevertheless), I get asked for advice from time to time from upcoming newbies who have one singular goal in mind: how to take my job away from me.

This happens in every facet of the business. Writers are asked how to get a good agent. Actors are asked how to get in to see a certain producer or casting director. White male actors are asked why they're not more diverse in their ethnicity.

In my case, I'm asked how to get on certain shows, or how to get booked as a sitcom warm up, or how to break into the church market.

In every scenario, I'm struck by the Indiana Jones quote. Every single person is asking the wrong question!

In show business, it's not "How do I get more people to look at my web site?" It should be, "How do I get better?" Period.

In the comedy world, it's not whether or not you have five, 10 or 45 minutes of material. Is any of your material actually funny?

In the acting world, it's not whether or not you have a good head shot, or demo reel or resume. Can you act? Do I believe you? Can you pretend to cry or die without making me giggle?

These are the basics, people!

A talent manager one time gave the best advice I've ever heard about how to get a major Hollywood agency interested. He said, "Get really famous. Then we'll come to you."

The same essential problem faces every human on the planet today. We are all asking a lot of questions, but are they the right ones?

I'll bet dollars to doughnuts (which, by the way, I have no idea what that even means) that the majority of the following queries have come out of your mouth...

How do I find the right girl or guy?

How do I get the right job?

How do I get more people to like me (or my page)?

Where should I live?

When and how should I ask for a raise?

How much money do I need for retirement?

Will I get asked to the dance (or party or big event)?

How can I look like that?

Why do I look like this?

Who do I have to sleep with to catch a break?

Why is everyone else absolutely wrong about absolutely everything?

It's not that any of these questions are bad in and of themselves. There are a million and one good questions. Questions that we need to answer in order to navigate through life. Fine. Deal with them. But don't spend all your time on questions and situations that are sometimes, at best, distractions.

The problem is that we get stuck on any number of *good* questions and we either skip, miss or avoid the *best* question.

While the question itself is easy, the answer to it can take a lifetime of reflection.

It should come as no surprise to anyone that I believe we are put on this planet to serve God, not the other way around. That's why I think our endless questions about our careers, relationships and money fall short of *the* question.

Once that question is asked, then life's priorities fall in line. But as I said, asking the question is the easy part. Discovering the correct answer and shifting your priorities accordingly can take a lifetime.

This is the Best I've Got

I'll admit it, I don't have a good testimony (the Christianese version of 'story'). I came from a loving family. I don't have a drug habit, I never woke up in a pig sty (my mother's declaration of the state of my messy room notwithstanding), I'm not currently in prison.

It's fairly depressing when you're a Christian trying to convince other people that Jesus saves and your conversion story puts nuns to sleep.

A few years ago another comedian found himself in the same boat and conveniently invented a past life where he said he was a reformed high priest for Satan. Man, did that sell like hotcakes!

While I would love to make boat loads of money and drink after the show and have affairs on the road like he did, he already took the best idea. So all I'm left with is stupid honesty. Sorry to let you down. For my next book I'll try to do better.

At this point I'm sure you won't be shocked by my admission that I'm not an intellectual by any means. Despite that, I tend to operate more from my head than from my heart. I always thought I was "less-than" because whenever I'd share the epic scope of my life, no one ever seemed to break down in tears.

So, I guess I'll have to live without having a drug addiction testimony or parents who dropped me off on the corner until I was farmed out to an adoption agency and went through foster care where I was brainwashed to sell flowers at the airport.

None of that happened. I'm just a normal guy with normal issues like anger, lust and pride. Oh, and coveting. And shading the truth to benefit me. Might as well throw gossip in there too. Fine, greed! I fall short in every area you can think of!

Despite the fact that my sins aren't sexy, they have still managed to screw up my life in major ways.

In all honesty, I'd be nowhere without the saving grace of God.

Checking Two Boxes

For me, the fact that Christianity works comes down to two checked boxes.

I was not a Christian growing up. I was raised in a Christian home, but I had not fully accepted my parent's faith. I was certainly close. I went to church, I knew the Apostle's Creed, I did all the right stuff, but in Young Life terms, I was still 18 inches away. (That's the approximate distance between your head and your heart.)

One of the problems I had was that everyone kept telling me that Jesus loved me. Well, so did my parents. What's the big diff? Because of that, I was fine. I didn't particularly need to add another person who loved me. Obviously, as a teenager, I wasn't plagued by deep thoughts.

One of the precepts of the Bible is that God not only foreknew us, but that He also predestined us. For what, only He knows, but He made each of us for a purpose. Whether or not we fulfill that purpose is one of the great quandaries of life.

God dramatically shifted my life from one path to another with a simple box on my SATs in high school.

As far as I was concerned, I was going to Indiana University about 10 minutes after I graduated. Both my dad and my sister went there, and they had a great swim team.

What it had to offer towards my education, I hadn't a clue.

Regardless, that was the box I checked on my SAT. They would send my scores to I.U., and I hoped that I did well enough on the test to insure my acceptance. That was the extent of my plan. My back up plan was, "what's for lunch?"

But the Scholastic Aptitude Test's instructions said we were supposed to check *two* boxes. I hadn't given another school an ounce of thought, because I knew where I was going. Since Ohio was the next state over, I figured that would be an easy drive from home, so I checked Ohio University. Yes, I'm an idiot.

That simple up and down stroke of a number 2 pencil on a standardized test late in my junior year changed my life forever.

I did well enough on the test for Ohio University to recruit me. Indiana totally ignored me, which I have yet to fully get over.

What both surprised and impressed me was that O.U. seemed to have everything I was looking for, such as an excellent radio and television department that allowed underclassmen to actually touch the equipment.

I discovered that I.U. only let their grad students work on the equipment. Point Ohio.

See, I came from a great high school. They had a career center that housed a radio and tv studio track that I'd been on for the previous two years. I wasn't about to go to a school where I'd have to wait for four more years just to do what I was already doing.

When I say O.U recruited me, I mean to say they actually came to my house! Not the whole university, but two of their representatives. I.U. was just an hour and a half south, and they didn't even bother to invite me on a double date.

Anyway, against my will, my plans changed and I found myself, all alone, in a small little town in south eastern Ohio.

My first class was an introduction to telecommunications. I had a previous introduction in high school, but the class was required, so I went. That's where I spotted a very cute brunette seated in the middle of the auditorium.

As fate would have it, this same adorable brunette was in my next class, an introduction to comedy writing.

For some reason, most of my Freshman classes in college seemed to involve very expensive introductions. "Robert, meet grammar." "Grammar, meet Robert. Now pay us your tuition."

Back to my point. This young girl sat in the front row while I started off in the back. Each week I moved up one row until I was sitting cattycorner right behind her. Subtle, huh?

You must understand I was, at this point, painfully shy and insecure. I was so uncomfortable in my own skin that when I talked to girls one-on-one, I tended to slip into an English accent. Yes, I did that! What's worse is that I had absolutely no idea I was doing it. If my future wife hadn't pointed it out, I'd probably still be doing it today!

Because of my morbid fear of girls, I couldn't get the nerve to ask this young girl out. At this time of my life, when it came to the opposite sex, I was a confirmed agnostic. I believed they existed, I just had no personal conversion experience.

But out of the blue this young girl broke her leg! What a stroke of luck! Her bad fortune was my window of opportunity! To my mind, since she broke her leg, I figured she'd be holed up in her dorm room with nothing to do and no way to get around town.

I got up the nerve to ask her out (she said yes), went over to her dorm, put her on my back, crutches and all, and walked her uptown to the movie theater.

That first date will go down in the record books as the best first date of all time. We saw a Looney Toons retrospective and laughed our heads off. Then we got a pizza and ate it on the steps of the courthouse. Then I carried her back to her dorm, we talked until two or three in the morning and after a good night kiss, I ran on wings back to my dorm, with a short break in the campus park where I relieved myself against a tree because my bladder had been barking at me for several hours, as I was too embarrassed to excuse myself to use the rest room. Eventually I realized being shy and insecure was a complete waste of time, not to mention bad for my bladder, so I decided to drop it. (The shyness, not my bladder.)

There were more than a handful of ups and downs over the next few years, but eventually that cute brunette became my wonderful wife and gave me two absolutely adorable, wonderful brunette children.

All because I checked a box on my SATs.

The second box happened that same year. Josh McDowell, the writer of *More Than A Carpenter*, came to campus.

The first night, he talked about relationships, on the second he started talking about Christianity and on the third night he laid out all of the predictions the Bible made about both Jesus and the end times.

When he was done, a large group of volunteers handed out comment cards. On that card was a box to be checked if you wanted to hear more about Jesus. I didn't want to be rude, and I was intrigued, so I made my second life-changing check mark.

The concert organizer, Campus Crusade (now known as CRU), knew they had a live one, so they sent someone over to my dorm about 10 seconds after I checked the box. If memory serves, they were waiting at my dorm, drooling, before I even got there.

We talked for a bit, they closed the deal and I was ushered into the kingdom of God.

From that year on, I entered into the two defining relationships of my life.

Fun Fact: Approximately 70% of Christian teens entering college will leave their faith. The number of college students with *no* religious affiliation has tripled in the last 30 years, from 10% to 31%. Students identifying as LGBTQ+ are twice as likely as other students to identify as either atheists, agnostic or none. Bottom line: it's hard to be a saint in the university!

Two Influential Leaders

Two leaders of Campus Crusade had a profound effect on me. They were, admittedly, not the usual stuffed shirts one expected to find in the Cru ranks at that time. The married couple, Fred and Sue Trane, were fun loving and over the next few years helped me understand the basics of the faith.

Fred was a nut. There's just no other way to describe him. I think that's why we got along so well. If you don't know it, you can probably guess that Campus Crusade for Christ wasn't exactly renowned for recruiting wild party people. It had a reputation for leaning way over on the conservative side. After all, they weren't called Campus Crusade for Outrageous Parties.

In the anything-goes climate of the seventies, it's as if the organization walked directly into Sodom and Gomorrah and said, "Well, good golly, Miss Molly, who wants to stop having immoral sex and join us in an exciting game of canasta?"

If any organization could have been given a collective wedgie by the rest of the campus, this one was it.

Despite every reason to avoid them, not only did I join up, but I stayed! Because of Fred. He was fun. He laughed. He let me be me. He knew I was still forming and did his best to steer me onto the right path.

One story his wife Sue told our group will stay with me until I die. She's passed on, so if I get any of these facts wrong, she'll have to wait until I see her to correct me. Regardless, here's the gist...

A group of young, eager women on staff with Campus Crusade were on a weekend retreat somewhere in the mountains by Fort Collins, Colorado.

It was a lovely night so the women decided to take a hike after dinner. Splitting up, Sue's group went up the mountain, walking in and among the trees. The other group went down the mountain to hike by the river.

Out of nowhere, a storm descended upon them. This was a lightning storm accompanied by a deluge of water. Sue's group was very high up on the mountain, so they turned around and started making their way down through the muddy trails.

As they were surrounded by trees, they prayed with all their might for God to stop the lightning. For some reason, God did not appear to hear their urgent request. In fact, the lightning increased. The women redoubled their efforts. They reasoned that their prayers should certainly be heard as they were on staff of a respected Christian organization. Surely God knew who they were and would honor this request!

But the storm only got worse, and the lightning dangerously crackled over their heads all the way down.

By the time the women got back to the retreat center, they were drenched to the bone and depressed out of their minds! Where was God? Why had He ignored them! Yes, they all made it back safely, but barely! If any bolt had zigged instead of zagged, it could have hit a tree and one or more of them could easily have died!

On a weekend that was intended to bring the women closer to God, this was a soul crushing moment. Much like finding out your boyfriend didn't really like chick flicks! It was horrifying!

Concerned about the other missing women, Sue and the other dripping, depressed members of Cru gave a half-hearted effort to pray for their friends, but no one had any belief that their tone-deaf God would listen to these soaking women standing on such shaky faith.

Sometime later, when everyone was extremely concerned about the missing party, the second hiking group came bursting through the doors.

For some reason, their demeanor was much different than the first hiking party. These women were also soaked to the bone, but they were laughing, whooping it up and praising God!

Sue's party ran over to their friends, ready to lay out how much their faith had been shaken that night. They helped their friends dry off first, sure, but more importantly, they had to let their sisters know how distraught they were over the events of the evening.

Then the river hikers told *their* story. Unlike the women at the top of the mountain, they had been caught in a flash flood! There was only one place to cross the now raging river, but no one had any flashlights in order to see the rocks they needed to leap on in order to get across the water to safety.

When the lightning started, the women were overjoyed that their Father in heaven was looking out for their safety. Each time a bolt flashed across the sky, one more woman was able to see the rocks in order to get safely across the river.

The women prayed to God for the lightning to continue, and continue it did! So much so that every single woman made it across the river, no one slipped or fell in, and after much effort the whole party was able to trudge their way back up the mountain to the retreat center!

In a literal flash, Sue and her disappointed friends were given a life lesson about the sovereignty of God.

He sees the big picture. While we're crying out to our Father that life isn't fair and that circumstances are dragging us down, He's whipping up a lightning storm to help someone else make it home safely.

Sue summed it all by saying, "Not only did we see that God is so much bigger than our narrow-minded plans, and that He watches over all His children, but unfortunately, we also saw He seemed to like the other group of women a lot more than us."

Can I Get A Witness?

Not to be overly critical, but I do have a minor bone to pick with Cru concerning their insistence (in the 70s at least) on what is known in Christian circles as 'witnessing.'

Their motivation is perfectly understandable. Jesus commanded His followers to go to the ends of the earth preaching the good news. I'm not arguing that it should be done. I have a problem with how large organizations exert undue pressure onto their followers to accomplish that goal.

Sometimes I wish Jesus could have been a little more specific. Maybe He could have said something like, "Go ye therefore and preach my good news to all the world. But don't be idiots about it. Don't guilt people into it. They'll only resent you for it later. Remember it's called *good news* for a reason. Don't berate people. Do it in love. Maybe start up a relationship before you bring me up. If people think you actually care about them, they'll be more inclined to listen. If you're just doing to it to score points with me or to get another spiritual notch on your belt, please reconsider. Seriously. You'll only do more harm than good!"

Cru may do it entirely differently now, but when I was in college, they gave their wide-eyed converts little four spiritual laws pamphlets and sent them out to engage the populace in order to convert the world to Christianity.

We had the knowledge of toddlers and they fully expected us to tell horny college students that there was a better, more chaste, less drunken and rowdy way.

Me, I'm an introvert. I hate walking up to strangers and engaging them in casual conversation only to drop a bomb three seconds later. "Hi, how are you doing? Isn't it a beautiful day? Such a blessing from the Lord. Speaking of God, do you have a personal relationship with our Savior? I'll take the fact you're peeing on my shoe as a no." Yeah, it was like that.

I went to a conference in Chicago where the activity before lunch was for everyone to go outside and attempt to convert the entire city. They paired up hundreds of teens two by two and sent us out into the dead of winter to make converts for Christ!

This was nothing short of torture. I just couldn't do it. Neither could the young girl they paired me with. But we weren't allowed to come back to the conference until we'd witnessed to at least one stranger. I'm sure the early disciples used the same tactic; "No converts, no food!"

Reasoning that our parents would be disappointed if they were told their children froze to death on the streets of Chicago, my partner and I decided to do our appointed duty. We were mini martyrs suffering under the arctic winds blowing off Lake Michigan.

This is how it went down. After much fearful procrastination, I went up to a man and said,

"Hi, we don't want to do this. But we're with an organization that has told us to go out on the streets and witness to total stranger, and we're not allowed to go back until we do. Could we just share this with you so that we can get out of the cold?"

He smiled, acquiesced, told us he was a Buddhist and let us do our duty. I have no doubt he's in heaven today telling all who will listen how he was brought into the kingdom via apology.

It may well be the best evangelical tool God and man ever invented, but that was the first and last time I ever used the four spiritual law booklet.

Back in my college dorm some time later, I was complaining about this to my roommate. It was late at night, we were in our bunk beds ready for sleep and I started in. I laid out how I felt about witnessing and how it just felt wrong to do it to complete strangers and on and on and on.

Maybe he did it just to shut me up, but my roommate asked me why I was with Cru and why Jesus was so important to me.

I then shared with Jon my entire, albeit short, journey and why I believed down to my toes that Jesus really was the way and how frustrated I was that I seemed to be entirely incompetent in sharing what was supposed to be the most important thing in my life!

After a long beat of silence, Jon said, "Bob... Do you realize you just witnessed to me?"

And I said, "Huh, I guess I did."

If I have done any good in my life, it's usually after first making an entire mess out of my original goals. Eventually my roommate became a Christian and so did my girlfriend. She did it under threat of my leaving her if she didn't, but I think it still counts.

I tell you this to encourage you. Jesus even loves people who stumble, trip and fall as they attempt to follow Him. That's good, because it's the only way I know how to do it.

He Watches Over

Josh McDowell says that the best proof of our faith is not endless facts and figures, but our own personal stories.

One of my stories of faith is quite simple: it involves the births of our children.

Our first child was the definition of an unplanned pregnancy. We had only been married for a few months. Imagine being flat broke and then dip just slightly below that level. I had just graduated from film school, which means I was writing the next great American screenplay. Which means I was a waiter.

Mind you, my wife and I were taking precautions against any kind of fertilization. Apparently, that didn't matter, as we soon had proof positive we were pregnant.

Modern science could not prevent the creation of our child! Some may well point to God and His will, but personally I like to take credit. Despite the obstacles thrown at me, nothing could stop my power to impregnate my wife. Me strong like bull!

While we loved our daughter to death the minute we met her, as a young couple just starting out, this unforeseen development did not come as good news. Beyond the shock, we both knew beyond a shadow of a doubt that we couldn't afford this blessing.

It wasn't part of the plan. We had no insurance! It scared the pants off of us. Which, if I'm not mistaken, was how my wife got pregnant in the first place.

What we didn't know was that God knew about this pregnancy some 20 years before we did.

My wife's grandmother was a sweet little old lady named Mama Honey. Like us, she was flat broke. (I guess it runs in the family.) She lived with her daughter (my soon-to-be mother-in-law) and basically raised my wife.

The special ingredient in this long-gestating plot was that Mama Honey had a friend who had some money. My wife's grandmother told her friend to put her granddaughter in her will. She said, "Little Annie's going to need a bit of help some day."

Flash forward 20 years. The week before we found out we were pregnant, we got a letter from a lawyer in my wife's old home town of Toledo. In it was a check for $5,000 from Mama Honey's friend's estate.

My wife looked at it and said, "We're going to need this money for something." And $5,000 was exactly what it cost to cover the expense of delivering our first child. Yes, the cost has risen dramatically, but at that time, that was the exact number we needed.

I tell this story quite a lot and I'm still amazed at the skill and exquisite timing it took for God to pull off this stunt.

I'm probably the only person on the planet who gets excited every time he sees a letter from a lawyer sitting in their mailbox. The odds are extremely long that any of Mama Honey's close, rich friends are still alive, but I live in hope.

The story of our second child deals not with what happened in the past, but with what was planned for him in the future.

This time we were ready. We waited five years after the birth of our first before we were confident enough to stick our toe back into that water. Most conversations between new parents go something like this, "Our first one's still alive. Want to tempt fate and go for a second?"

We went for it, and within hours my wife was pregnant again. As I said, me strong like bull!

A week before our son was due to arrive, our daughter came

home with the chicken pox. This is the part where one must thank the public education system. Germs are today's version of Show 'n Tell. If one kid's got it, the whole class is guaranteed to take it home by that afternoon.

Concerned about the impending birth, my wife called her mom and found out she'd already had the dreaded pox when she was a child, so we were safe.

After my wife was comforted, I asked if any of Mama Honey's close friends had passed away recently. It never hurts to ask!

From that conversation and a talk with our doctor, we were confident we were out of danger, so we set about putting our daughter in quarantine and dabbing her ten thousand red spots with ointment.

A few days later, out of the blue, my wife walked into my office and declared in no uncertain terms, "We have to have this child today." When I asked why, she said, "I don't know why, but God says it has to be today."

When God speaks, it's a good idea to move, so, we called the doctor, went to the hospital, they induced and we had our son.

For those of you who have never had a child, let me just say that's really all there is to it. No muss, no fuss, no pain. Just walk in and within minutes they wheel you back out with a brand-new bouncing baby boy! It's exactly like you've seen on every sitcom!

At any rate, as if on cue, the very next day (our original due date) my wife caught the chicken pox. Again. I don't know how, but it happened. We didn't know it at the time, but if she'd had them when our son was born, he would have died. The Red Cross were called in. They flew in an emergency serum just in case. We were that close.

If my wife hadn't had the premonition to have our child a day early, I can only imagine the heart-wrenching conclusion.

Flash forward some 25 years to the day: our son graduated from the Los Angeles Police Academy. Today he's a cop in the gang unit. He puts his life on the line every day to help the disenfranchised and protect the innocent. To say I'm proud of him would be a gross understatement.

The point here is that our children may have been a surprise to us, but they were not to God.

He knew 20 years before our daughter was born that we were going to need financial help. And with our son He knew 25 years after his birth he was going to be a cop.

God not only saw them before the beginning of time and knit them together in their mother's womb some 14 billion years later, but He knew the circumstances surrounding their births and took care of them.

Personally, I'm sorry to say we stopped at two children. I wanted to have more just to see what miracles God would pull off.

But unfortunately, my wife's body was done. From that point on I couldn't come to bed unless I was wearing an entire wet suit. I could not have on enough protection. Like I said, strong like bull!

Fun Fact: God spoke audibly to Jesus three times (that we know of)! The first was after He was baptized by His cousin, John, in the Jordan river. The second was on a mountaintop at the Transfiguration (with special appearances by Moses and Elijah) and finally, again, just before He was crucified. After this last time Jesus said, "This voice was for your benefit, not mine."

Old Softie

Another proof of the positive effect of Christianity is the slow and gradual melting of my icy cold three-sizes-too-small Grinch heart.

I am not, by nature, an emotional person. I was raised in a culture of men who did not cry. Men were allowed to show emotion for three reasons: 1) Saluting the flag, 2) Watching *Old Yeller*, and 3) When the Cardinals won the series.

That was it. Crying at any other time made one highly suspect. Fortunately, times have changed, but that was my early reality.

Now, after having kids and watching my fair share of romantic comedies, I've become an old softie. I seriously never know when this is going to hit me.

My wife and I went out for dinner one night, and the restaurant had hired a special needs young woman as a hostess. Her spine and mouth were crooked and her fingers bent back so she had a hard time grabbing the menus.

I was so touched by this, I couldn't stop staring the entire meal.

That restaurant did what we're all supposed to do! We're called to help people help themselves. We should all give dignity to those who've been dealt a hard hand. Abraham Lincoln called it "the better angels of our nature."

I called the manager over to thank them for hiring the young girl and to my surprise, I couldn't get through it!

I started off with, "I want to..." And then I choked up. I started in again with, "I want to thank you..." and broke down again. I took a deep breath and did my best to rush through it, "I want to thank you for hiring..." And I lost it again, so my wife filled in for me. She's more versed in speaking while crying.

By the time the manager left, she thought I had special needs.

She sent the hostess over to give me a job application. So far, the money's been great!

Be B.O.P.

We are all travelers down life's highway. Some of us are sensible economy models, others are sleek sports cars, a few are big wheeled semis and the majority of us are just trying to not be road kill.

As one who has traveled down the road a-ways, like it or not, I like to think I've got some advice for the brand-spanking new believer. Or at the very least some cautionary tales for everyone else.

To my mind, Christianity comes down to three essential ingredients: Belief, Obedience and Perseverance, or, as I like to call it, B.O.P.

Christianity is incredibly simple, while, at the same time, is also unbelievably complex. It takes a lifetime to understand the basics and even after that there's still room for improvement!

Belief is first.

Just acknowledging who Jesus is doesn't cut it. This is more than acquiring the secret password to get in through the door. You can't say that you believe in Jesus and Buddha and Mohammad and Joseph Smith and the rest of their cronies equally. You must select from the multiple-choice test which one you will follow.

The biggest obstacle here can be described in one word: *feelings*. Feelings are great, no doubt. This would be a very pale world indeed without feelings. While I, myself, tend to hide mine behind a façade of sarcasm, I heartily acknowledge that feelings do exist and, on occasion, are actually useful.

What needs to be stated, however, is that feelings should never be given top priority when it comes to huge life decisions. Feelings, by their very nature, are not to be trusted.

Not that your feelings are sneaking around behind your back in order to bring you down.

"Anger, what are you doing?"

"Nothing."

"What are you holding?"

"Nothing."

"I can see it. What is it?"

"...A grudge."

"Drop it."

"I don't wanna."

"I said drop it!"

"You never let me have any fun!"

Or something like that.

While I may have ever-so-slight issues with Campus Crusade for Christ, one thing they told us will never leave my head. They had us all imagine a train on a track. The front engine pulling the load was labeled 'facts,' and the caboose pulling up the rear was labeled 'feelings.'

I have no memory what cargo this particular faith train was hauling, but I will never forget the life lesson this rudimentary example taught us, which was, basically, never get the two train cars mixed up! Facts come first, feelings should always pull up the rear. I certainly understand this may not be true 100% of the time, but it's a good general rule to live by.

With that in mind, despite what it may trigger in you, all evidence points to the fact that Jesus was a real, historical figure who claimed to be fully God and fully man.

He said He came to this planet for two very specific purposes; to introduce us to His Father and to die for our sins.

That heavily-documented-event may well stir up feelings in you, but those emotions, while not inconsequential, should take a back seat to the facts on hand.

When you look at the universe and everything science has uncovered about its creation, you get to decide whether or not you believe it was all planned or all just a happy twist of fate.

Your belief on that subject will determine a great deal of your worldview. Then you get to make another weighty decision about the Nazarene who lived a little over 2,000 years ago.

You get to look at all the evidence presented and decide for yourself if you're going to buy in or reject it like a bad rumor.

That being said, simply having belief in this life altering subject is not enough. Sorry to say it is merely the starting point.

Obedience comes in second.

This is the 'not-so-fun' part. No one wakes up wanting to obey someone else. We all want to do what we want when we want to do it!

But for all the parts of your life to work together smoothly here, you've got to put several of your own desires on hold more often than you'd like and do your best to obey God. Sometimes your wishes and His coincide. Other times not so much.

Generally, obedience gets a bad rap. It's looked upon as if it's the kid in the front of the class who reminds the teacher every day before the bell rings that they've forgotten to assign any homework.

If obedience were out on the playground, it would be the first one to be put in a head lock for a severe noogie.

But there is a very positive side of obedience: when you do it, you not only avoid punishment, but also sometimes dire consequences!

We all obey certain laws on the books for one very simple reason: we don't want to pay the consequences. If I were insanely rich, I wouldn't care about how many speeding tickets I got. At least not until they pulled my license. Then I'd care a lot.

The real issue of obedience goes back to that bastard step child, *feelings*! We want to act on our impulses! Our impulses feel good! We have a hard time denying our impulses! We *neeeeeed* to give in!

Here's a modicum of hope: neural pathways in your brain (that tell us what we neeeeeed!) can be changed over time. If you establish positive habits, you will soon find that your impulses tend to scream at a softer volume the longer you manage to deny them. (The urge for chocolate and Chicago pizza being the notable exceptions.)

This is what the Apostle Paul was talking about in Romans chapter 12 when he urged everyone to renew their minds. This is how effective change takes place. And it starts with obedience.

If that word makes you balk, drop it like a hot potato. Instead, tell yourself you're not submitting to a higher authority, but that you're in general agreement with the world's top Life Coach. Make semantics work for you!

Perseverance is the final piece of the puzzle.

The Bible calls this life a race. We are urged to run it to the best of our ability and, above all, to finish well. You can start off excited about all that God has shown you. But after a really tough weekend of trials and tribulations, one can get rather tired and want to give up.

Life is a marathon. If you show up wearing boogie board shorts and flip flops, after a few miles you're going to get some serious chafing and blisters.

This is where we desperately need God's help. He knows it's a long haul. When you're in pain or need support or are hanging on by a thread, life feels as if it's never going to end. Conversely, when everything is going well, that state of euphoria seems to evaporate into a mist in a matter of moments.

Recently a news report came out about a popular comic who fell from grace because of sexual impropriety. This should come as no surprise in our post-Harvey Weinstein era, but this one hurt because the fallen comic was not just a very funny guy but also a professing Christian.

He was a popular comedian whose sexual addiction was unceremoniously publicly uncovered. It may have been just another blip on the screen to the majority of people out there, but to me, it was a serious kick in the gut.

Here's a guy who had the belief part of the equation down pat but fell short in both the obedience and perseverance categories.

I was incredibly saddened by the news. I can't imagine what it's like to be both wildly popular and handsome. The temptations must have been overwhelming! Sometimes I'm very thankful that fame passed me by. Regardless, I still wish I were better looking.

Not to gang up on another guy, but the biblical poster child for this section is the legendary Samson. This guy had it all but threw it away because of unbridled lust. He's another in a long line of guys who had the 'B,' but couldn't be bothered with the 'O' or the 'P.'

Like most of us, Samson was under the misguided belief that he could continue to disobey God without consequences. What most of us don't realize about God is that while He is more patient with us than we deserve, even He has His limits.

It might be public humiliation at the hands of the Philistines, or it might be in the court of public opinion on social media. Either way, it's a hard lesson to swallow.

If you need help in the area of obedience or perseverance, there is a treasure trove of great advice throughout the Bible, especially in both Proverbs and the Psalms.

It's Hard, But It's Good

The Church at Rocky Peak's pastor Michael Yearly says that God's word can be compared to a guardrail. It offers both protection and direction. It keeps us from veering off the path and careening down into the ravine, but only if we stay on the straight and narrow.

You should know that having a faith won't keep you from experiencing tragedies. Just because you love God will in no way gain you a get-out-of-jail card. What it will do is help you get through your tragedies with a peace that passes understanding.

God never promises anyone a trouble-free life. What He does promise is that He will be with you every step of the way. If that's enough, you will find great comfort in it. If you want more, you may want to prepare for a lifetime of disappointment.

One thing I can guarantee you is that God will never stop

working on your character. If you want a true friend and confidant who will never stop urging (and pushing) you to become the person whom you're destined to be, this is the religion for you.

While this may sound like it's all too much, the bottom line is that the Christian religion gives us hope.

Hope of a better tomorrow.

Hope for a life free from fear and anxiety.

Hope that all of our trials will pay off some day and that all of our pain will be nothing more than a dim memory.

Hope that when we get to the other side, we'll honestly say we are glad God put us through all the tests He did.

I believe that when we look back at our lives, most of us will be like that famous scene in Steven Spielberg's *Schindler's List* where Schindler breaks down saying, "I should have done more!"

Until then, be B.O.P.

Fun Fact: When a woman nurses her child, her brain releases a neurochemical called oxytocin, which emotionally bonds her to her child. Unfortunately, when anyone watches porn, the same neurochemicals are also released, bonding them to those images, rather than to another human. This explains why 68% of Christian men are reportedly addicted to pornography. The repeated viewing has literally changed the physical structure of their brains.

The Goal

Everything I've stated up to now was just leading up to this: Christianity has a bottom line. It has a goal. And that goal is for you to serve your fellow man (and woman and various and sundry others with increasingly more complicated identities).

If you've been looking for a reason to exist, if you wake up wondering what your purpose is in this life, this is it. It is to serve.

God could certainly throw down a miracle or three every time we needed help, but He's come up with a different system. He wants His children to get out and do their best to make this a better world.

And while you're doing that, be a good ambassador. That's your other job. Be a good representative of God.

When you destroy someone's faith by hurting or manipulating them, you've just helped to destroy God's reputation.

Very few people can separate God from His people. I wish they could because, were it left up to me, I'd revoke some of His children's credentials. There are a lot of very poor ambassadors roaming around out there.

C'mon, people, represent!

Your goal is not to make a lot of money. It's not to be famous. It's not to die with the most toys. Your goal is to be a good soldier willing to carry out the General's orders (even if it's KP duty, if that's your assignment) so that when you die and meet your Maker, He can say, "Well, done, good and faithful servant."

Notice He's not going to say, "Good and faithful CEO who controlled others through manipulation." He didn't say, "Good and faithful demanding movie star." And He's never going to say, "Fantastic! We got another narcissist! Come on in!"

There's a reason He said "servant."

With that in mind, this is the question you should ask every single morning for the rest of your days. When you wipe the sleep out of your eyes, and after you go through your list of urgent To Do's, and after you have a good breakfast and plan out your lunch and dinner, and after you scroll through the morning news and every post of your social media, you might consider asking, "How can I serve You today?"

Then figure out how to spend your limited resources of time, talent and treasure to accomplish whatever task He sets out before you in order to make this broken world a better place.

Lunch with a Lesbian

With that in mind, I'd like to tell you the story about the time I went out to lunch with a lesbian. (It was actually just to get a coffee, but I'm a sucker for alliteration.)

Okay, a little unpacking. A young performer saw me at a show, thought we had a lot in common (we both like women) and suggested we meet over coffee.

This was one of my favorite phone calls to my wife, ever. "Honey, can I have lunch with a lesbian? Please! You know nothing's going to happen!"

But here's where it gets interesting. The performer did some research on me. She said, "I see you perform in churches and I wasn't sure you'd want to be seen with me."

That made me so sad.

First, it's how we label each other. She labels herself through her sexual preferences. That's her choice. I'd say she's cute, effervescent and bubbly. But she leads with 'lesbian.'

My generation never did that. I didn't lead with, "Hello, I'm a desperately needy, uncoordinated, inexperienced heterosexual." I didn't need to. It was painfully obvious.

I told her that as a Christ-follower, it's my job to be a good ambassador. And that means to extend grace and mercy to everyone I meet, regardless.

I also said that if Jesus has a problem with her sexuality, He can talk to her about it. That was above my pay grade.

A few of my Christian friends disagreed with me on this. They sent me scriptures about not associating with people of ill repute. Yes, they actually did.

In response, I told them that if I only had lunch with perfect people, I wouldn't be able to eat with anyone! I couldn't eat with me!

If you're going to cherry-pick scriptures, what about the one about loving your neighbor as yourself, or that all have fallen short of the glory of God, or that no one is righteous, no not one, or before you complain about the speck in your neighbor's eye, you might consider taking the log out of yours.

That's right, two can play the 'can you top this scripture' game!

Because I'm pretty sure Jesus *didn't* say...

"Zacchaeus! You Roman sympathizer! Stay up in that tree!" "What? This woman was caught in the act of adultery? Stone her now!"

"Father, smite them, they know not what they do."

Anyway, my lesbian lunch was delightful. Next week I'm having brunch with a Buddhist, mojitos with a Mormon and supper with a Scientologist.

The Ultimate Question

It's taken a while to get here, but that's pretty much it. That's my pitch.

In a nutshell, God made the universe, the world and you. He's taken credit for it all and wants you to pay Him the respect He believes He deserves. You do this not by beating yourself up. Not by pretending you don't have any problems. Not by spending the rest of your life racking up good deeds. No, all you have to do is accept His free gift of grace.

If you're now seeing red over the fact that you had to wade through the previous pages to get to that very simple conclusion, I fully accept your warranted wrath. However, in my world, without the proper set up, the punchline never works.

Despite the process to get here, the question remains: what are you going to do about it?

We have all been given an amazing gift. To waste our time here on earth would be the greatest crime of all.

When philosophers ask, "What's it all about? Why are we here?" I think the answer's as plain as the wondrously created noses on all of our faces.

I see a grander purpose for our existence than just mere survival. I can't see building this whole she-bang just so humanity can fritter away their years thinking only of themselves.

It's as if we are all, regardless of how much is in our bank account, children of extreme privilege. To be blunt, we owe something to the world around us. We need to get out of our comfort zone and help those who seem to be having a hard time.

I'm not saying you have to solve the homeless problem (although, if you can, please come out to L.A., as we need you desperately!), but maybe you could call an old friend. Or write a card to your mother. Or take someone out to lunch! Or clean up the trash on your street. There are a million ways to make the world a better place for all of us.

Remember the old saying, "Many hands make light work?" Well, if eight billion people made that kind of effort every day, this place would turn around in a heartbeat!

Putting all of that aside, where do you fall when it comes to the ultimate question?

†††

Fun Fact: While many claim Jesus talked more about money than any other subject, if you look at the context of what He's saying, it doesn't hold up. Jesus' top topics were about 1) God and His kingdom, 2) faith and salvation, 3) hell and 4) how easy today's kids have it compared to when He grew up!

An Eternal Evite V

The Bottom Line

Not long ago I was down in San Diego for a gig. It wasn't a 'hell' gig per se, but it was definitely Hades adjacent. The night was hot and sticky, people were sweating, the air was close, and I had to follow some very dirty comics who closed their acts with material that would make Lenny Bruce blush. Needless to say, I survived, but I did not give the best performance of my career.

As I drove away, I quite naturally rationalized my mediocre showing. But the next morning I woke up with a condemning thought: it was as if God was in my brain saying, "You did that on your own last night, didn't you?"

That was my 'coulda had a V8!' moment. Instead of praying for the people in the crowd and using my time to lift them up, I did the whole show on my own. For me. And I got the appropriate response.

I forgot to invite my partner on stage with me. While that sounds super spiritual, it's really quite rational.

I have looked at the evidence and have drawn conclusions from my lifetime of experimentation. I do better when my goal is to do the show for others. When I'm in my head, I'm not communicating and rarely having fun.

The way I phrase it is to simply 'Invite God In.' Invite Him in to whatever you are doing. Whenever you're doing it. He knows He is the source of our strength. That's the way He made us. You cannot do it on your own.

354

Another example of what we need to pay attention to is called the 'armor of God.' It's in Ephesians 6.

Every day before I go out my door I make sure my hair and teeth are brushed, put on appropriate clothes, double check my zipper, put on my glasses, throw down a fast breakfast because I don't want to start off with low blood sugar, check my email and phone messages, then go over our individual schedules with my wife. And after all that I feel I'm ready to face the day.

What I more often than not forget to do is invite God along for the ride. Even though He has explicitly told me to put on my spiritual armor, 99 times out of a hundred, I neglect to put it on.

As I said, I identify as an idiot.

Imagine you're on the football field in the middle of a game wearing a T-shirt, shorts and sandals and you keep getting hit by the opposition. After you get knocked down for the umpteenth time, you look over at the coach and call out in frustration, "Why do I keep getting hit?"

The Coach shakes his head, then calls back, "Put—On—Your -Uniform!"

The ultimate mistake of humanity is that we tend to go out into the world and engage in battle without the tools we have been given and then blame everyone else around us (especially God) when we get knocked down.

The Four Loves

C.S. Lewis has some wonderfully dense thoughts about what the Bible lays out as the four loves.

In today's culture, we combine all types of love into one big, unwieldy mess. It's much easier to talk about a subject, love especially, when we take the time to define exactly what we're talking about.

C.S. Lewis agrees with this assessment and recorded a series of radio broadcasts where he talked about inviting God into each of the four types of love, be they eros, storge, phileo or agape.

As he explains it, the passion of eros (erotic love) will subside over time. We all get weary of doing good in agape (selfless, altruistic love). Our children and friends tire us out in both storge (parental love) and philia (brotherly/sisterly love).

But if we invite God in to each of the loves, they will not only get better, but they will become what God intended all along.

While the occasional relationship may start off great, eventually the passion fades, reality raises its ugly head and we find ourselves either bored, irritated or ready to quit. Mr. Lewis suggests we invite God into the process.

When love fades, it is an indication that you need help. You cannot do it on your own. You were not meant to! Don't you see? While you are beating yourself up that you're a bad parent, lover or friend, God is on the side saying, "If you'd like, I can help with that."

We all need to invite God in. He's the juice we need to keep our lives going.

I am a prideful, competent man. Because I can handle the basics, I have made the huge mistake of thinking I can do life on my own. Yes, I believe in God, but I'm embarrassed to say I only come to Him when I need Him.

My conclusion is that I cannot do this on my own. I need help. Yes, I have my community. Yes, I have my wife. Yes, I have many people in my life who are willing to help me as long as I offer to buy them lunch afterwards.

I'm grateful for all that. But more than all that I need the help of my Father. I need to invite God in. It is an act of will that I must repeat daily. Sometimes hourly.

On my own I can do nothing. With His help, I can accomplish the tasks He has set out for me. Which in itself is rather strange. He gives me His spiritual To Do list, then waits for me to ask Him to help me knock off the list one by one.

Even though I know all this, I keep forgetting!

After I fail for the quadrillionth time, instead of trying it again by myself, I need to remember that I have a helper. He is on the side always patiently waiting for me to invite Him in. He's such a gentleman that He will never intrude.

Why?

Here, at the end of our journey, one rather large question still remains.

I have spent quite a lot of time looking at the big questions of life from both the scientific and religious angles. I hope I have clarified a few murky areas, but I must beg your indulgence with a final whopper of a puzzler.

I have to wonder why God went to all this trouble in the first place? Why did He even bother?

When one even tries to fathom the complexity of creating an entire universe, then our particular life-sustaining rock within that cosmos, then our exquisitely finely tuned bodies living on that life-sustaining rock within said universe, it leads me to one inevitable conclusion: all of this must be extremely important.

One doesn't just whip up a universe on a whim. It takes some forethought and planning with a serious end goal in mind.

When I step back and look at the big picture, this is how I see it: as strange as it may be for mere mortals to comprehend, I believe before the creation of our home and time and space and all of that, God was faced with a dilemma.

As a triune God, He was in a perfect relationship with Himself. God, Jesus and the Holy Spirit got along swimmingly, but something was missing. He would not be fulfilled until He was in relationship with other beings. He had perfected love, but He would not be satisfied until He found a way to share that love.

That, my friends, appears to be the ultimate purpose of life.

As a counterbalance, our culture is lousy with examples of what love *isn't*!

When Stephen Stills told us to "love the one we're with," he was just trying to con some young star-struck hippie into a heavy make out session.

When *Love Story* said that "love means never having to say you're sorry," an entire generation reacted in unison with a confused, "I'm sorry, what?"

Poor Tina Turner must've still been angry at Ike when she called love a "second hand emotion."

Billy Joel said he loved his first wife just the way she was, but three wives later, he may well have regretted ever writing that song.

Lastly, when Whitney Houston sang her heart out telling us that the *greatest* love of all was to love *ourselves*, she was dead wrong!

However, I do think Curly came really close in *City Slickers* when he told Billy Crystal's character to find "that one thing."

Selfless love is the theme running throughout the entire Bible! Page after page tells us to love God and our neighbor as we love ourselves, that there's no greater love than to lay down your life for a friend and on and on and on.

It's a little tiresome that this love thing always seems to be directly tied to sacrificial love. How about if we give selfish love a little shout out, huh?

When all this mess is eventually wrapped up, God's stated goal is to be in heaven with several billion of His creation, both human and angel, all living in perfect harmony, with no evil, whining or tears in sight.

To achieve that goal, God went to an unbelievable amount of trouble, the most dramatic of which was to sacrifice His only Son. But that's what true love does. It does whatever is necessary.

I believe God's trying to show us by example that true fulfilment will only come from loving others so completely that you pour yourself out for that person or persons.

Every parent knows this. Most every mom or dad will go to great lengths to keep their child safe from harm. Their goal is not to work long hours or to pay for a math tutor to help their child pass first grade.

Those are the things people do to achieve their goal, which is to see their offspring grow into who they are meant to be so that they can enjoy a relationship with each other and sit around at Christmas sipping eggnog complaining about kids these days!

I believe God is patiently waiting for a few billion of us slow learners to catch on to that particular clue!

Our ultimate fulfillment will never come from money, fame or success. Especially if we sacrificed relationships along the way to get those prizes.

True love doesn't think of itself. Like it or not, in the paradoxical world of Christianity, our happiness is tied up in how well we love others. Happiness is actually a by-product of loving sacrificially.

And as God has said repeatedly, you'll never learn how to truly love unless you allow Him to help you.

We spend our lives learning that selfishness is wrong, that mercy love and compassion will always trump hatred, but the entire trip will be wasted if it doesn't lead you to God's ultimate wish for you: to see and know who He is and to accept Him as your own.

Your Turn

So, now, big surprise, it's your turn. You get to make a decision. Not that you have to do it now. You can ruminate on this for as long as you'd like. But if you happen to see a logging truck barreling towards you on the freeway, I'd say a very quick prayer, because you're about to meet your Maker.

I am not a psychic, but I suspect you're frustrated from trying to do everything on your own

I suspect you're frustrated that the world is not going the way you'd like it to go.

I suspect you need just as much help as I do. Maybe you're not as big of an idiot as I am. Good for you.

Maybe you actually remember to put on your spiritual armor as you go out into the world.

Maybe you'll never make a mistake again (but somehow, I doubt it).

Maybe you're just lonely.

Maybe you're like me and don't want to accept this faith, but the avalanche of facts has overwhelmed you to the point where you can see no other option.

I have hopefully shown you miracle after miracle that God has done for you and for me. You get to determine whether what I and countless others like me have said over the years makes enough sense.

When you follow the evidence, where does it take you?

If it's not too much trouble, in another minute or so, you'll be done with this book. That would be a perfect time for you to take a moment and meet the Creator of the universe. He's patiently waiting for you to come to the end of yourself.

Instead of reiterating the thoughts of others, I'll just use His words…

Apart from me you can do nothing. I am humble and gentle. Take my yoke upon you for my burden is light. I am the light of the world. No one comes to the Father but through me. If you are humble and believe, I will come into your heart. Nothing can separate you from the love of Christ. Now there is no condemnation for anyone who believes. My peace I give to you. You can do all things through Christ who strengthens you.

Heavy stuff, huh? Maybe not as awe-inspiring as how God made the universe, but pretty darn close!

Get the peace that passes all understanding! Ask Him into your heart and your life will never be the same!

Good luck on your journey. I hope to see you on the other side.

Recipe—Heaven

1. Greet relatives.
2. Stand in line to meet Jesus. Repeat, "I do believe in God, I do believe in God" until He hugs you.
3. Have every tear wiped away along with sickness, nausea and phlegm.
4. Get new name and perfect body.

5. Gain perfect knowledge.
6. Learn to fly, levitate and travel through dimensions.
7. Get keys to new mansion.
8. Attend marriage of the Lamb. Banquet to immediately follow (Sit in the back. Wait to be called up front). Admire Michelangelo's new statues in hall.
9. Watch creation video (on loop).
10. Visit Bible-Land amusement park. Go through Ten Plagues Hall of Horrors, ride the Red Sea roller coaster, challenge Samson to contest of strength and watch Thomas in one man show, "I Doubt it!"
11. Spend decade in Puppy Park petting and rolling around with thousands of puppies.
12. Attend Humble Olympics. Team Captains Billy Graham and Mother Teresa.
13. Tour Martyrs Museum.
14. Receive working assignments for next millennium.
15. Greet everyone you see with, "Way to go! You made it!"

Fun Fact: There will come a day when the purpose of the universe will no longer be a mystery. No matter how God did it, or
how long He took to create our current home, He says a better
one waits for us. Whether it's in another dimension or some far
away realm hidden from our eyes, He claims the streets are paved
with gold, each of us gets to live in a mansion and the leaves from
the tree of life will heal the nations. Not to mention there are lots
and lots of banquets. If His current creation pales by comparison,
I can hardly wait!

Acknowledgements

I would be remiss if I did not thank a few of the people who helped shape this tome.

My first readers who slogged through a lot of sloppy thinking and rabbit trails: Jamie Alexander, June Colson and Christy Conder.

The scientist who double checked my facts: Perry Lanaro.

The editor who corrected my endless confusion with colons and semi-colons: Rita Warren.

The publisher who took a chance on a comedian: Mike Parker of WordCrafts Press.

And of course, my wife, Anne, who has patiently listened to every idea, notion and dream of mine for over four decades now.

I appreciate you all! Now on to the next one!

Bibliography

1. *The Science of God*, by Gerald L. Schroeder
2. *Why the Universe Is the Way It Is*, by Hugh Ross
3. *The Creator and the Cosmos*, by Hugh Ross
4. *The Case for Miracles*, by Lee Strobel
5. *Astrophysics for People in a Hurry*, by Neil DeGrasse Tyson
6. *The Language of God*, by Francis S. Collins
7. *The Miracle of the Scarlet Thread*, by Richard Booker
8. *The Privileged Planet*, by Guillermo Gonzalez and Jay W. Richards
9. *Evaluating Story: A Christian Look at Film, TV and Theater*, by Sean Gaffney
10. *How the Body Works*, Penguin Random House books, various authors
11. *Mere Christianity*, by C.S. Lewis
12. *Evidence That Demands a Verdict*, by Josh McDowell
13. *The Case for Christ*, by Lee Strobel
14. *The Reason for God*, by Timothy Keller
15. *Walking with God through Pain and Suffering*, by Timothy Keller
16. *This is Your Brain on Music*, by Daniel J. Levitin
17. *The Bible*

About the Author

Not many comedians make the cover of *The Wall Street Journal*, have warmed up thousands of audiences for Hollywood's top sitcoms, are a staple on SIRIUS radio's *Laugh USA*, or have released eight comedy projects.

Robert G. Lee is a seasoned comic who comes armed with a refreshing clean relatable act. He's been entertaining audiences behind the scenes on Hollywood sitcoms such as *Golden Girls*, *Wings*, *Old Christine* and *One Day at a Time* for over three decades!

Whether delivering laughs nationwide on his *DryBar* comedy special or writing punchlines for produce on *Veggie Tales*, Robert's clever, slice-of-life observational material along with his impish and punchy storytelling style is always a guaranteed audience pleaser.

Now, with his first book, *What's the Big Idea? A Comedian Explains God, the Universe and Other Minor Stuff*, he's taking his comedic sensibilities from the stage to the page.

If you'd like to follow Robert on any number of social media sites, please go to www.RobertGLee.com. If you'd like him to entertain at your event just email him @ info@robertglee.com. If you want to berate him for any reason, please scream into your pillow and then let it go.

Also Available From

WordCrafts Press

Trusting God Through Testing Times
   by Jill Grossman

I Am
   by Summer McKinney

Pondering(s) Too
   by Wayne Berry

Written That You May Believe
   by Rodney Boyd

I Wish Someone Had Told Met
   by Barbie Loflin

More Devotions from Everyday Things
   by Tammy Chandler

www.wordcrafts.net

Made in United States
North Haven, CT
25 March 2022

17525042R10224